SCREENING INTEGRATION

SCREENING
INTEGRATION

RECASTING MAGHREBI
IMMIGRATION IN
CONTEMPORARY FRANCE

EDITED AND WITH AN INTRODUCTION BY
SYLVIE DURMELAT AND **VINAY SWAMY**

UNIVERSITY OF NEBRASKA PRESS
LINCOLN AND LONDON

Chapter 6 was previously published in Mireille Rosello, *The Reparative in Narratives: Works of Mourning in Progress* (Liverpool: Liverpool University Press, 2010). Reprinted with permission.

The editors are grateful to Marianne Begemman and the Office of the Dean of Faculty at Vassar College and to the Graduate School at Georgetown University for providing the funds to prepare the index for this volume.

Library of Congress Cataloging-in-Publication Data
Screening integration: recasting Maghrebi immigration in contemporary France / edited and with an introduction by Sylvie Durmelat and Vinay Swamy. p. cm. Includes bibliographical references and index. Includes filmography. ISBN 978-0-8032-2825-2 (pbk.: alk. paper)
1. North Africans in motion pictures. 2. Immigrants in motion pictures. 3. Social integration in motion pictures. 4. Assimilation (Sociology) in motion pictures. I. Durmelat, Sylvie. II. Swamy, Vinay.
PN1995.9.N66S38 2011
71.430944 — dc22   2011010518

Set in Bulmer by Kim Essman. Designed by Nathan Putens.

CONTENTS

ACKNOWLEDGMENTS

By definition, a volume such as this is the fruit of collective labor. Our most sincere thanks go to the contributing authors, whose incisive and original reflections compel us to share their insights with the reader. As with many projects, this one too began with a day of reflection in 2007, organized by Carrie Tarr in conjunction with "Beur Is Beautiful," a retrospective she curated for ArteEast's CinemaEast Film Festival in New York City. We thank Livia Alexander and Rasha Salti of ArteEast and the French Cultural Services for organizing and cohosting the festival under the aegis of which we first met. To Carrie, we are very thankful not only for her indefatigable work as a pioneer in the field but also for her generosity and effort in bringing together scholars as well as filmmakers, allowing us to engage with the general public. Her encouragement was instrumental in urging us to undertake this project. Publishing a book is akin to filmmaking: this work too is a product of the commitment and combined efforts of several individuals and institutions who, although neither authors nor editors, lent their support and expertise in invaluable ways. Without them this volume would not have materialized. We thank Heather Lundine and Bridget Barry of the University of Nebraska Press for their interest in the project and for their guidance through the publishing process. Our sincere thanks to Lona Dearmont for meticulously copyediting and to Paulina Velasco for proofreading the manuscript. We are very grateful to Louisa MacKenzie and Mark McKinney for giving us valuable feedback at various stages of the project. Devin Griffin's eye for detail helped us immensely with preparation of the manuscript, and Susan Wilson's technical support with illustrations was essential. Last, but not least, we are indebted to the Gabriel Snyder Beck Fund at Vassar College and the Graduate School of Arts and Sciences at Georgetown University for providing research support for this volume.

SCREENING INTEGRATION

INTRODUCTION

Sylvie Durmelat and Vinay Swamy

Integrating into Mainstream French Cinema?

Since the early 1980s, French citizens of Maghrebi immigrant descent have actively engaged in making a cinema that foregrounds their experiences.[1] Likewise, as protagonists, they now play central roles on the French screen. The volume of this production, the increased visibility and professional recognition it enjoys, its sizable viewership as indicated by box office entries, and the historical span it covers, make of this cinema a phenomenon to contend with in its own right. In addition, the representations and interventions in sociocultural debates it proposes render this cinema a complex object of study. Maghrebi-French filmmakers, as they have been named by some British and American scholars, moved away from the activist, marginal cinema of the 1980s (*Ils ont tué Kader* [1980], the documentary by the Collectif Mohammed; *C'est Madame la France que tu préfères?* [1981], a short film by Farida Belghoul) and gained access to the means of production of mainstream French film industry in the 1990s. For instance, Yamina Benguigui's *Mémoires d'immigrés* (1997) benefited from the financial support of commercial film sponsors such as Canal+

as well as state-funded institutions such as the CNC and the FAS.[2] In 1999 Djamel Bensalah's comedy *Le ciel, les oiseaux et . . . ta mère!* demonstrated the commercial viability of this kind of filmmaking with over 1.2 million entries at the French box office in 1999 alone.[3] Filmmaking by and about descendants of Maghrebi immigrants has since gained international appeal, as evidenced by the 2006 nomination of *Indigènes* by Rachid Bouchareb for an Academy Award (Oscar) for the Best Foreign Film in the year of its release. *Indigènes* was not only tremendously successful at the French box office (almost 3 million entries in 2006 alone), it also spurred a national debate on the history of North African participation in the French army during the Second World War (see Mireille Rosello's chapter in this volume). France's own Académie des Arts et Techniques du Cinéma has also begun recognizing the impact of filmmakers and actors of Maghrebi descent: for the second time in the span of three years, a film by Abdellatif Kechiche was awarded four César prizes (the French equivalent to the Oscars). His 2007 immigrant tale, *La graine et le mulet*, won for best film, best director, best screenplay, and most promising actress (Hafsia Herzi) in February 2008. Kechiche's success is all the more remarkable given that in 2005 his second feature film, *L'esquive* (2004), swept awards in the same categories, with Sarah Forestier for most promising actress. Such acclaim, garnered at both national and international levels, seems to indicate that films by directors and actors of North African descent have not only gained mainstream recognition but have now also reached a critical mass.

Yet such recognition has not necessarily afforded easier access to the funds required to finance large-scale projects, because being a better established filmmaker does not necessarily mean that one is, or even feels, integrated into the (French) film industry. For instance, Kechiche has recently expressed bitter feelings about what he perceives to be the continued rejection of actors and directors of Maghrebi immigrant origin by mainstream cinema (Kechiche 2007). Such comments reflect the difficulties he has experienced in gathering the funds necessary to produce his films, and echo remarks made by others (Ghorab-Volta 2007). Although there is no one model that accounts for the experience of the various filmmakers studied in this volume, as Carrie Tarr has noted (2005, 11–12), the one common feature of the films from the 1980s and early 1990s was that they were mostly made on a very low budget, cobbled together from atypical sources. Malik Chibane, for instance, struggled for six years to find funding before finally succeeding in making his first feature-length film, *Hexagone* (1994). Nevertheless, such production and the associated filmmakers have become successful in finding a place in the distribution circuits and networks of French cinema, where they can express their voices and partake in what Jean-Michel Frodon has termed "national projection" (1998). The once struggling director Chibane is now the president of the Société des Réalisateurs de Films (SFR, the Society of Filmmakers).[4]

Since their emergence in the early eighties, these films have attracted the interest of cinema critics and scholars alike. From the start, issues of definition were prevalent, similar in this respect to the corresponding discussions regarding the use and meanings of the word *Beur* (to which we will return below), or the attempts to characterize a *Beur* novel or literature. In the early 1990s critics defined "a *Beur* film" as "one which was made by a young person of North African origin who was born or who has spent his or her youth in France, and which features beur characters" (Bosséno 1992, 49).[5] This definition, although somewhat restrictive because it is entirely based on ethnicity, was meant to distinguish this nascent filmic expression from the films made by "first-generation *émigrés* [that] date from before the emergence of the beur phenomenon in the 1980s" and from films "which feature immigrants and beurs but were directed by filmmakers of completely French origin" (Bosséno 1992, 48). Any objection to the undue primacy given to ethnic labels has been borne out, given that the porosity of this grouping of films as defined above has only increased today (see Alec Hargreaves's chapter in this volume). Hence, it is clear that such parameters used to determine the corpus could be problematic, if not altogether self-defeating, and need a more expansive reading.

Fahdel (1990, 147) and Bosséno further stated that these films do not constitute "a veritable cinematic 'school'" (1992, 49). Rather, for Bosséno and others, their one distinctive feature is an ensemble of "genres and themes" such as the choice of comedy, the naturalist vein and documentary feel of social-realist cinema, the depiction of social margins, the strong emphasis on integration, and the relative absence of women and religion (Bosséno 1990; Dhoukar 1990; Fahdel 1990). In 1990 Bosséno concluded that this was a cinema of transition, yet one that had inspired mainstream filmmaking to rediscover and explore urban peripheries and suburbs as fertile social and imaginary spaces at a time when escapism and the heritage film were dominant in mainstream French film production (Austin 1996; Powrie 1997; Tarr

2005). And indeed, in 1995, critic Thierry Jousse in *Positif* coined the term "*banlieue* film" to account for the grouped release of such films as *Hexagone* (Malik Chibane 1994), *La haine* (Matthieu Kassovitz 1995), and *Etats des lieux* (Jean-François Richet 1995), which depicted the life of marginalized suburban (mostly) male youth in French housing estates. Although labels such as *Beur* and *banlieue* cinema overlap, and may well be temporary, they have highlighted the contributions of films that have renewed the images of immigrants and their descendants by providing a perspective from within the North African immigrant experience. Michel Cadé (2004), for instance, credits this corpus with the creation of more complex characters of North African (immigrant) origin: from shadows in the backdrop of colonial films, they have now become the focus of films by directors of various origins.

Female characters and directors of North African immigrant descent have also gained visibility and made their voice heard since the mid-1990s with films such as *Souviens-toi de moi* (Zaïda Ghorab-Volta 1995), *Sous les pieds des femmes* (Rachida Krim 1997), and Yamina Benguigui's groundbreaking documentary triptych, *Mémoires d'immigrés: L'héritage maghrébin* (1997). The emphasis is not on youth alone either, and directors have made narrative forays into their parents' past — rehabilitating their heretofore neglected and despised experiences as poor migrants — in films such as *Vivre au paradis* (Bourlem Guerdjou 1999) and *Inch'Allah dimanche* (Yamina Benguigui 2001). For Cadé, as for Bosséno earlier, this vein of filmmaking upholds integration in France. The return to the country of origin, for instance, is not depicted as a viable nor a desirable option for the protagonists in these films, despite the hurdles — racism, xenophobia, unemployment — they describe but also tend to minimize.

In 2005 Carrie Tarr published the first comprehensive study of this corpus. Based on articles written from 1992 to 2003, Tarr's work documents the history of "*Beur* and *banlieue* filmmaking" from "the margins to the mainstream" (2005, 3). Although Tarr agrees with Bosséno and Cadé that integration is undeniably taking place in "this particular period of French/film history" (2005, 12), her book mostly focuses on the complex interactions of *Beur* filmmakers and characters with mainstream discourses on Frenchness. Her main concern is to analyze how the films gathered under the categories of *Beur* and *banlieue* cinema (or filmmaking as she puts it [11]) negotiate the pressures of French republican, universalist ideology and to what extent they can represent and address questions of ethnic, gender, and social differences on screen.

Tarr's cogent analysis of the main themes and challenges faced by the filmmakers of North African descent could not, given the publication date of *Reframing Difference* (2005), take into account some significant developments in the recognition of the cinema made by and about descendants of Maghrebi immigrants as part of mainstream production in the first decade of the new millennium. Our collective volume not only enters into conversation with *Reframing Difference*, but it also builds on the foundation laid by that monograph to emphasize the multiple ways in which the categories of *Beur* and *banlieue* cinema are both being expanded and tested. In what follows, we present a brief overview of the sociohistorical conditions in which these films have been produced in order to contextualize how this cinema has become established while, at the same time, the categories used to define it continue to be contested.

Enduring Specificities or Persistent Stigmatization?

The North African migration cycle saw its heyday during the so-called *Trente Glorieuses* (the period that approximately corresponded to the post–Second World War economic boom that lasted until the oil crisis of 1973–74). That cycle has long since ended, and the generation of parent-migrants is now aging and dying. Yet recounting, shaping, and circulating that generation's stories and memories play a crucial role in contemporary negotiations and conflicts over the place and role of their descendants within France. Indeed, this cinematic production demonstrates that actors and directors of Maghrebi descent have moved beyond being mere subjects by becoming the authors and producers of their own history. This volume posits that it is their specific history of (post)colonial migration and its contested legacy that distinguish these filmmakers, actors, and characters. As such, *Screening Integration* builds upon the notion that ethnicity is not based on essentialist differences between children of immigrants and "majority French" but rather it is a relational, shifting concept, informed and shaped by a historical — legacy, in this case that of colonialism, and by the "set of social relations and discourses" that cultural producers have experienced in France as a result of this specific history (Tarr 2005, 13).

If the present volume focuses specifically on migration from North Africa in its different forms, there are several reasons why the North African experience in France, while by no means unique, remains distinct. Descendants of Maghrebi immigrants, after three or four generations in some cases, are still being set apart from mainstream French society, as opposed to offspring of

European migrants, who often become "invisible." Many factors can help explain this situation. For one, migrations from North Africa constitute the largest and oldest mass emigration from France's colonies.[6] Algeria's conquest started in 1830 and Algerian workers began to work in France at the end of the 19th century (Sayad 1999, 103; Zehraoui 1999, 121–22). Migration trends intensified with the First World War, when colonial labor was needed in the armament industry and on the battlefront. These trends continued after the Second World War, during the *Trente Glorieuses*, and even increased during the Algerian War and after Algerian independence. During the colonial period, the systematic displacement and internment of the Algerian rural population in "camps de regroupement" by the French army marked the beginning of a large-scale rural exodus that made Algerians available for migration. This military operation was designed to "protect" the locals from the FLN (Front de Libération Nationale, the insurgent group that led Algeria to independence) and to cut the latter off from much-needed resources. However, it exacerbated what colonization had started with the spoliation of Algerian lands for European settlers, making Algerians readily available as labor for the metropolitan market (Bourdieu and Sayad 1964). As such, contrary to popularly held beliefs, immigration from North Africa was anything but a voluntary and purely economically motivated migration.

In this case, colonial racism and the long unacknowledged trauma of the Algerian War, along with the mostly unexamined and paradoxical imperial heritage of the Republic (Shepard 2006, 269–72), explain in part why the descendants of North African immigrants are still considered to be illegitimate citizens of France. Moreover, the fact that North African migration to the ex-colonial metropole continued, despite the newly gained independence of the countries of origin, further blurred the lines between former colonial subjects and potential new citizens, thus increasing cultural anxieties about the status and place of the formerly colonized and their heirs.

Although Polish, Italian, Spanish, and Portuguese migrants have experienced difficulties similar to those of migrants from North Africa (the nostalgic yearning for home, as well as forms of economic exclusion and spatial segregation in [sub]urban areas), as Marie-Claude Blanc-Chaléard notes, the "context of integration" was markedly different (1999, 167). Large numbers of colonial migrants arrived and settled down as the period of unbridled economic prosperity of the *Trente Glorieuses* reached its peak. Therefore, unlike the Italians for instance, they did not fully benefit from the integrationist effects of prosperity, and suffered most from the consequences of the economic crisis in the 1970s (Blanc-Chaléard 1999, 170), with the accompanying crumbling of working-class-based political associations and organizations, which had fostered the assimilation of previous migratory groups. Furthermore, male colonial migrants were sought after as a temporary labor force, while their families were deemed less desirable than those of European migrants who arrived during the Industrial Revolution and in a period of demographic decline. The wives and children of those earlier migrants had been welcome as cheap labor and potential soldiers, respectively (Blanc-Chaléard 1999, 168). On the contrary, in the context of the demographic expansion of the baby boom, (ex)colonial migrants were deterred from bringing their families by strict regulations on housing and by implicit but nevertheless clear preferences given to intra-European immigration, for migrants from the (ex)colonies were considered to be "subjects of an inferior race" (Blanc-Chaléard 1999, 168). Consequently, in the wake of the *regroupement familial* policy of 1973, far from formalizing the settlement of North Africans and their children in France, the new official stance created an artificial split between *immigration de travail* (work-based immigration) and *immigration familiale* (family-based immigration). This distinction has further contributed to singling out the descendants of North African migrants and designating them as undesirable, or *inassimilables*. In their specific case, the relationship of domination to which all immigrants are subjected through pressures to assimilate was exacerbated by the colonial heritage. More recently, in the aftermath of the September 11, 2001, attacks, resistance toward Islam, already part of an enduring colonial racist rhetoric, has been reactivated and even intensified as conflicts in the Middle East often elicit new transnational affiliations and identifications — of a political, social, and religious nature.[7]

Going Beyond *Beur* and *Banlieue* Filmmaking

However foundational the particular historical background described above might be, it does not entirely define or encompass the cultural productions that originate from the migrant experience. No doubt North African immigration has a strong identity — and characters, directors, and actors testify to their specific history and experience of migration and (re)settlement. Yet the films studied here also emphasize the fact that North Africans in France share social and cultural trajectories with migrants of other origins, such as sub-Saharan Africans and their descendants, as well as with French citizens of working-class backgrounds. Insofar as they experience similar kinds of urban segregation, and religious and cultural discrimination, the descendants of North Africans and of migrants from other regions face similar obstacles to making their voices heard. In this respect, the films in question create diverse portraits of working-class cultures and neighborhoods in contemporary France, which include, but also go beyond, particular cultural specificities. Furthermore, in the 1990s, the descendants of North African immigrants consolidated the significant symbolic and political capital gained in the 1980s, which allowed them to explore new ways of belonging while continuing to express difference — cultural or other — and thus trace new paths to defining and inhabiting Frenchness.

In this light, *Screening Integration* aims to foreground the contribution of such filmmakers, actors, and producers in order to show the extent to which their works represent both an integration that is presented as desired by all concerned and yet is sometimes hindered by invisible barriers that still separate this group from the majority population in France. This volume also seeks to demonstrate how the concerns of artists of Maghrebi origin have moved beyond some of the most basic issues surrounding immigration. Indeed, for the descendants of Maghrebi immigrants, the majority of whom are legally French citizens, many of the questions posed by their immigrant parents (such as the option of returning to their homeland) do not have the same resonance or applicability.

Therefore, it is not surprising that actors and filmmakers of North African descent have moved away from topics and characters strictly related to their socioethnic and historical heritage. The career of director Rachid Bouchareb (see the chapter by Alec Hargreaves) and that of the actor Sami Bouajila, who has become mainstream enough to play both ethnically marked and unmarked characters (see the chapter by Murray Pratt and Denis Provencher), provide prime examples of this move. A similar opening of the field is visible when we take into account the films by North African émigré directors (see the chapters by Patricia Geesey and Will Higbee) or directors of non–North African heritage (see the chapters by Michel Cadé, Pratt and Provencher, Carrie Tarr, and Darren Waldron) such as Philippe Faucon and Thomas Gilou.[8] All these directors demonstrate that migrants and their offspring play an integral part in the construction of contemporary France. Foregrounding their experiences helps us better understand current French public debates. In this respect, integration is indeed being reframed and recast, as the contributors to this volume demonstrate in many ways.

Revisiting Integration

In paying attention to the politically charged history of the term "integration" in France, it should be noted that this term is not any more neutral than "assimilation," and has indeed become a highly polemical and politicized term in France.[9] Although it is said to measure belonging, as these films testify, integration is a process fraught with paradoxes and contradictions. Moreover, in the French context, integration has not always been the privileged (political) term of choice for describing the situation of immigrants. Alec Hargreaves has noted that the French state used the terms "insertion" and "assimilation" before preferring the current term, "integration" (Hargreaves 1995, 195–96).[10] Indeed, assimilationist policies were especially promoted during the heyday of the French colonial empire of the Third Republic (1870–1940) as part of the ideology of the *mission civilisatrice* (civilizing mission), and continued de facto in the post–Second World War period, during the *Trente Glorieuses* and beyond. The assimilationist model persisted despite the growing visibility of the immigrant population of non-European heritage in hexagonal France, but it nevertheless came under pressure to undergo significant changes to better accommodate the cultural specificities of the newer populations.

For instance, should immigrants abandon their cultural and religious practices in order to espouse a so-called French identity? In an attempt to respond to such questions, successive French administrations began to shift from a policy of assimilation to a more self-reflexive approach often labeled "integration," a term that reflected a growing public consciousness of cultural diversity and the right to cultural difference, even though the latter would still be subsumed within the so-called universalist principles of the Republic. Moving from thinking in terms of assimilation to integration also shifted the burden of adaptation from the state to migrants and their offspring. It initiated an ambiguous blame game whereby the latter have to want to integrate, and have to demonstrate this desire endlessly through their words and actions, despite renewed hurdles and public debates that point to their perceived persistent foreignness (Sayad 1999). The official espousal of this new approach was signaled by the creation of institutions such as the Haut Conseil à l'Intégration (HCI [High Council on Integration]) in 1989 by then prime minister Michel Rocard (of the Socialist Party) to observe and report to the prime minister the state of integration of foreigners and French citizens of "foreign origin" in France.[11] Therefore, although integration aids the nation-building project in that it aims to create citizens from immigrants, over the last decades of the twentieth century, promoting such a policy has also forced successive French governments to redefine the relationship between universalist republican precepts and differences based on class, ethnicity, sexuality, and gender. Nevertheless, while the creation of the HCI represents, for instance, a concerted effort to move away from the assimilationist-style approach of the 1960s and 1970s, the current policies on integration have been critiqued as new avatars of assimilation by several vocal activists who emerged in the wake of the 1980s *Beur* movement (Battegay and Boubekeur 1993; Bouamama 1994).

What becomes apparent is that as polemical as the hegemonic discourse on the subject in the political realm might be (Weil 2002), it rarely includes perspectives of those who are the subject of the integrative measures taken by the state. As open as newer state structures such as the HCI might seem toward instituting and ensuring equality among all citizens of France, their policies often remain formal injunctions. For example, following a July 2006 law, new immigrants applying for long-term residency in the family-based category are now required to sign a Contrat d'accueil et d'intégration (Agreement for Settlement and Integration), which stipulates that new residents have to agree to French republican notions including *laïcité* and equality with respect to male-female relationships (La documentation française 2007).[12] In this light, a focus upon such institutional responses to integration-related issues tells only a partial story.

The contributors of *Screening Integration*, by focusing on how cinematic fiction portrays the many ways in which individuals and groups of Maghrebi descent perceive and experience integration, are able to explore the interactions between on-screen representation of social experiences and political discourses, as well as individual and collective interpretations of what being integrated can mean. Although the films studied here document contemporary social issues, we recognize that cinema is not to be taken as a direct mirror reflection of the times.

Furthermore, whether films are deliberate in delivering messages or present issues in a tentative or less explicit fashion, whether mainstream or independent, they are products of a complex process of negotiation between various competing, and sometimes contradictory, demands. They may vacillate between the need to ensure viability through commercial success and the desire to make the voices of non-mainstream French citizens heard. Or these films might hesitate between the need to address the concerns of various marginalized groups and the impetus to uphold the logic of French republican discourse and ideology as inherently viable. In this, as realist as some of the fiction films analyzed in this volume might be, and although some of them might employ documentary techniques (voice-over commentary in Chibane's *Hexagone*) or an amateur cast (Kechiche's *L'esquive* or Ameur-Zaïmèche's *Wesh wesh, qu'est-ce qui se passe?* [2001]), they nevertheless have to wrestle with the various competing interests enumerated above.

The socio-realist agenda of numerous directors of films studied here stems mostly from the desire to represent hitherto neglected experiences and to compensate for the deficit of images about immigrants and their families, their everyday lives, and the spaces they inhabit. Yet cinema also uses the tools of fiction and representation to explore what could be and should be, a projection into the future, either idealized or feared. Indeed, through the fiction of narrative constructs, complex personal and social realities are being cinematically fashioned: they do not give viewers access to an unmitigated truth of the times. Rather, as Michel Cadé rightly notes, films afford glimpses, and open windows, into how the people of a specific time period consider and represent their times (2004, 111).

The title of this volume thus resonates in at least four different registers. First, and most evidently, *Screening Integration* refers to cinema as a medium for expression of social and political concerns. Second, by inherently screening *for* integration in films, authors in this volume choose to explore the different ways in which the concept of integration operates in contemporary France. Third, these chapters highlight how integration is itself a screening process that can either exclude or include, and through which differences are created, maintained, and/or displaced. By recasting the politics and received narratives of Maghrebi immigration, the films discussed in this volume attempt to make visible the different screens (political, social, cultural) that have hindered the very integration promoted by the French republican ideology. Finally, it must be noted that the integrationist ideology that seeps into most discourses on immigration and integration in France cannot but permeate the productions of filmmakers who have grown up to become professionals in that country. Consequently, the ultimate screen — that is to say, the ideology that animates such a process—sometimes remains not only untouched but is also (inadvertently) reproduced, as Cadé, Durmelat, Rosello, Tarr, and Swamy argue in this volume, by the films analyzed here.

The Ever-Recurring Naming Game

One of the objectives of *Screening Integration* is to underscore how, despite enduring obstacles, the economic, religious, cultural, and symbolic integration of this group and its members into the French mainstream is well under way. Yet as the texts written by contributors to the present volume testify, the labeling of Maghrebi immigrants and their descendants remains a thorny issue. Indeed, although at the conclusion of his essay in this volume Michel Cadé states that "there will not be a third generation," critics today are still caught between the need to define and name the specificity of the social group on which they focus, and the desire to avoid repeating the stigmatization that comes with labels that always fall short of simply calling the sons and daughters of migrants "French."

To be sure, this brief overview is in part a reflection of the situation in France, where the label "French" does not always easily include the descendants of North African immigrants. So critics and scholars are left with the burden of finding terms and designations that allow as much flexibility as possible while reflecting the complexities and various sentiments of the people whom these denominations are meant to designate. To this end, each contributor of this volume explains his or her use of terms. However, a few words here to cast light on the complex naming game will help us elucidate the nature of the challenge.

Although the term *Beur* is less than satisfactory for various reasons, including the fact that some of its designees do not accept it (Reynaert 1993; Hargreaves 1997; Durmelat 1998), it still circulates today in the media and among those it designates, along with other, sometimes regional, related terms, such as *Rabza* or *Rebeu*. So *Beur*, although dated, remains a highly recognizable and practical term. It is short and deceptively easy to use. Scholars have often used it within quotation marks or have chosen to italicize it both to indicate a critical distance as well as to avoid lengthy periphrases that can sometimes make for awkward syntax in English.

On that note, expressions such as "children of Maghrebi heritage," "descendants of Maghrebi immigrants," or "French citizens of Maghrebi origin" to translate the French *issus de l'immigration* or *d'origine maghrébine* have been used in an attempt to be more descriptive and to avoid terms such as *Beur* that are sometimes perceived as more loaded. However, these periphrases nevertheless beg the question of how long such qualifiers are necessary before a French citizen's particular genealogy no longer needs to be taken into account. In other words, while some citizens of recent immigrant heritage acquire an unquestioned full status as French citizens, requiring no further qualification (due to the lack of stigmatization of their perceived ethnicity), others, such as those of Maghrebi descent, have an additional, unacknowledged yet verbalized hurdle to negotiate in order to claim full citizenship. Therefore, terms such as *issus de l'immigration* are misleading insofar as they are mostly used to designate descendants of Maghrebi origin, thereby glossing over several other (earlier or concurrent) migrations, such as those from eastern Europe, Italy, or Portugal, all of which, as Gérard Noiriel has shown, have been integral to the formation of contemporary France (1988, 1996). Other geographically based euphemisms such as *les jeunes des banlieues* (suburban youths) or *les jeunes des quartiers* (youths from the housing projects) replace the ethnic marker by a (sub)urban stigmatization that clearly identifies disenfranchised, ethnic minority youths.

In the new millennium, the term "Maghrebi-French" has gained currency mostly in British and American scholarship and evidently mirrors the American-style hyphenated identity that indicates the dual heritage of the French-born descendants of Maghrebi immigrants. However, as Lisa Lowe (among others) has argued (1996), such a hyphenation can itself be problematic. The choice, although practical, tends to conflate two national histories and social realities, which may share commonalities but are inevitably different. Hyphenated identities are not recognized as such in the French public space, where the term "new French" has been used in some instances (Brouard and Tiberj 2005). Other social commentators systematically refuse all the qualifications and epithets that are habitually used to designate (and often stigmatize) them. For instance, *Le Monde* journalist Mustapha Kessous writes: "On dit de moi que je suis d'origine étrangère, un beur, une racaille, un islamiste, un délinquant, un sauvageon, un 'beurgeois,' un enfant issu de l'immigration. . . . Mais jamais un Français, Français tout court" [They say that I am of foreign extraction, a *Beur*, scum, an Islamist, a delinquent, an uncouth youth, a *Beurgeois*, a child of immigration. . . . But never French, just French] (Kessous 2009). On the one hand, his desire to be "Français tout court" [just French] is a clear protest against the persistent resistance to consider descendants of Maghrebi immigrants to be truly French. On the other hand, it also appeals to, and thus perpetuates, the republican dream of a national society in which ethnic differences are considered to be irrelevant to interactions in the public sphere.

The contributors to this volume wrestle with some of the same underlying issues as the filmmakers, actors, and characters of the films analyzed here: how determinant is the ethnic factor in defining the identity of these films? Ought we not to recognize that in many ways the films are already a part of the national production and distribution circuits anyway? For the moment it is clear that we, as scholars, have trouble engaging with these films without giving them a label or grouping them as a corpus. Although some, such as Kessous, might argue that it is time to just call them French, such a move could be called integrationist and seen as absorbing all differences under a mythical national umbrella. Therefore, at present, we still find ourselves hanging between such unsatisfactory notions as *Beur* cinema and French cinema.[13] Yet we cannot deny that this filmic production is part of the history of French cinema at large and that it also contributes to the production and development of contemporary French culture and history. Therefore, in this volume each essay defines its use of any label not only to contextualize it but also to avoid the reification that would result in a homogenization brought about by an editorial privileging of one (or more) term(s). In this way, the provisionality of any defining term used by each author is maintained.

Although the approaches used in this volume to analyze filmmaking by and about descendants of Maghrebi immigrants in France are varied, the contributions can nevertheless be loosely grouped. The opening chapters, by Alec Hargreaves and Michel Cadé, give us an overview of this cinematic production over the last three decades. Hargreaves argues for a vision wider than that indicated by either the terms *Beur* or *banlieue*. His reading articulates how the cinema made by those he calls Maghrebi-French filmmakers can be best understood, not as stretched within a bipolar, and still less a binational, perspective. Rather than be torn between France and Algeria or between France and Morocco, Hargreaves argues that this cinema takes a "glocal" outlook. That is to say, these films identify on the one hand with local spaces (the *banlieues*) and on the other hand with global space and influences that culturally, commercially, and politically transcend national spaces. For his part, Cadé surveys this production to consider the place of religion (Islam) on the French (national) screen. If Islam is not as present as one might expect in a cinema that "ought to" make room for it, Cadé suggests that it is as though directors of Maghrebi origin downplayed its presence, because they have internalized the standard French interpretation of it as a marker of cultural difference, and that internalization and consequent effacement are corollaries of their mimetic desire to integrate.

The next two chapters focus on a new brand of road movies that redefine what it means to return home and put pressure on the assumed polarity between home and host countries. Will Higbee's contribution studies films that explore the trope of the myth of return — a long-held desire to reintegrate into the society of origin, especially prevalent in the generation of immigrant parents — as experienced by later generations, whose metropolitan French upbringing affords them a certain distance from the country of origin of their parents. Focusing on *Ten'ja* (Legzouli 2004), *Bled number one* (Ameur-Zaïmeche 2006), and *Exils* (Gatlif 2004), Higbee suggests that these films reappropriate the road-movie genre in order to reflect on the meaning of displacement and belonging, and ultimately to allow space for intercultural exchange between the Maghreb and France through the figure of the traveler with North African roots.

Belonging, we discover in Hakim Abderrezak's essay, does not necessarily imply integration into metropolitan France. His close reading of Djamel Bensalah's 2005 comedy, *Il était une fois dans l'oued*, not only provides a springboard for reflection on the relationship between France and Algeria but also puts to the test clichés on North Africans, (return) migrations, and France's particular, quasi-obsessive integrative impetus. In a comic reversal of roles, the film's protagonist is a Frenchman who, drawn to Algerian culture, crosses the Mediterranean southward as a clandestine immigrant and claims to be an Algerian to achieve his dream of becoming an Arab grocer. Abderrezak's reflections on Bensalah's film and its ambivalent use of stereotypes and caricatures thus reframe long-standing discussions regarding immigration, integration, and citizenship.

If the films analyzed by Higbee and Abderrezak foreground the physical return to the Maghreb, collective memories and the retelling of the past are the focus of the next two chapters. Sylvie Durmelat puts into historical and political perspective the relative absence of the Algerian War of Independence in films by and about Maghrebi immigrants and their descendants. She highlights how these cinematic (re)visions of the war — from passing references to historical reenactments — not only propose a renewed understanding of the often-overlooked role of the Algerian migrants in the war, but also offer a corrective to both Algerian and French national histories of the war. Furthermore, she argues, cinematic commodifications of Algerian immigrants' war experiences invite viewers to both identify with immigrants, all the while stressing that they cannot be readily assimilated in an unquestioned French, or Algerian, national genealogy. Such cinematic (re)visions open the possibility of writing a transnational, French-Algerian history of the war, one that accounts for the continued (post)colonial entanglement of the two nations, for the memory of this war involves more than just the French (Re)public.

Mireille Rosello interrogates the treatment of that history through her critical analysis of the production and reception of Bouchareb's *Indigènes*, which sparked a general discussion of the role of Maghrebis in the Second World War. Her use of the term "event of memory" allows Rosello to go beyond reading *Indigènes* as a film about memory itself and/or about an historical event, as it purported to be. Instead, she interprets the film's release and reception as constituting a specific occasion when the construction of memory itself is rendered visible. She theorizes the distinction between the politics and the ethics of events of memory in order to analyze the relationship between one specific *event* of memory (a film, a speech, a new testimony) and what constitutes a given *moment* of memory (which determines the parameters of what can be debated).

Indigènes is not the only film that has incited debate on the image of the French nation. As Carrie Tarr and Geneviève Sellier explain in their respective essays, films about the French state school system and its ethnically diverse students have captured the public's attention and provided much fodder for debate about that institution, because of its status as a privileged site of nation (re)building. Tarr's essay assesses the extent to which films that represent the French secondary school system question an education based on the ideals of republican universalism and therefore "indifferent to difference." Both chapters highlight the increasing awareness of France as a multiethnic space, in which the Maghrebi component is but one, albeit significant, element (see their discussion of *L'esquive* and the 2008 film *Entre les murs* by Laurent Cantet). Sellier's analysis of Jean-Paul Lilienfeld's 2008 film, *La journée de la jupe*, renders this shift explicit. Her focus on this film in particular draws our attention to the ways in which gender, ethnicity, and religious tensions form a nexus around which that cinematic school drama constructs its response to current-day French politics of integration. Reading how the film attempts to relaunch the career of Isabelle Adjani — a well-known French star whose Maghrebi-German heritage is not so well known — allows Sellier to demonstrate how the (token multicultural) protagonist she plays becomes a vehicle for a islamophobic, supposedly feminist, integrationist message that borders on racism. Although the film's seemingly feminist message purports to uphold women's freedom to dress as they please in the face of the violent and threatening machismo of youths of nonmajority French heritage, Sellier suggests that it produces a reductive and narrow vision of female agency and reinforces stereotypical racist perceptions about (young) men of African origin.

Space — whether public or private, intimate or open — and its feminine appropriation are highlighted in Patricia Geesey's essay. For her, cinematic space is defined by the specific ways in which female characters of Maghrebi descent circulate and navigate various visual and diegetic spaces and are able (or unable) to negotiate borders defined by traditions, social exclusion, and class and gender differences. She underscores how the increased mobility of female characters, and their ability to turn these spaces into places to inhabit as their own, embody their undeniable acquisition of power and agency.

Whereas Geesey is concerned with feminizing or feminized cinematic space, Darren Waldron's chapter on the intersection of sexuality and ethnicity in Liria Bégéja's *Change-moi ma vie* (2001) and Amal Bedjaoui's *Un fils* (2003) expands the notion of gendered space through an exploration of transgendered and transvestite identities, and the "queering" of the ethnic on the French screen. Using the notion of gender performance, Waldron's essay examines the extent to which cross-dressing protagonists imbricate both masculine and feminine codes of gendered behavior and the inflections of ethnicity on their performed identities. In a similar vein, Murray Pratt and Denis Provencher posit the possibility of a new French masculine belonging through an examination of Sami Bouajila's career as an actor since the early 1990s. By situating the sexualities and sensitivities of Bouajila's characters within the specific sociocultural geographies evoked by films in which he stars, their analysis suggests that Bouajila's roles allow for new reconfigurations of the image of the *garçon arabe* as a sign of integration of the (young) *Beur* male into the French national family.

Whereas as Pratt and Provencher focus on the career of a single actor in order to highlight how the integration of characters of Maghrebi origin also implies a reframing of our understanding of masculinity, in the volume's final essay, Vinay Swamy examines the work of one director, Malik Chibane, to comprehend the evolution of his approach to the integrative project of the French Republic. Chibane is remarkable because of his consistent public presence, over almost two decades, as filmmaker and commentator on radio and television. In particular, by focusing on what Chibane has retroactively named *La trilogie urbaine* — comprising his films *Hexagone* (1994), *Douce France* (1995), and *Voisins, voisines* (2005) — this chapter examines the ideological underpinnings that undergird Chibane's perspective on the identity-formation and integration of descendants of Maghrebi (and other) immigrants in suburban France. Spanning over two decades, the work of this director indicates that the stories of these migrants and their offspring — continually (re)told — are undeniably integral to the narratives that make up contemporary France.

As the chapters collectively demonstrate, the scope of this body of films includes a rich multiplicity of genres, locales, and means of production. The films foreground varied subjects, ranging from the suburban to the glocal, from the myth of return to comic reversals of home and host countries, and from an occluded history to explicit explorations of a contested past. Relatively homogeneous depictions of the parents' "immigrant" generation have now branched out to nuanced representations of their children's performance of gender and sexual identities; the school as a space for mythical assimilation has become a cinematic site where ethnic, social, and gender differences are played out. All these transformations are integral to the filmmaking by and about descendants of Maghrebi immigrants, whose stories are now being heard and have the capacity to initiate change in the way the French perceive themselves and tell their collective history. By shedding light on such cinematic moments, these essays demonstrate that screening the ongoing process of integration plays a key role in recasting Maghrebi immigration in contemporary France.

Notes

1. The title of this volume refers deliberately and specifically to the Maghreb, although, following usage in the French language, we do use the adjectives "North African" and "Maghrebi" interchangeably in this introduction. The latter term designates a specific region within North Africa, located in western northern Africa, south of the Mediterranean, and known in Arabic as *Maghrib* (West). In English, "the Maghreb" technically refers to five countries: Morocco, Algeria, Tunisia, Libya, Mauritania, and the disputed

territory of Western Sahara. In French, the *Maghreb* is usually more narrowly understood to designate the former French colonies of Morocco, Algeria, and Tunisia, north of the Atlas Mountains, and in contrast with the territories to the east, known as the *Machrek* (sometimes transliterated from the Arabic as *Mashreq* or *Machreq*). Given the long (post) colonial history of the Maghreb, it is, as we understand it in this volume, not just a geographical region that comprises Morocco, Algeria, and Tunisia. It designates as well a political and cultural territory whose borders are also shaped by historical phenomena such as immigration to France.

2. Created by law in 1946, the CNC or the Centre national du cinéma et de l'image animée (the National Center of Cinematography and the Moving Image, formerly known as the Centre National de la Cinématographie) funds and promotes French cinema and is run under the aegis of the Ministry of Culture. Since funding Benguigui's documentary, the FAS (Fonds d'Action Sociale pour les travailleurs immigrés et leurs familles) was renamed Fonds d'Action et de Soutien pour l'Intégration et la Lutte contre les Discriminations (FASILD) in 2001, and in 2006 it became the Agence nationale pour la cohésion sociale et l'égalité des chances (ACSÉ). This state agency uses part of the taxes collected from immigrant workers to fund and sponsor a variety of cultural and social projects aimed at and/or organized by migrants, their children, and their associations to promote integration, fight discrimination, and prevent (juvenile) delinquency.

3. Unless otherwise stated, French box office figures are from the Council of Europe's Lumière database on admissions of films released in Europe, available online at http://lumiere.obs.coe.int.

4. SFR is a union of filmmakers that actively contributes to the CNC's decisions to fund films (*l'agrément*). It also codirects the BLOC (Bureau de Liaison des Organisations du Cinéma [Liaison Office for Cinema Organizations], which promotes cinema as an industry) and actively participates in the efforts of other professional organizations in the film industry such as the FERA (Fédération européenne des réalisateurs de l'audiovisuel [European Federation of Audiovisual Artists]) and the Coalition française pour la diversité culturelle, a coalition that promotes cultural diversity.

5. Bosseno's 1992 article, published in English in *Popular European Cinema*, is the translated and expanded version of a shorter text that came out in *CinémAction* in 1990.

6. Migration from North Africa reached its peak during the 1960s and 1970s, and was only to a limited extent directly organized by the French state. In contrast, immigration from Martinique or Guadeloupe (two of the oldest French territories, colonized well before the French Revolution) to mainland France only began much later, in the 1960s. In fact, it was initiated by the state with the creation in 1963 of a specific administrative entity for the Caribbean called the BUMIDOM (Bureau pour le développement des migrations dans les départements d'outre-mer [Office for Migration from the Overseas Departments]) after the departmentalization of 1945 officially turned colonial subjects from those islands into citizens with full voting rights.

7. On the subject of Islam and colonial Algeria, see Anna Bozzo (2005); the recurring debates on the *hijab* have been thoroughly documented by Françoise Gaspard and Farhad Khosrokhavar (1995) and John R. Bowen (2007).

8. Whereas Kechiche, Chibane, and Bouchareb, among others, were either born in France or immigrated as children with their parents, émigré directors such as Merzak Allouache chose as adults to move to France for political reasons. Because the latter were socialized and came of age in North African countries and not in France, they bring to the screen a different sensibility, perspective, and capital of experiences. Besides, contributors also include directors such as Thomas Gilou and Philippe Faucon (who was born in Morocco) who are neither descendants of Maghrebi immigrants nor exiles but whose subject choice and focus on the colonial heritage in France make their films germane to our discussion. For more on directors in exile, see the chapter by Will Higbee; for more on Gilou and Faucon, see the chapter by Michel Cadé.

9. As Sylvie Thénault (2005) remarks, the term "integration" entered into circulation during the Algerian War of Independence to refer to the French government's efforts and projects to use economic development, industrialization, mass schooling, infrastructure building, and so on to bring Algeria and Algerians to the same level of development as metropolitan France. The objective was to turn Algerians away from the Front de Libération Nationale and entice them to favor Charles de Gaulle's proposed "association" with France, rather than choosing independence.

10. The term "insertion" implied primarily the introduction of new immigrants into the economic context, without taking into consideration, for example, the cultural context of either the immigrants' countries of origin or of France. By contrast, "assimilation" implied an obliteration of immigrant cultures to refashion the individual as "purely" French. Based on the ideology of assimilation, the crucible model of forging new French men and women prevailed over much of the twentieth century (Noiriel 1988).

11. This formal distancing from earlier assimilationist policies is clear in the HCI's opening remarks of its 2001 report, which explicitly acknowledge France's assimilationist logic in the following terms:

Jusqu'à une période récente, il paraissait entendu que le problème de l'intégration des Français d'origine étrangère ou des étrangers vivant en France ne se posait plus. Les lois républicaines suffisaient pour leur assurer lentement mais sûrement la plénitude de leurs droits sociaux dans la communauté française, la seule qui soit reconnue. [Until recently, it was understood that integrating French citizens of foreign descent or foreigners living in France was no longer a problem. Republican laws were sufficient to ensure that they acquired, slowly but surely, their full social rights within the French (national) community, the only community to enjoy official recognition.] (HCI 2001)

12. Furthermore, the HCI goes so far as to recommend a pragmatic approach, including twelve criteria (using twenty-three statistical parameters) by which to measure the extent to which immigrants and their descendants have integrated into French society (Cour des Comptes 2004). The perhaps unintended effect of such an approach that codifies integration is that it creates a problematic teleology, suggesting that those who integrate will progressively become more "French," even though the very concept of Frenchness, as the HCI itself acknowledges, is constantly evolving ("toute culture évolue et . . .

il n'existe pas de culture définitivement figée" [all cultures evolve . . . there is none that remains fixed forever] [HCI 2004, 112]) as it takes into account the different sociocultural influences of the day.

13. On the subject of labeling this cinema as *Beur*, see Alison J. Murray Levine (2008).

References

Austin, Guy. 1996. *Contemporary French Cinema*. Manchester: Manchester University Press.

Battegay, Alain, and Ahmed Boubekeur. 1993. *Les images publiques de l'immigration*. Paris: CIEMI/L'Harmattan.

Blanc-Chaléard, Marie-Claude. 1999. "L'intégration des Italiens hier; quels enseignements pour aujourd'hui?" In *Immigration et intégration, l'état des savoirs*, ed. Philippe Dewitte, 165–72. Paris: La Découverte.

Bosséno, Christian. 1990. "Un cinéma de transition." In "Cinémas métis, de Hollywood aux films beurs," ed. Guy Hennebelle and Roland Schneider. *CinémAction* 56:146–47.

———. 1992. "Immigrant Cinema: National Cinema — The Case of Beur Film." In *Popular European Cinema*, ed. Ricard Dyer and Ginette Vincendeau, 47–57. London: Routledge.

Bouamama, Said. 1994. *Dix ans de marche des beurs, chronique d'un mouvement avorté*. Paris: Desclée de Brouwer.

Bourdieu, Pierre, and Abdelmalek Sayad. 1964. *Le déracinement: La crise de l'agriculture traditionnelle*. Paris: Les Éditions de Minuit.

Bowen, John R. 2007. *Why the French Don't Like Headscarves: Islam, the State and Public Space*. Princeton: Princeton University Press.

Bozzo, Anna. 2005. "Islam et république: Une longue histoire de méfiance." In *La fracture coloniale: La société française au prisme de l'héritage colonial*, ed. Pascal Blanchard, Nicolas Bancel, and Sandrine Lemaire, 77–84. Paris: La Découverte.

Brouard, Sylvain, and Vincent Tiberj. 2005. *Français comme les autres? Les citoyens d'origine maghrébine, africaine et turque*. Paris: Presses de la Fondation Nationale des Sciences Politiques.

Cadé, Michel. 2004. "Une représentation en éclats: Les Maghrébins dans le cinéma français." In *Maghrébins de France*, ed. Mohand Kellil, 111–34. Toulouse: Privat.

Cour des Comptes. 2004. "L'accueil des immigrants et l'intégration des populations issues de l'immigration." Cour des Comptes Report, November. http://www.ccomptes.fr/fr/CC/documents/RPA/AccueilImmigrants.pdf (accessed September 10, 2009).

Dhoukar, Hedi. 1990. "Les thèmes du cinéma beur." In "Cinémas métis, de Hollywood aux films beurs," ed. Guy Hennebelle and Roland Schneider. *CinémAction* 56:152–60.

La documentation française. 2007. "Le contrat d'accueil et d'intégration: Un parcours obligatoire, condition d'une installation durable." July 3. http://www.vie-publique.fr/actualite/dossier/integration/contrat-accueil-integration-parcours-obligatoire-condition-installation-durable.html (accessed October 7, 2009).

Durmelat, Sylvie. 1998. "Petite histoire du mot beur: Ou comment prendre la parole quand on vous la prête." *French Cultural Studies* 9:191–207.

Fahdel, Abbas. 1990. "Une esthétique beur?" In "Cinémas métis, de Hollywood aux films beurs," ed. Guy Hennebelle and Roland Schneider. *CinémAction* 56:140–51.

Frodon, Jean-Michel. 1998. *La projection nationale: Cinéma et nation.* Paris: Odile Jacob.

Gaspard, Françoise, and Farhad Khosrokhavar. 1995. *Le foulard et la république.* Paris: La Découverte.

Ghorab-Volta, Zaïda. 2007. "The Experience of a Maghrebi-French Filmmaker: The Case of Zaïda Ghorab-Volta." Trans. Martin O'Shaughnessy. *Cinéaste* 33 (1): 22–23.

Hargreaves, Alec. 1995. *Immigration, "Race," and Ethnicity in Contemporary France.* London: Routledge.

———. 1997. *Immigration and Identity in Beur Fiction: Voices from the North African Immigrant Community in France.* Providence RI: Berg. First edition 1991.

HCI. 2001. "Les parcours d'intégration." HCI Report, La documentation française. http://www.ladocumentationfrancaise.fr/rapports-publics/014000758/index.shtml (accessed September 12, 2009).

———. 2004. "Le contrat et l'intégration." HCI 2003 Report to the Prime Minister, La documentation française. http://www.ladocumentationfrancaise.fr/rapports-publics/044000033/index.shtml (accessed September 12, 2009).

Jousse, Thierry. 1995. "Le banlieue-film existe-t-il?" *Cahiers du cinéma* 492:37–39.

Kechiche, Abdelattif. 2007. "Interview avec Abdellatif Kechiche." Dossier de presse. http://www.lagraineetlemulet-lefilm.com/presse/index.html (accessed June 1, 2009).

Kessous, Musthapha. 2009. "Moi, Musthapha Kessous, journaliste au *Monde* et victime du racisme." *Le Monde*, September 23. http://www.lemonde.fr (accessed September 25, 2009).

Lowe, Lisa. 1996. *Immigrant Acts: On Asian American Cultural Politics.* Durham NC: Duke University Press.

Murray Levine, Alison J. 2008. "Mapping Beur Cinema in the New Millennium." *Journal of Film and Video* 60 (3–4) (Fall/Winter): 42–59.

Noiriel, Gérard. 1988. *Le creuset français: Histoire de l'immigration, XIXe–XXe siècles.* Paris: Seuil.

———. 1996. "French and the Foreigners." In *Realms of Memory: Rethinking the French Past*, ed. Lawrence D. Kritzman, trans. Arthur Goldhammer, 1:146–78. New York: Columbia University Press.

Powrie, Phil. 1997. *French Cinema in the 1980s: Nostalgia and the Crisis of Masculinity.* Oxford: Clarendon Press.

Raynaert, François. 1993. "Y a-t-il une culture beur?" *Le Nouvel Observateur*, December 2–8, 34.

Sayad, Abdlemalek. 1999. *La double absence: Des illusions de l'émigré aux souffrances de l'immigré.* Paris: Seuil.

Shepard, Todd. 2006. *The Invention of Decolonization: The Algerian War and the Remaking of France.* Ithaca NY: Cornell University Press.

Tarr, Carrie. 2005. *Reframing Difference: Beur and Banlieue Filmmaking in France.* Manchester: Manchester University Press.

Thénault, Sylvie. 2005. *Histoire de la guerre d'indépendance algérienne.* Paris: Flammarion.

Weil, Patrick. 2002. *Qu'est-ce qu'un Français? Histoire de la nationalité française depuis la Révolution*. Paris: Grasset.

Zehraoui, Ashène. 1999. "Les Algériens de l'immigration à l'installation." In *Immigration et intégration: L'état des savoirs*, ed. Philippe Dewitte, 121–27. Paris: La Découverte.

Filmography

Ameur-Zaimèche, Rabah, dir. *Wesh wesh, qu'est-ce qui se passe?*, 2002.

——, dir. *Bled number one*, 2006.

Bedjaoui, Amal, dir. *Un fils*, 2003.

Bégéja, Liria, dir. *Change-moi ma vie*, 2001.

Belghoul, Farida, dir. *C'est madame la France que tu préfères?*, 1981.

Benguigui, Yamina, dir. *Mémoires d'immigrés: L'héritage maghrébin*, 1997.

——, dir. *Inch'Allah dimanche*, 2001.

Bensalah, Djamel, dir. *Le ciel, les oiseaux et . . . ta mère!*, 1999.

——, dir. *Il était une fois dans l'oued*, 2005.

Bouchareb, Rachid, dir. *Indigènes*, 2006.

Cantet, Laurent, dir. *Entre les murs*, 2008.

Chibane, Malik, dir. *Hexagone*, 1994.

——, dir. *Douce France*, 1995.

——, dir. *Voisins, voisines*, 2005.

Collectif Mohamed, dir. *Ils ont tué Kader*, 1980.

Gatlif, Tony, dir. *Exils*, 2004.

Ghorab-Volta, Zaïda, dir. *Souviens-toi de moi*, 1995.

Guerdjou, Bourlem, dir. *Vivre au paradis*, 1999.

Kassovitz, Matthieu, dir. *La haine*, 1995.

Kechiche, Abdellatif, dir. *L'esquive*, 2004.

——, dir. *La graine et le mulet*, 2007.

Krim, Rachida, dir. *Sous les pieds des femmes*, 1997.

Legzouli, Hassan, dir. *Ten'ja*, 2004.

Lilienfeld, Jean-Paul, dir. *La journée de la jupe*, 2008.

Richet, Jean-François, dir. *Etats des lieux*, 1995.

1

FROM "GHETTOES" TO GLOBALIZATION

Situating Maghrebi-French Filmmakers

Alec G. Hargreaves

In the quarter century since second-generation Maghrebis in France first began making full-length feature films, there has been a vigorous and ongoing debate about how best to categorize and label them. The two most commonly used labels — "Beur" and "banlieue" cinema — are grounded respectively in ethnic and social markers that are specific to the multiethnic fabric of contemporary French society (Hargreaves 1999; Tarr 2005). Others, such as "postcolonial," "diasporic," "transnational," and "accented" cinema, embrace the work of filmmakers of diverse origins in many different countries and are not unique to filmmaking in France by directors of Maghrebi origin (Naficy 2001; Shohat and Stam 2003). There is disagreement not only over the relative merits of different labels but also over the corpus of work denoted by each of these terms. These disagreements stem in part from a lack of consensus concerning the most salient aspects of films when it comes to categorizing them. Are films best categorized and labeled with reference to the ethnic origins of their directors, their diegetic content (i.e., their story lines), or the location of production companies and/or target audiences? Depending on whether "Beur" cinema is understood to reference films that are *by*, *about*, or *for* an ethnically defined group, the corpus denoted by this label varies considerably. Similar variations mark the use of other terms employed in this debate. My purpose in this chapter is less to argue for or against particular labels (though I will endeavor to clarify these in the course of my analysis) than to situate more clearly the body of work at issue in this debate. While delineating the cinematic corpus discussed here with reference to the ethnicity of its directors, second-generation Maghrebis raised in France by immigrant parents, I will argue that diegetically and intertextually (i.e., in its allusions to and borrowings from other films) this body of work extends far beyond ethnic markers of this kind.

Ethnicity and Transnationalism

In this context, the second generation of Maghrebis is to be understood as that raised in France by immigrant parents from the Maghreb. Most second-generation Maghrebis were born in France while others were brought there at a young age by their parents. What they all have in common is that they were born of Maghrebi immigrants and spent their formative years in France, of which most are citizens. Their backgrounds and early experiences distinguish them both from Maghrebi émigrés who came to France as adults after spending their formative years on the other side of the Mediterranean and from majority ethnic French citizens with no ancestral connections with the Maghreb. In the work of émigré directors such as Merzak Allouache, their country of origin generally retains a foundational referentiality that distinguishes it from films by second-generation Maghrebis, for whom France is "home" in a more fundamental sense than for migrants who have settled there as adults. Thus films such as Allouache's *Salut cousin!* (1996) and *Chouchou* (2003) tend to be framed by the experiences of characters "discovering" France after migrating from the Maghreb whereas it is the southern, rather than the northern, side of the Mediterranean that appears unfamiliar in films such as *Cheb* (1991) and *Bled number one* (2006), directed by Rachid Bouchareb and Rabah Ameur-Zaïmeche, respectively, second-generation Maghrebis who spent their formative years in France. At the same time, the cultural heritage of second-generation Maghrebis and the discrimination that they often suffer in France distinguish them from their majority ethnic peers. Although, as we shall see, feature films directed by second-generation Maghrebis are by no means confined to a narrowly defined ethnically based optic, they draw on firsthand knowledge of minority ethnic cultures and experiences that are not directly shared by majority ethnic directors such as Mathieu Kassovitz and Eric Rochant, who in films such as *La haine* (1995) and *Vive la République* (1997), respectively, have featured second-generation Maghrebis among their characters. For analytical purposes it is therefore useful to distinguish movies directed by second-generation Maghrebis — also referred to here as Maghrebi-French — from those of North African émigrés or majority ethnic French directors, though there are of course many areas of overlap between them.

Most of the discussion surrounding the films made by second-generation Maghrebis has tended to situate their work in relation to the nationally bounded spaces of France on the one hand and, on the other hand, the formerly colonized territories of North Africa — Algeria, Morocco, and Tunisia — which gained independence from France half a century ago. This is true not only of analyses constructed around the categories of "Beur" and "banlieue" cinema but also in the deployment of other terms. To view these films in a "postcolonial" optic is to situate them with reference to France's former domination of North Africa, the resistance movements that led to the creation of independent nation-states, and the continuing legacy of that dynamic (Sherzer 1996; Chibane and Chibane 2003). Just as a "diasporic" vision situates expatriate migrant populations and their descendants in relation to a common homeland, located in the present case in North Africa, so "accented" movies are defined as those made by "deterritorialized" filmmakers "in dialogue with the home and host societies and their respective national cinemas" (Naficy 2001). Yet if the films made by second-generation Maghrebis may in many respects be viewed as "transnational" (Shohat and Stam 2003), this term needs to be understood in more senses than one. These films cut across the binary logic of nationally defined spaces not simply or even primarily in the sense that they have a foot in each of two national camps. No less importantly, from the very earliest of these films through to the present day, sub- and supra-national spaces have also been powerfully present. While national boundaries are undoubtedly salient, these films are in many ways "glocal" in nature, focusing most commonly (though not always) on urban localities that, by virtue of their ethnic and cultural hybridity, are linked to spaces that are global rather than binational in reach.

These localities are commonly known in France as "banlieues," a term that since the 1980s has been transformed by media usage from a generic term for suburbs into a synonym for chronically disadvantaged multiethnic suburban areas (Hargreaves 1996). Such areas have also been described in media and political discourse as "ghettoes," suggesting that they are in danger of becoming sites of ethnic segregation comparable to those seen in the United States, though they are seldom as large or as dominated by a single ethnic group as in certain American cities. These spaces are Janus-faced. On the one hand, because of their high levels of social disadvantage, with chronic rates of unemployment and poverty, they are often regarded as dead-end spaces. On the other hand, the ethnically diverse nature of the populations concentrated in these spaces makes them richly multicultural. The horizons spanned by this cultural diversity are not limited to the regions in which immigrant minorities have their origins. While migrants often remain deeply nostalgic for their countries of origin, their descendants, born and raised in the country of settlement, are generally less narrowly focused. In contemporary France, as in other places, the mass media bring into the homes of virtually every part of the population a diet of information and entertainment that to a significant degree emanates from outside the country. Anglophone spaces, above all the United States, have long dominated globally circulating cultural flows of this kind, which often exert a powerful attraction among younger members of minority ethnic groups. That attraction is visible in many aspects of "banlieue" culture, including language, dress codes, music (notably hip-hop), and street art such as "tagging" (i.e., graffiti). Thus even when the action takes place entirely in the physically closed space of the "banlieues," films set in this milieu need also to be seen as located in wider, global spaces. Moreover, in their cinematic practices filmmakers raised in this milieu are often influenced by American models and from a very early stage North America has featured as a real or imagined location in some of their most significant films.

Another transnational space, increasingly seen as a global rival to the United States, is that of Islam. While generally less visible than American popular culture, Islam also helps to frame the work of filmmakers of Maghrebi descent. It is striking that when the protagonist in Ismaël Ferroukhi's *Le grand voyage* (2004) is pressed by his Moroccan immigrant father to accompany him on a pilgrimage from the south of France to Mecca, the road movie that ensues takes them by land across multiple borders en route to Saudi Arabia. The tensions that divide father and son have less to do with nationally defined spaces (France versus Morocco) than with personal values and beliefs embedded in rival transnational cultural models (American-style materialism versus the spirituality of Islam). Similarly, when Islam is referenced in other films by second-generation Maghrebis — generally in a passing fashion, as in Mehdi Charef's *Le thé au harem d'Archimède* and Youcef Hamidi's *Malik le maudit* (1997), and sometimes in more extended ways, as in Malik Chibane's *Douce France* (1995) and Yamina Benguigui's *Inch'Allah dimanche* (2001) — it serves to mark a sense of personal morality and codes of interpersonal behavior grounded in a collective system of transcendent belief that is not inherently national in nature. While the supranational reach of the Islamic faith is generally alluded to only fleetingly in these films, it nevertheless implicitly helps to frame them and is sometimes seen more explicitly, as in *Le grand voyage*, where the contrast in values between father and son is played out in a journey across a space that extends far beyond the national boundaries of France and Morocco.

It is of course true that the majority of films by Maghrebi-French directors are set in France and more often than not in the "banlieues" or similar disadvantaged milieux. It is equally true that their protagonists are often shown to be struggling to find a place for themselves in French society in the face of prejudice and discrimination. Crucially, however, while many around them seek to force upon them an ethnic straitjacket framed in terms of nationally defined identities, the protagonists in these films evince little interest in such categories other than for pragmatic purposes. Except for those who migrate from one country to another — as did first-generation Maghrebis now living in France — the life opportunities of most people are to a large extent bounded by the national space in which they reside. With little, if any, interest in "returning" to the home country of their parents, where living standards are lower and cultural codes are less familiar than those in France, most second-generation Maghrebis have no other practical option than to seek a future for themselves in the country where they were born and raised. To the extent that they depict co-ethnics in France, it is therefore no surprise if films by Maghrebi-French directors often address the challenges involved in staking a claim to a place in French society. But this does not mean that their vision is limited to a nationally bounded polarity in which "France" represents a monolithic alternative to "Algeria" or "Morocco." The aspirations and actions of the protagonists in these films are informed, rather, by value systems that are not fundamentally national in nature though for practical purposes their realization is sought within the boundaries of French society.

When the work of Maghrebi-French filmmakers is read within this optic, it can be seen to possess a greater underlying unity than might appear from the different labels under which it has been categorized. As I will show in the remainder of my analysis, it has never been valid to reduce their films to either a "Beur" ethnicity or a narrowly defined notion of the "banlieues." Moreover, while these films may be read in varying degrees as "postcolonial," "diasporic," or "accented," none of these labels, insofar as they foreground nationally defined spaces, does full justice to the underlying contours of this body of work.

Re-Visioning "Beur" and "Banlieue" Cinema

If, as indicated above, there are valid analytical reasons for distinguishing second-generation Maghrebis from other ethnic groups, it is far from easy to find a universally acceptable way of labeling this group. Initially adopted as a self-designating neologism by second-generation Maghrebis in the 1970s, the word "Beur" became contaminated by media usage in the 1980s closely linking it with the stigmatized "banlieues," which led many of those to whom it was applied to reject the term. Writers, filmmakers, and other artists of Maghrebi origin commonly object to it because they feel it tends to separate or ghettoize their work instead of allowing it to be considered as part of "French" or other, wider, cultural categories (Reynaert 1993). For this and other reasons, the term "Beur" is avoided here except when referencing its use by others, with quotation marks serving to remind the reader of its problematic status. "Maghrebi-French" has in recent years acquired some currency in Anglophone countries, though not without considerable ambiguity. In particular, it has sometimes blurred the distinction between émigrés from North Africa and people of Maghrebi descent born and raised in France. As used here, "Maghrebi-French" is to be understood as referencing only the second of these groups. While recognizing that some of those designated in this way object to any label — including "second-generation Maghrebis" and "Maghrebi-French" — which distinguishes them from the rest of the population in France, for analytical purposes we cannot manage without terms of this kind if we acknowledge, as I believe we must, that this group — and the filmmakers and other artists who have emerged from it — share cultural and social characteristics that distinguish them in significant ways from the majority ethnic population.

The first full-length feature films by Maghrebi-French directors — Charef's *Le thé au harem d'Archimède* and Bouchareb's *Baton Rouge* — were released in 1985. Set in the bleak housing projects of the Paris "banlieues," featuring a "Beur" co-protagonist and written and directed by the son of Algerians, *Le thé au harem d'Archimède* was quickly hailed as a work of "Beur" cinema. Rachid Bouchareb's *Baton Rouge* attracted far less publicity on its release a few months later. This may in part have been because *Baton Rouge* was made on a shoestring budget by an unknown director, unlike *Le thé au harem d'Archimède*, which was directed by an author who had already made a name for himself with a widely publicized first novel a couple of years earlier and which benefited from the support of a distinguished producer, Constantin Costa-Gavras. Yet the two movies should in many ways be viewed together for they represent from the outset the two faces of the glocal dynamic that was subsequently to characterize much of Maghrebi-French filmmaking. While Charef's film highlights the dead-end localities around which the notion of "banlieue" cinema would coalesce ten years later, Bouchareb's is much more upbeat in tone and is set mainly in the United States, though its trio of protagonists hail from a Paris "banlieue" to which they eventually return. Together, the two films show how, from their earliest films onward, the works of Maghrebi-French directors span spaces that are far more diverse than those suggested by the ethnic marker "Beur."

In the 1990s, public debate in France focused increasingly on what, during his successful 1995 presidential election campaign, Jacques Chirac famously called "la fracture sociale," that is, the divisions between the haves and the have-nots. Ethnic minorities remained prominent on the "wrong" side of this dividing line, which in media and political discourse had become located in the "banlieues." Mathieu Kassovitz's film *La haine*, released in 1995 to worldwide critical acclaim, spurred talk of "banlieue" cinema, in which ethnic specificities appeared less central than social disadvantages and class divisions. Instead of focusing on a single ethnic group (as "Beur" cinema had been assumed to), "banlieue" cinema was understood to be more multiethnic in nature, typically focusing on a black-blanc-beur (black-white-beur) trio — as in *La haine* — rather than on a single minority ethnic protagonist. The films that most obviously helped shift the terms of the debate in this way were the work of majority ethnic directors such as Kassovitz, François Richet, and Thomas Gilou, but the "banlieue" label also came to be applied in varying degrees to the work of Maghrebi-French directors (Jousse 1995; Videau 1995).

Interestingly, Maghrebi-French directors such as Malik Chibane, whose work was initially labeled as "Beur" cinema, have come to align themselves more readily with banlieue-related, rather than ethnically based, categories. The characters foregrounded in Chibane's first two feature films, *Hexagone* (1994) and *Douce France* (1995), were almost exclusively second-generation Maghrebis, leading many to classify these as "Beur" films. But when they were remarketed in 2008 as part of a triple-movie DVD compilation that also included Chibane's most recent film, *Voisins, voisines* (2005), the umbrella name given to the set was "Trilogie urbaine." When Chibane was asked during a recent discussion to comment on the relative merits of a range of labels — "Beur," "postcolonial," "diasporic," and so on — with reference to his work, he expressed a firm preference for categorizing it as "cinéma urbain."[1] "Urbain" is in this context to be read as an adaptation of "banlieue" designed to throw off the negative connotations often associated with the latter in political and everyday discourse. Like "banlieue," the term "urbain" has acquired a glocal resonance, evoking at one and the same time a specific type of urban locality and globally circulating cultural currents that Chibane and others consider to be exemplified in American film culture (*Les cultures urbaines* 2002).[2]

This does not, of course, mean that nationally framed concerns are absent from Chibane's films. The tower block in which *Voisins, voisines* is set is called "Bâtiment F." Chibane has stated that in choosing this name, he intended "F" to be understood as an allusion to France.[3] The tower block serves as a microcosm of the ethnic diversity within French society, showing — like Chibane's previous films — how marginalized minorities can and should be incorporated into the wider social fabric. This process of incorporation should not be understood as assimilation into a preexisting mold requiring minorities to abandon cultural and other markers originating outside France. In line with the multiethnic nature of the "banlieues," such markers — associated in *Voisins, voisines* with characters originating in North and sub-Saharan Africa, southern Europe, India, and elsewhere — are present throughout the movie, which simultaneously evokes the micro-spaces of the "banlieues" and transnational forms of universalism, a notion exemplified in a line sung by Moussa, the rap artist whose songs serve as the guiding thread holding the film together: "On est tous du même pays quand vient la nuit" [We all belong to the same place when night falls]. The "pays" [place] evoked here is to be understood not so much as France as the human condition, the shared nature of which becomes apparent when surface differences visible during the day are effaced in nocturnal comings and goings involving the multiethnic cast of characters.

In casting Moussa, Chibane auditioned rappers from many different ethnic backgrounds and eventually selected Insa Sané, who is of West African origin, to play the role. Chibane was looking not so much for a specific ethnicity as for a talented performer whose songs evoked both the nitty-gritty concerns of life in the "banlieues" and a wider sense of universalism. Rap music, originally created by African Americans in the "ghettoes" of U.S. cities, is inherently multicultural, blending an African rhythmic heritage with American popular culture, and is deeply marked by the socially disadvantaged milieux in which it was forged. The multicultural span of rap has been greatly expanded in France, where performers and audiences have always been more multiethnic than was originally the case in the United States. If in some strands of French rap — such as the soundtrack in *Voisins, voisines* — social protest is muted in favor of a more lyrical tone, rap continues in many ways to serve as an emblem of the "banlieues" and all that these connote at both sub- and supra-national levels (Cachin 2007; Durand 2007).

Looking back from our current vantage point, it is possible to read the cosmopolitanism of *Voisins, voisines* as an extension of the black-beur-blanc trio commonly associated with "banlieue" movies, a trio that may in turn be seen to have been foreshadowed in many of the films originally classified as "Beur" cinema. Although made by a Maghrebi-French director, the earliest such film, *Le thé au harem d'Archimède*, features dual protagonists of different ethnic origins — Madjid (Kader Boukhanef), of Algerian descent, and Pat (Rémi Martin), his majority ethnic ("white") working-class buddy, who share the same problems and basically similar responses to them — together with secondary characters spanning a range of other ethnic groups.[4] The action is driven not so much by cultural or ethnic specificities as by social disadvantage, exemplified in near-exclusion from the labor market and confinement to dilapidated housing projects in the "banlieues." In these respects, *Le thé au harem d'Archimède* set the template for key aspects of "banlieue" cinema a decade before that label became current following the release of *La haine* in 1995. A similar preoccupation with social marginalization rather than with the specificity of a particular ethnic group marks many of Charef's later films, such as *Miss Mona* (1987) and *Marie-Line* (2000). Although made by a Maghrebi-French director, these cannot in diegetic terms be described as "Beur" movies.

Rachid Bouchareb's Global Vision

The work of Rachid Bouchareb, the most productive and — thanks to the worldwide success of his 2006 release, *Indigènes* — best-known Maghrebi-French director, also extends far beyond the question of Maghrebi-French ethnicity. His début movie, *Baton Rouge*, features a trio of protagonists. While two of these are Maghrebi-French, the third is "white." Like the protagonists in *Le thé au harem d'Archimède* and *La haine*, these characters share in the social disadvantages that characterize the "banlieues." But where Madjid, Pat, and the black-blanc-beur trio in *La haine* remain trapped in the "banlieues," making only temporary forays into better-off parts of Paris, the protagonists in *Baton Rouge* seek to surmount their problems by traveling to the United States, where most of the movie is set. While they of course carry with them preoccupations forged in the context of the "banlieues," it is highly significant that in seeking solutions to their problems they turn neither to France nor to the Maghreb but to a space with which they have no ancestral connections. The United States attracts them, like many other young men and women in the "banlieues," for at least three reasons. First, it offers an escape route from a majority ethnic gaze that tends to stigmatize minority ethnic youths as inherently alien to French society, perceiving them as extensions of their parents' (or grandparents') country of origin even when it means little to them. Second, the United States is seen as a country in which, through its civil rights movements and affirmative action programs, minorities have been afforded far greater opportunities than in France. Third, through its economic strength and domination of global media, the United States has projected an image on the world stage as a trendsetter that has carried enormous appeal in popular culture, especially among young people.

In numerous films by Maghrebi-French directors, as in the eyes of young people in the "banlieues" more generally, American popular culture in its black, white, and Hispanic variants represents a way out of the closure that is seemingly forced upon them by ethnic and social marginalization in France. Dreams of success in a society where foreign origins may be supposed not to matter are typified by the aspirations of the eponymous protagonist (Samir Guesmi) in *Malik le maudit*, who longs to make a new life on the other side of the Atlantic with a beautiful Canadian air hostess. If the white-skinned flight attendant, like the city of Baton Rouge in Bouchareb's film of that name, represents the dream of America as a land of opportunity irrespective of skin color or ethnic background, we see at other times affinities that point rather toward the Black Atlantic, understood as a culturally hybrid site of resistance to racist domination (Gilroy 1993).[5] It is no accident that rap music, which originated among African Americans, was quickly taken up by minority ethnic groups in the French "banlieues" and often features in the soundtracks of movies set there. Neither is it by coincidence that Brian de Palma's *Scarface* (1983), recounting the American success story of Cuban-born gangster Tony Montana (Al Pacino), enjoys a cult following among minority ethnic youths in the "banlieues" (Bui 2005) and is repeatedly alluded to, alongside other American movies such as Martin Scorsese's *Taxi Driver* (1976) and Spike Lee's *Do the Right Thing* (1989), in *La haine*.

As some of these intertextual references suggest and as the protagonists in *Baton Rouge* discover, the American dream may appear less realizable when tested on the spot, but this has not prevented it from enjoying enormous potency among young inhabitants of the "banlieues" and in many other parts of the globe where people feel trapped in a dead-end world. Through the characters and situations depicted in *Baton Rouge* and other films, Bouchareb constantly questions the validity of ethnic and social hierarchies in determining life chances. While ethnic markers are present in all his work, and often powerfully so, it should be noted that few of them revolve around a polarity between France and the Maghreb and many are set in other countries. Far from being preoccupied with the fates of narrowly defined Maghrebi-French characters or situations, Bouchareb's vision is much more global in scope, blending the specificities of a wide range of social and ethnic milieus with an underlying concern for universal principles of individual freedom and equality.

Only three of Bouchareb's feature films — *Cheb* (1991), *L'honneur de ma famille* (1997), and *Indigènes* (2006) — can be characterized basically in terms of a polarity between the Maghreb and France. Far from being locked into that polarity, Bouchareb has shown himself to be at least as interested in the United States as in the Maghreb. His 1994 film *Poussières de vie* is about Amerasian children left behind by the American troops who fathered them during the Vietnam War. Set entirely in Vietnam, though shot in Malaysia, *Poussières de vie* passed almost unnoticed in France although it received an

Academy Award nomination for Best Foreign Film in 1996. *Little Senegal*, released in 2001, is set almost entirely in the United States and primarily in New York City, where it explores tensions between long-established African Americans and immigrants who have recently arrived from West African countries formerly colonized by France.

The American dimension of Bouchareb's oeuvre is by no means wholly detached from the kinds of issues — ethnic, cultural, and political — faced by young North Africans and other postcolonial minorities in France. There is, for example, a very close underlying similarity between the tensions explored in *Cheb* with reference to the experiences of the young adults born to Algerian migrants and later forced to return to the home country of their parents, and those of young Amerasians abandoned to a hostile Communist regime in Vietnam. But it would be wrong to read these other locations as mere ciphers for France or the countries in which France's immigrant minorities originate. On the contrary, Bouchareb is clearly interested in exploring horizons beyond the seemingly closed world of the "banlieues." In line with this, both *Cheb* and *Poussières de vie* emphasize the sterility of dragooning young people into closed and, still worse, state-regimented notions of national identity.

Although *Indigènes*, which focuses on the role of colonial troops in liberating France from the Nazi occupation, is set almost entirely in North Africa and France with a small transitional portion in Italy, the cinematic models on which Bouchareb drew in this film were primarily American. He and his crew openly acknowledged that in shooting the battle scenes for *Indigènes*, they were particularly mindful of Steven Spielberg's Hollywood blockbuster *Saving Private Ryan* (1998), with which many critics have noted similarities. Thematically, Bouchareb was inspired by films such as Edward Zwick's *Glory* (1989) highlighting the previously neglected role of African Americans in U.S. history.

The most commercially successful movie to date by a Maghrebi-French director, *Indigènes* illustrates how far filmmaking by second-generation Maghrebis has come since its early days in the mid-1980s. Back then, it was very difficult for young directors from disadvantaged backgrounds to raise funds for their films, most of which were shot on shoestring budgets with only limited releases. While the "Beur" label gave a certain kind of visibility to such films, it also tended to marginalize them in relation to mainstream French cinema. Since the late 1990s there has been a veritable revolution with a growing number of Maghrebi-French actors playing leading roles in mainstream box office successes. It was their emergence that was the key to enabling Bouchareb to make *Indigènes*, which he had first conceived back in the mid-1990s. Because the film called for relatively expensive historical reconstructions and battle scenes, it needed a much larger budget than any Maghrebi-French director had yet been able to mobilize. When Jamel Debbouze, the son of Moroccan immigrants, overtook Gerard Départdieu as the best-paid actor in France while starring alongside him in Alain Chabat's *Astérix et Obélix: Mission Cléopâtre* (2002), Bouchareb seized the opportunity to enlist the support of Debbouze and three other "bankable" Maghrebi-French stars, whose names could now be used to drum up financial support on a scale that would not previously have been possible. Even before shooting began in 2005, the film was already front-page news, with *Le Monde*'s weekly color magazine devoting a cover story to "Nos stars beurs" (2004), that is, the quartet of second-generation Maghrebis who, together with Bernard Blancan, cast as a Pied-Noir (European settler) sergeant, would subsequently receive collectively the Best Male Actor award at the 2006 Cannes Film Festival. *Indigènes* went on to garner an Academy Award nomination for Best Foreign Film and wide audiences in the United States and around the world (Hargreaves 2007).

Bouchareb's 2009 film, *London River*, is set in London in the wake of the terrorist bombings of 2005. The principal characters — Ousmane (Sotigui Kouyaté), a Muslim of sub-Saharan African origin from France, and Elizabeth Sommers (Brenda Blethyn), a Christian from the Channel Islands — meet by chance in London while searching for a son and a daughter, respectively, who have been missing since the terrorist attacks. It turns out that their children had been living together. If the issues examined in the film are by no means irrelevant to Maghrebis in France, who by virtue of their Muslim heritage are often regarded with suspicion by majority ethnics fearful of Islamist extremists, Bouchareb's agenda is clearly global rather than parochial in scale. The way in which his characters meet and discover their interconnectedness despite differences of ethnicity, language, and religion betokens a sense of universalism similar to that at work in Chibane's *Voisins, voisines*.

The global optic apparent in these recent movies is not a new phenomenon in Maghrebi-French filmmaking. As my analysis has shown, it was already evident in the very earliest such films and has been powerfully present throughout the evolution of this body of work. The many labels that have been applied to these films — "Beur," "banlieue," "postcolonial," "diasporic," and so on — all have a certain pertinence but none captures the full span of them. Referring to similar forms of complexity with reference to émigré Algerian filmmakers in France, Will Higbee proposes the notion of a "cinema of transvergence" that positions movies at one and the same time "within the context of specific national cinemas" and on a "transnational level [spanning] the relationship between the global and the local" (Higbee 2007). While "transvergence" may not necessarily be the most apposite term, a multipolar approach of the kind proposed by Higbee has much to commend it with reference not only to the movies of émigré filmmakers but also to the work of directors of Maghrebi descent born and/or raised in France, whose horizons are at one and the same time locally grounded, nationally referenced, and globally minded.

Notes

1. Remarks made by Malik Chibane during a seminar hosted by the Winthrop-King Institute for Contemporary French and Francophone Studies at Florida State University, October 7, 2008.

2. Remarks made by Chibane at Florida State University, October 7, 2008.

3. Remarks made at Florida State University, October 7, 2008.

4. "White," like "black" or "beur," is to be understood not as an objectively existing skin color, "race," or cultural essence but as a socially constructed ethnic category that, because it informs significant aspects of social perceptions and relations, has to be taken into account in analyses of cultural representations dealing with questions of ethnicity. The quotation marks placed around these terms serve here as reminders of the need to retain a critical distance toward them.

5. On the affinities that many minority ethnic artists in France feel with the Black Atlantic and the ways in which this has helped them reshape the cultural "mainstream" in France, see Hargreaves (2005, 2009).

References

Bui, Doan. 2005. "Tony Montana, idole des quartiers." *Le Nouvel Observateur*, November 17.

Cachin, Olivier. 1996. *L'offensive rap*. Paris: Gallimard.

Chibane, Malik, and Kader Chibane. 2003. "Le cinéma post-colonial des banlieues renoue avec le cinéma politique." *Mouvements* 27–28:35–38.

Les cultures urbaines. 2002. *Les cultures urbaines, 2000–2001: Dossier de presse*. Paris: ADRI.

Durand, Alain Philippe, ed. 2007. *Black, Blanc, Beur: Rap Music and Hip-Hop Culture in the Francophone World*. Lanham MD: Scarecrow Press.

Gilroy, Paul. 1993. *The Black Atlantic: Modernity and Double Consciousness*. Cambridge MA: Harvard University Press.

Hargreaves, Alec G. 1996. "A Deviant Construction: The French Media and the 'Banlieues.'" *New Community* 22 (4) (October): 607–18.

——. 1999. "No Escape? From 'cinéma beur' to the 'cinéma de la banlieue.'" In *Die kinder der Immigration/Les enfants de l'immigration*, ed. Ernstpeter Ruhe, 115–28. Würzburg: Königshausen and Neumann.

——. 2005. "Street Culture: Dead End or Global Highway?" In *Migrant Cartographies: New Cultural and Literary Spaces in Post-Colonial Europe*, ed. Sandra Ponzanesi and Daniela Perolla, 205–16. Lanham MD: Lexington.

——. 2007. "*Indigènes*: A Sign of the Times." *Research in African Literatures* 38 (4): 204–16.

——. 2009. "Beyond Postcolonialism: Globalization and Postcolonial Minorities in France." In *Empire Lost: France and Its Other Worlds*, ed. Elisabeth Mudimbe-Boyi, 37–46. Lanham MD: Lexington.

Higbee, Will. 2007. "Beyond the (Trans)national: Towards a Cinema of Transvergence in Postcolonial and Diasporic Francophone Cinema(s)." *Studies in French Cinema* 7 (2): 79–91.

Jousse, Thierry. 1995. "Le banlieue-film existe-t-il?" *Cahiers du cinéma* 492:37–39.

Le Monde 2. 2004. "Nos stars beurs." November 20.

Naficy, Hamid. 2001. *Accented Cinema: Exilic and Diasporic Filmmaking.* Princeton NJ: Princeton University Press.

Reynaert, François. 1993. "Y a-t-il une culture beur?" *Le Nouvel Observateur*, December 2–8, 34.

Sherzer, Dina. 1996. "Race and Matters of Race: Interracial Relationships in Colonial and Postcolonial Films." In *Cinema, Colonialism, and Postcolonialism: Perspectives from the French and Francophone Worlds*, ed. Dina Sherzer, 229–48. Austin: University of Texas Press.

Shohat, Ella, and Robert Stam, ed. 2003. *Multiculturalism, Postcoloniality, and Transnational Media.* New Brunswick NJ: Rutgers University Press.

Tarr, Carrie. 2005. *Reframing Difference:* Beur *and* Banlieue *Filmmaking in France.* Manchester: Manchester University Press.

Videau, André. 1995. "Cinéma: Les banlieues sont de sortie." *Hommes et migrations* 1192 (November): 60–64.

Filmography

Allouache, Merzak, dir. *Salut cousin!*, 1996.

——, dir. *Chouchou*, 2003.

Ameur-Zaïmeche, Rabah, dir. *Bled number one*, 2006.

Benguigui, Yamina, dir. *Inch'Allah dimanche*, 2001.

Bouchareb, Rachid, dir. *Baton Rouge*, 1985.

——, dir. *Cheb*, 1991.

——, dir. *Poussières de vie*, 1994.

——, dir. *L'honneur de ma famille*, 1997.

——, dir. *Little Senegal*, 2001.

———, dir. *Indigènes*, 2006.

———, dir. *London River*, 2009.

Chabat, Alain, dir. *Astérix et Obélix: Mission Cléopâtre*, 2002.

Charef, Mehdi, dir. *Le thé au harem d'Archimède*, 1985.

———, dir. *Miss Mona*, 1987.

———, dir. *Marie-Line*, 2000.

Chibane, Malik, dir. *Hexagone*, 1994.

———, dir. *Douce France*, 1995.

———, dir. *Voisins, voisines*, 2005.

De Palma, Brian, dir. *Scarface*, 1983.

Ferroukhi, Ismaël, dir. *Le grand voyage*, 2004.

Hamidi, Youcef, dir. *Malik le maudit*, 1997.

Kassovitz, Mathieu, dir. *La haine*, 1995.

Lee, Spike, dir. *Do the Right Thing*, 1989.

Rochant, Eric, dir. *Vive la République*, 1997.

Scorsese, Martin, dir. *Taxi Driver*, 1976.

Spielberg, Steven, dir. *Saving Private Ryan*, 1998.

Zwick, Edward, dir. *Glory*, 1989.

2

HIDDEN ISLAM

The Role of the Religious in *Beur* and *Banlieue* Cinema

MICHEL CADÉ

French cinema has had little if any interest in portraying Islam, a religion that was only minimally present in metropolitan France before the Second World War (Cadé 2006, 1058–75).[1] Relegated to shabby spaces—grudgingly conceded to the Maghrebi immigrants of the postwar period—it was nearly invisible at the national level.[2] Thus, Islam has hardly been a part of the *projection nationale* (Frodon 1997). In colonial cinema, Islam was reduced to a set of signs associated with the picturesque—mosques silhouetted against the sky, gestures of prayer—which were more or less linked to the traditional and the quaint (Benali 1998). In French cinema at large, Islam remained unspoken as well as unseen and was ignored as an element in the identity of the rare immigrant workers glimpsed in films in which the action took place in France.

While Maghrebi immigrants became more visible in the cinema of the 1970s, due to the primarily militant perspective of many of these films (often with negligible ticket sales), references to Islam were neglected, perhaps in an effort not to alienate spectators (Cadé 2004). Both the social and cinematic contexts changed in the 1980s. The election of François Mitterrand as president of the Republic in 1981, the rise in power of the National Front in the 1983 municipal elections, the March of the *Beurs*—those young people of Maghrebi descent born or raised in France—against racism and for equality that same year, and the formation of SOS Racisme in 1984 (Becker and Ory 1998) coincided with the release of the first films directed by young *Beur* directors, the most exemplary of which remains Mehdi Charef's *Le thé au harem d'Archimède* (1985). Since then a *Beur* cinema has continued to evolve, characterized as much by the origins of its directors as by the situations dramatized, and is generally tied to the difficulties of life in the *banlieue* or in the rundown neighborhoods of certain urban centers. As a result, a new genre of French cinema can be delineated: *banlieue* filmmaking, as evoked by Carrie Tarr (2005), relies for its dramaturgy mainly on the difficulties experienced by young people of Maghrebi origin (or of sub-Saharan African descent, for the latter often share with the former the same religious affiliation) in integrating into French society. Its filmmakers are not necessarily of Maghrebi descent but generally bring a particular focus to the problems posed by the integration of minorities of diverse ethnic origins into French society. Among these filmmakers are Thomas Gilou—who has successively focused on the insertion of immigrants of sub-Saharan, Maghrebi Muslim, Maghrebi Jewish, and Latin American origins into the national community—and Philippe Faucon, who was born in Oujda, Morocco, in January 1958 and is married to a woman of Maghrebi origin.[3] The authority of these directors to cinematically represent the *banlieue* and the problems of its inhabitants over the last thirty years cannot be called into question without endorsing a notion of ethnic legitimacy that would radically break with the terms of the French social consensus. I will therefore not distinguish among the diverse ethnic origins of the filmmakers in constituting the corpus that serves as the basis for this study, even while observing that the majority of them in France today would be called French (though some, such as Merzak Allouache, are not) of Maghrebi descent to whom the *banlieue*-born substantive *Beur* has frequently been affixed.

A preliminary observation: of the some 130 French films produced between 1981 and 2003 that Carrie Tarr has identified as more or less corresponding to the categories considered above (2005, 213–18), to which it would be appropriate to add some fifteen or so films made since then, more than half do not evoke the Muslim dimension of their protagonists, and some, such as Malik Chibane's *Nés quelque part* (1997) or Coline Serreau's *Saint Jacques*

... *La Mecque* (2005), even try to subsume Islam into a kind of syncretism founded on the more or less clearly affirmed dominance of Christianity. In this respect, one cannot overlook that Abdellatif Kechiche — the French filmmaker of Maghrebi descent who is the current darling of the French media and has also achieved considerable success with the public[4] — does not allude in the least to Islam (other than, in quasi-imperceptible fashion, on the soundtrack of his most recent film).[5] Nevertheless, all three of his films — *La faute à Voltaire* (2000), *L'esquive* (2004), and *La graine et le mulet* (2007) — foreground an environment where characters of Maghrebi descent play a central role.[6] As for those films that do devote a few shots to Islam, they do so, almost without exception, in an incidental way, for only a few minutes at best out of the hour and a half of a feature-length film.

A Discrete and Generational Islam

Along with this quasi-invisibility of Islam in French cinema (no doubt preferable to its rare caricature as in, for example, Alexandre Arcady's *L'union sacrée* [1986]) is the expression of a generation gap that does not help to give a very dynamic image of the Muslim faith.[7] In *Beur* and *banlieue* cinema, religious practice in its most conventional aspects, as well as in those that verge on superstition, is ordinarily associated with the generation of immigrants. Examples include Madjid's mother, Malika, in *Le thé au harem d'Archimède*; Staf's father and Slimane's mother in Malik Chibane's *Hexagone* (1994); Djamel and Nordine's mother in Thomas Gilou's *Raï* (1995); Alilou's uncle in Merzak Allouache's *Salut cousin!* (1996); the father of the injured boy in Ariel Zeitoun's very popular *Yamakasi, les sept samouraïs des temps modernes* (2001); Samia's parents in Philippe Faucon's *Samia* (2001); Réda's father in Ismaël Ferroukhi's *Le grand voyage* (2004); and Brahim's grandmother in Mahmoud Zemmouri's *Beur, blanc, rouge* (2006). Paradoxically, with the exception of *Le grand voyage*, the few works whose stories provide a more important role for Islam (among others, Malik Chibane's *Douce France* [1995], Mahmoud's Zemmouri's *100% Arabica* [1997], or even, with some reservations, Rabah Ameur-Zaïmeche's *Dernier maquis* [2008]) involve young people practicing religion, specifically those who belong to what is sometimes improperly called the second generation of immigration, or *Beurs*, to use a controversial but nonetheless widely used term. The first group of films dramatizes the stories of immigrants and sheds light on the attachment to the country of origin through fidelity to religious beliefs (as well as by foregrounding the myth of return). The second group, which features the children and grandchildren of immigrants, takes into account a renewed interest in Islam, which sometimes manifests itself in fundamentalist form. Although the 1995 terrorist attacks in the Paris Metro station of Saint-Michel was a violent expression of extreme fundamentalism in the heart of French society, the on-screen representation of such radical forms remains limited, if not watered down, as in the "ostentatious" wearing of the headscarf and the fight against Raï music, portrayed in *Douce France* and *100% Arabica*, respectively. However, the impact of these two films was quantitatively negligible: *Douce France* had ticket sales of 18,273 and *100% Arabica* 154,000, whereas *Yamakasi* had more than 2.4 million entries.[8] Tony Gatlif's *Exils* (2004), Djamel Bensalah's *Il était une fois dans l'oued* (2005), and Rabah Ameur-Zaïmeche's *Bled number one* (2006) — to which one could add Rachid Bouchareb's *Cheb* (1990), Gaël Morel's *Les chemins de l'oued* (2003), and Hassan Legzouli's *Ten'ja* (2005) — constitute a slightly different category, in that the relationship with Islam is inscribed in a reverse exile: the return to Algeria or Morocco. But the different categories of works listed above hardly allow one to construct a chronology founded on typologies of relationship with Islam. The character of Malika in *Le thé au harem d'Archimède* is echoed twenty years later in a comedic vein by the grandmother of *Beur, blanc, rouge*, while, beginning in 1995, the issue of Islamic fundamentalism continues to appear in *Beur* cinema, although admittedly in such a discrete manner that it amounts to denial.

The on-screen representation of religion of any sort is never a simple matter. Indeed, the heart of the religious resides in the relationship the believer maintains with divinity, a relationship that is personal and invisible unless devalorized into empty words; religious practice alone can provide a visual manifestation for it. It is therefore through ritual practices in their most characteristic and thus visually manifest forms, whether individual or collective, that cinema attempts to translate the unshowable. When it comes to Islam on screen, one must point out at the outset that a patriarchal chauvinism haunts this cinema: from *Raï*, Zaïda Ghorab Volta's *Souviens-toi de moi* (1996), *100% Arabica*, or *Samia*, through Yamina Benguigui's *Inch'Allah dimanche* (2001), Coline Serreau's *Chaos* (2001), *Bled number one*, and *Beur, blanc, rouge*. More generally, one has to distinguish between religious values and what is simply a matter of tradition. Thus in *Inch'Allah dimanche*, the heroine, Zouina, is persecuted by her mother-in-law, Aïcha, mostly out of a tradition in which the mother of a son is an absolute tyrant to his wife. Islam, in this case, serves as mere a posteriori justification for a set of customs that predates it (Latiri 2003). Similarly, in *Samia*, Samia's brother — a young man mistreated by a society that refuses to recognize him — relies on seemingly religious views to justify going against his parents' will and subjecting his sister to his own. Through the exercise of traditional male power, he hopes to recover a dignity denied on a daily basis; religion serves only as a pretext here. The male chauvinism or machismo featured in Italian and Spanish, not to mention Greek, cinema is a cultural characteristic that owes little to Islam and everything to old Mediterranean ways that subordinate women within both social and familial structures. Although, in general, one must take into account interpretations of the Koran that attempt to align it with Middle Eastern and Mediterranean patriarchal traditions such as the headscarf, social rather than religious factors are at work.

Along with dietary prohibitions, shared in part with Judaism, prayer appears in cinema as the principal marker of Islam, no doubt because it is compatible with the usual representation of Christianity, the dominant religion in the French cultural context, and because its gestures are sufficiently distinct from Christian practice. Whether the prayer is individual (Malika in *Le thé au harem d'Archimède*, the injured child's father in *Yamakasi*, the young Algerian immigrant in *Exils*, Yacine's father in *Il était une fois dans l'oued*, Réda's father in *Le grand voyage*) or collective (*Douce France*, *Le grand voyage*, *Bled number one*, *Dans la vie*, *Dernier maquis*), it represents the believer's submission to God (except when it is likened to a fundamentalist appropriation of faith as in *Salut cousin!* and *100% Arabica*). This submission is represented in the very way scenes of prayer are filmed, generally with a high angle shot. By including prayer within sequences of significant shots, the editing of these films makes it clear that the act is more than merely anecdotal. Consider the sequence in *Le thé au harem d'Archimède* in which Pat and Madjid prostitute one of the women living in their housing project to immigrant workers living in nearby trailers: after a few shots showing the start of the transaction and its completion, Pat, accompanied by the young woman, opens the door of a trailer; the following shot shows him frontally, from the occupant's point of view, while we hear the words of a prayer, *Allahu Akbar*. A high angle shot frames the face of a man wearing a turban, and follows the movement of his kneeling body as it leans forward. In the following sequence, which ends with a long shot, the man pursues the three accomplices, insulting them in Arab and French. The man who prays rejects commercial sex, and in his diatribe, attempts to reestablish the human values that Islam advocates here. In *Le grand voyage*, the father's prayer not only affirms a spiritual relationship that remains inaccessible to the son, Réda, but also forms part of a collective act on the journey to Mecca, of Muslim fraternity, of the *ummah*. The contemplative simplicity of the religious act in *Dans la vie* and especially the beauty of the chants in *Dernier maquis* — which may remind Catholic spectators (the majority in France) of Gregorian chant — establish a new vision of Islam as a peaceful religious practice far from the stereotypes too often dominant in French society. Likewise, the denunciation of hypocrites in *Salut cousin!*, in *100% Arabica*, or in the final sequence of *Douce France* does not call into question the dignity of sincere prayer. In *Salut cousin!*, Alilou is astonished by the naiveté of the Parisian Muslims when he discovers that the imam of the mosque his uncle attends is an old friend from Algiers, but Alilou refuses to get into a pointless argument. When a believer in *100% Arabica* discovers the malevolence of the imam, he does not renounce prayer. Instead, he decides to pray by himself from then on.

Allusions to Ramadan (*Samia, La nuit du destin, Il était une fois dans l'Oued*) or to Eid, the Festival of Sacrifice (*Hexagone, Inch'Allah dimanche, Dans la vie*), are less frequent: while they form a part of the visualization of Islam in the cinema, they nonetheless retain a superficial character. The central role of the Koran, touched on in *Hexagone, 100% Arabica*, and in *Il était une fois dans l'oued*, is also generally neglected. Funeral rites, which are evoked fairly often, are treated somewhat differently. Either they are inscribed within a tragic context in which young people who have mostly lost touch with Islam return to their religious roots for their last voyage (*Hexagone* and *Raï*), or they signify the end of a discreet but clearly religious journey for characters belonging to the generation of immigrant parents. As members of that generation age and begin to die, the latter scenario has appeared in a number of recent works. Examples include the burial of the father in Jean-Pierre Sinapi's *Vivre me tue* (2003); the son's initiation to his roots in *Ten'ja* as he escorts his father's body to his native village in the south of Morocco (though religion admittedly does not have a great deal of importance here); or M. Malouf's stubborn search for a Muslim burial plot for himself in *Voisins, voisines* (Chibane 2005). No doubt special attention should be given to the son in *Le grand voyage*: crushed by grief in Mecca as he washes his dead father, he rediscovers age-old gestures he did not realize he knew. But filial piety in *Vivre me tue* and *Ten'ja* has more to do with witnessing the passing of a generation, and with the sons' belated understanding of their fathers' hard destiny, than with a return to religious practices from which the sons remain just as distant after their fathers' deaths as before.

Integrationist Discourse and the Rare Representation of Islam's Centrality

A few rare films have tried to place Muslim religious worship at the center, or at least not entirely at the periphery, of their stories. By means of a dramaturgy intended to be didactic, *La nuit du destin* was the first to try to explain Islam and its rituals to spectators, who are represented in the film by a well-intentioned police inspector. The film's failure with the public (less than five thousand spectators) indicates that the French public was not ready for this sort of initiation. In *Douce France*, Malik Chibane had more success in portraying seemingly opposing characters, the sisters Souad and Farida, to depict the complex relationships that young *Beurs* have with their parents' culture and more generally with Islamic culture. The only film to deal with the question of the headscarf (aside from a brief allusion in *Beur, blanc, rouge,* an audacious appropriation in Pierre Jolivet's *Zim and co.* (2005), and the mere acknowledgment of its existence in *Dans la vie*), *Douce France* plays on appearances and pretense to give Islam a notable and positive role, not without denouncing hypocrites and hypocrisy. However, it remains anchored in a more cultural than religious domain.

Without doubt the most notable work in this respect is Ismaël Ferroukhi's *Le grand voyage*. An ordinary young man from the *banlieue*, in love with a non-Muslim woman, is obliged to accompany his aging father on a pilgrimage by car to Mecca. The fifth pillar of Islam is rarely evoked in French cinema other than by its name, hadj, employed occasionally in the characterization of a few pious characters, or more recently as a secondary plot in *Dans la vie*. So, making the pilgrimage the subject of the film was audacious to say the least. Approaching his subject with remarkable austerity, Ferroukhi refuses the temptation of the picturesque and privileges long traveling shots on anonymous highways, low-light bivouacs, and closeups of the two protagonists. Only the two pearls of Islam, Istanbul and Mecca, receive a more sumptuous representation. *Le grand voyage* is the story of an initiation into Islam; prayer, the reading of the sacred book, almsgiving, and the pilgrimage are its integral components. Of the five pillars, three are portrayed on screen here. Although Réda is initially indifferent, he does become interested in the pilgrimage in which he now finds himself a participant. It brings him closer to his father rather than to an Islam that, in Turkey, does not appear to him in a very flattering light. Once he arrives in Mecca, he does not participate in prayer any more than in the rituals of pilgrimage. And once he has accomplished the funerary rites for his dead father, the only other Islamic obligation, perhaps the most universal one, that he will respect is that of almsgiving, even if one may interpret it as more a matter of respect for paternal example than for his father's religion. Indeed, despite his minimal resources, Réda's father had given alms to a poor woman during the voyage. The filmmaker allows us finally to draw our own conclusions about this journey through a world and a religion of which he gives both a positive and nuanced image while avoiding any didacticism or proselytism. But if *Le grand voyage* won the Luigi de Laurentis prize at the 2004 Venice Film Festival, and had a certain success in North America and Britain, it found only a small audience in France (76,501 entries since 2004). The absence of salient national references, a somewhat contemplative style, highly skillful but intentionally unsuspenseful editing, a cast not known to the general public, and an unusual subject can account for, without fully explaining, the failure of this beautiful film in France.

Likewise, though less centered on Islam, Tony Gatlif's *Exils* takes the form of a road movie. The pilgrimage to Algeria of the confused daughter of a *harki* and the son of a French militant partisan for Algerian independence culminates with the soft violence of a trance in an encounter with Muslim heterodoxy, Maghrebi maraboutism, and Sufism (foregrounded also by *Bled number one*). These reveal the diversity of a religion often experienced in France as monolithic. In France, Islam is primarily Maghrebi, that is, Maliki Sunni, though with ethnic and cultural variants, but it is not the only form practiced (Withold de Wenden 2006); mystic Sufi and Shiite communities have also become established (Geoffroy 2006). Most non-Muslim French are unaware of this diverse, even divided, Islam and have instead a general and perfectly artificial notion of "Islam" largely formed by colonial and neocolonial thinking (Arkoun 2006).

If placement of the Muslim faith at the center of the narrative is the criterion, there are only three exceptions to the relative silence about Islam in all the films released between 1985 and 2007. These exceptions do not prevent one from legitimately questioning why *Beur* and *banlieue* filmmaking, which should have been the most sensitive to France's second most important religion, has been discreet in portraying Islam. It is all the more surprising given that two non-*Beur* films have made Islam the main theme of their narration.

The first and older of the two films, *Black mic-mac* (Gilou 1986), recounts the adventures of a community of immigrants from black Africa in an old working-class district of Paris. Faced with the administrative harassment of Parisian bureaucrats, the community calls on a sainted marabout who comes directly from his village to the new Babylon. The very respectful staging of the prayer scenes, the absence of derision in the treatment of the sainted man, and the depiction of faith moving mountains make this film, which has no pretensions to do anything more than entertain, one of the least biased presentations of Islam in French cinema. The second, François Dupeyron's *Monsieur Ibrahim et les fleurs du Coran* (2003), a great popular success (324,366 entries since 2003), is an attempt to bring to the screen Sufi mysticism within a comedy, and at the very least, provide a more nuanced image of Islam.

The paucity of representation of Islam in a cinema where its presence would seem natural can be attributed, in general, to the difficulty of portraying religious devotion on screen but also the daily practice of religious rites, which risk testing the spectator's patience. Although they are increasingly present (mostly in news programs) on television, religious rites seem to have disappeared from the big screen. However, even if one sets aside the many mawkish old Catholic films, the success of Alain Cavalier's *Thérèse* (1986) — which ponders the life of Carmelites — and Thomas Gilou's 1997 hit *La vérité si je mens!* — which takes place in "le Sentier," the picturesque Parisian Sephardic district — show that there is no taboo in representing religious aspects of society, as does indeed *Monsieur Ibrahim et les fleurs du Coran* with Islam. On the other hand, it is true that Thomas Gilou, a filmmaker attentive to the evolution of French society, has indeed chosen to portray, in a superficial though insistent way, religious aspects of the ethnic groups he depicts (Muslim in *Black mic-mac*, Jewish in *La vérité si je mens!*). Yet the fact that in *Raï*, a *banlieue* film with *Beur* protagonists, he chooses to downplay Islam in favor of a few, rare evocations of superstitious practices says a lot about the incapacity of *Beur* and *banlieue* filmmaking, with a few rare exceptions, to take Islam into account. Films such as *Le thé au harem d'Archimède*, *Raï*, or Mathieu Kassovitz's *La haine* (1995), whether presented as somewhat despairing social portraits or as cries of revolt (*Ma 6-T va crack-er* [Jean-François Richet 1997]) or as possible solutions to the problem of integration into society,[9] all have a common goal: the integration of *Beurs* and *Rebeus* (Arabs) into French society, while accepting, albeit with some nuances,

France's declared refusal of ethnic and religious particularity. Often considered a marker of difference — particularly by those who reject the presence of a Maghrebi population in France (a group represented essentially by an extreme right that until the presidential elections of May 2007 consisted of approximately a fifth of the electorate) — Islam has been hidden in order to encourage a smoother on-screen assimilation. Moreover, the same desire for a "cinema of integration" explains the absence of Islamic fundamentalists, except in the films of Mahmoud Zemmouri and Merzak Allouache, both of whom, it is worth recalling, are Algerian directors, and whose films take place entirely or in part in Algeria.

This largely integrationist discourse of *Beur* and *banlieue* cinema would seem to have its legitimacy: in effect, it is one of the characteristics of cinema to be at the avant-garde of social change and to sketch out an image of a possible future. However, by denying the specific religious dimension of French of Maghrebi descent, and in effacing that element of their identity, this discourse contributes to maintaining them in a marginal position, condemned as they are to being represented only by their social position. If the relationship with Islam can at first glance seem more salient in films produced since 2000, a careful study of them reveals that this is the case only when the films take place beyond French borders, thereby eliminating the problematic of integration.

From (an Islam in) the Margins to (Islam as) a Mode of Integration

In this respect, *Le grand voyage* is exemplary: Islam can be experienced only in Muslim territory. The split noted above between the banal images of travel in Europe and the caressing beauty of the shots devoted to the mosques of Istanbul embodies this proposition; moreover, one finds a juxtaposition of the same sort in *Monsieur Ibrahim*.

The return to North Africa has the same effect of revealing an Islam that remains off camera and virtually invisible in the films set in France. Such a split also appears in *Exils* and *Il était une fois dans l'oued*. In the latter film, set at the end of the 1980s, physical distance is compounded by temporal separation. Such an eclipsing of Islam according to the geographical setting seems most palpable in the works of Rabah Ameur-Zaïmeche.

In *Wesh wesh, qu'est ce qui se passe?* (2002), a *banlieue* film and Ameur-Zaïmeche's first feature in which he himself plays the hero, Islam is utterly absent, but in *Bled number one*, shot entirely in Algeria, Maghrebi varieties of

Islam along with maraboutism govern daily life. By contrast, his most recent film, *Dernier maquis*, appears to give Islam a larger role. In a pallet factory and garage in the Parisian *banlieue*, the boss, Mao (an uncommon diminutive for Mohammed and no doubt an allusion to the Great Helmsman), who is a good Muslim, offers his workers a mosque in the workplace. Whether the product of a sincere love for Islam or merely an employer's ruse, the project splits the workers, who with few exceptions are also Muslim, but from diverse backgrounds. The conflict does not come from the proposed mosque per se but from Mao's selecting the imam without consulting the Muslim employees. The workers from sub-Saharan Africa, recent immigrants organized according to the structure of a traditional village (their representative to Mao is the village chief), accept the mosque and the imam designated by the owner. However, the workers of Maghrebi descent born in France have quite a different reaction. These employees, most of whom are Muslim — one of them is even a new convert paradoxically ready to play the role of imam, and another one refuses any religious belief or practice — work in the garage, the company's most complex industrial structure, which employs skilled labor. They belong to the aristocracy of the working class and demand the autonomy due them as citizens, even in the religious domain. Though not for the most part hostile to setting aside space for religious practice at work, they are radically opposed to the employer's co-optation of such a place of worship. What comes to light finally, according to Rabah Ameur-Zaïmeche himself, is that "class struggle is always the engine of history" (Ameur-Zaïmeche 2008). Borne by images of great formal audacity, *Dernier Maquis* uses the symbolism of color with consummate artistry. Long dolly shots of the piled-up pallets turned into mobile factory walls offer an exact visual counterpart to the false openness of Mao's proposal. The red of the pallets, along with the blue and white of the trucks — color of revolt and color of exploitation — form the complement that reminds us of the tricolor French flag and signifies the absence of a divide between adherence to Islam and allegiance to the French nation. In a less subtle way, this is also shown by the presence of two Muslim believers of apparently European descent. This meditation on Islam, inserted into a Marxist analysis of the means of production at the very site of the production of surplus value, to use the film's terms, shows that the "banal" dimension of Muslim faith is beginning to be portrayed on screen in *Beur* and *banlieue* cinema.[10]

One can see the confirmation of this observation in Philippe Faucon's 2008 film, *Dans la vie*, where, in the mode of realist comedy, Islam and

Judaism are made to enter into dialogue through the intermediary of two elderly women. But as in *Samia*, Faucon's intentions go beyond this plot line, if in a less dramatic way. He ponders the existence of diverse conceptions of Islam in France. Without radically opposing them, he endeavors to compare Halima and Ali's tolerant Islam with a more rigid one, the Islam of most of their relatives, that places importance on the headscarf and displays a certain distrust toward the surrounding society. Though we can easily see which type of Islam the filmmaker prefers, his approach is nonetheless not completely black and white. Halima and Ali's tolerance of others, particularly other people of the book (Jews and Christians), is facilitated by the confidence they draw from their roots. As immigrants from Algeria, they experience Islam as a kind of constant, the least questionable constitutive element of their identity; the temptation to be something else does not even enter their awareness. Such is not the case for their children, or nieces and nephews, who are born in France and belong to a social group whose foundation is not primarily influenced by Islam. To conserve their religious identity in the heart of their French identity, they have to engage in a kind of cultural and religious exaggeration. To be sure, other choices are possible, if not obvious. Salima, one of the couple's daughters, cohabits with a man of African descent of undisclosed religious affiliation and has herself an attitude toward religion that can be described as secular. In response to her cousin who wears a headscarf, she exclaims, "Religion is a personal choice, it isn't transmitted, it isn't hereditary." Nevertheless, through her work she affirms her double identity as a woman who is both religious and independent. When Salima meets practicing members of her family, she takes off her makeup and does not drink or smoke or let them know she lives with a man. The intelligence of *Dans la vie* is to establish these differences within the Muslim community and to find their resolution there as well. Woven into Faucon's film, without ever reducing its interest, are the meaning of the pillars of Islam, the importance of an imam's advice, the redemptive significance of the pilgrimage to Mecca, and the rules for living that one can extrapolate, sometimes in contradictory ways, from the Koran. The importance given to the closeup framing of little groups, through the attention given to each face, as during a collective prayer at the mosque, suggests individual choice rather than collective pressure in religious matters.

Thus, until recently, French cinema has constructed an Islam of exile or return without paying attention to what is now a well-established reality: Islam in France is characterized by, among other things, an attempt to organize a French Islam (Lochon 2004). Indeed, this constituted one of the most surprising blind spots of *Beur* and *banlieue* cinema. But the most recent productions seem to be moving toward making its appearances on screen more routine. To be sure, two films do not foretell how Islam will be represented in the future, but they indicate nonetheless a new attention to an important aspect of the Maghrebi-French community. It is not necessary to make Islam the only, or even the most important, marker of French citizens of Maghrebi descent — some of these citizens are secular, and religious practice in this community displays the same decline as in society as a whole (Boyer 2006, 777).[11] No one doubts that the "integration" so fervently desired by the filmmakers is occurring, or perhaps has already occurred, when directors no longer hesitate to show, as Rabah Ameur-Zaïmeche and Philippe Faucon do each in his own way, French citizens going to the mosque to pray on Friday nights as others go to Mass on Sundays or to the synagogue on Saturdays. Cinema is not a reflection of society; it is one of society's views of itself, an idealized one. If cinema sometimes lends a certain importance to religious practices, it is because such practices are, within their accepted limits, the paradoxical guarantors of republican liberty. The absence of Islam on screen was less a matter of a reverence for the secular, never completely acknowledged (with the exception perhaps of Abdellatif Kechiche), than of the fear of stigmatizing a group by portraying it as different. The recent change of direction seems to signify that, in cinema at least, French citizens of Maghrebi descent can now affirm their identity as French at the same time that they assert themselves as Muslim.[12] There will be no "immigrants of the third generation."

Translated from the French by Alexander Price.

Notes

A much shorter version of this article appeared as "La religion musulmane dans le cinéma *beur* et 'de banlieue'" in *Perpignan: L'histoire des musulmans dans la ville* (2005).

1. The representation of religion of any type has never been an important theme in French cinema. For further reading on this subject, see Boitel and Hennebelle (1988), Hennebelle (1996), and Cadé (2006).

2. Although France was a "land of immigration" during the interwar period, migration to France was mostly from other European nations. In the 1936 census, Maghrebis amounted to only 87,000 out of a foreign population of 2,198,000 people — a little less

than 4 percent (Atouf 2004, 86). In 1954 there were 227,108 Maghrebis, and they constituted 12.9 percent of the foreign population, reaching 410,373 in 1962, 19 percent of the foreign population (Atouf 2004, 267, 390).

3. Gilou, born in February 1955 in Boulogne Billancourt, then a working-class suburb of Paris, has depicted the difficulties of integration of West Africans in *Black mic-mac* (1985), of Maghrebis (and the children of Maghrebis) in *Raï* (1995) and in *Michou d'Auber* (2007), of Sephardic Jews coming from North Africa after 1962 in *La vérité si je mens!* (1997) and *La vérité si je mens! 2* (2001), and of Latin Americans in *Chili con carne* (1999). Faucon directed *Samia* in 1991 and *Dans la vie* in 2007, both situated within the Maghrebi communities in Marseille and Toulon, respectively. His feature film, *La trahison* (2006), deals with the Algerian War.

4. In 2000 Kechiche's *La faute à Voltaire* won an award for best first work at the Venice Film Festival; in 2005 *L'esquive* won four Césars, including best film; *La graine et le mulet* received the Special Jury Prize at Venice in 2007 and the Prix Louis Delluc in Paris the same year; in 2008 it received Césars for best director and best film. When *La graine et le mulet* was released, *Les cahiers du cinéma* put it on the cover of the December issue and devoted twelve pages to criticism and interviews having to do with the film. The magazine's old rival, *Positif*, also announced the release of the film on its cover, along with other films, and gave it eight pages.

5. Hamid, the musician, commenting on the refusal of the authorities to accept the opening of Slimane's restaurant, exclaims, "And it's not as if it's a mosque!" In the application to the bank for a loan, Rym and Slimane mention that the restaurant will be a place for communal and familial celebrations such as circumcisions, which, one might note in passing, could apply to Jews as well. In any case, these two allusions last no longer than thirty seconds in a film of more than two hours!

6. It is true that Abdellatif Kechiche privileges a mix of characters of Maghrebi and other diverse origins, including long-established French citizens as well as descendants of Italian immigrants, or even recent immigrants from eastern Europe.

7. I have shown elsewhere that quite often a character's adherence to Islam is reduced to a few meager signs, such as dietary prohibitions and the wearing of ostensibly Islamic jewels like the hand of Fatima (Cadé 2006, 1058–75).

8. These statistics are drawn from the BIFI database.

9. See, for instance, films such as *Baton Rouge* (Rachid Bouchareb 1985), *Bye-Bye* (Karim Dridi 1995), *Marie-Line* (Mehdi Charef 2000), *De l'amour* (Jean-François Richet 2001), *Chouchou* (Merzak Allouache 2003), *L'esquive* (Abdellatif Kechiche 2004), or, with reservations, *Beur, blanc, rouge*.

10. It is worth pointing out, however, that if *Dernier maquis* garnered considerable critical praise when it was released, it had only a mediocre success at the box office: 19,960 tickets sold in France during its first two weeks, with forty-two copies in circulation (*Le Film Français*, November 2008).

11. The percentage of French of Maghrebi descent and Maghrebis in France who practice Islam is estimated to be 30 percent, while the estimated rate for West Africans is 60 percent. If around 65 percent of Muslims in France observe Ramadan, only 10

percent regularly go to the mosque. From what I can tell, in a single generation, the rate of religious practice among Muslims in France seems to be tending to match that of the French population as a whole.

12. Several comedies and dramas that came out shortly after this chapter was written seem to confirm this tendency and the conclusions of this chapter. For instance, see *Adieu Gary* by Nassim Amaouche (2009), *Neuilly sa mère* by Gabriel Julien Laferrière, based on an original idea by Djamel Bensallah (2009), and *L'Italien* by Olivier Baroux with the actor Kad Merad (2010).

References

Ameur-Zaïmeche, Rabah. 2008. "Conférence de presse à Cannes." *Le Monde*, May 16. http://www.lemonde.fr (accessed June 1, 2008).

Arkoun, Mohammed. 2006. Introduction to *Histoire de l'islam et des musulmans en France du Moyen Age à nos jours*. Paris: Albin Michel.

Atouf, Elkbir. 2004. "Les Marocains en France de 1918 à 1965: L'histoire d'une immigration programmée." Thèse de doctorat, Université de Perpignan.

Becker, Jean-Jacques, and Pascal Ory. 1998. *Crises et alternances 1974–1995*. H119. Paris: Éditions du Seuil.

Benali, Abdelkader. 1998. *Le cinéma colonial au Maghreb, l'imaginaire en trompe l'œil*. Paris: Éditions du Cerf.

Boitel, Philippe, and Guy Hennebelle, eds. 1988. "Le film religieux." *CinémAction* 49.

——. 2004. "Une représentation en éclats: Les Maghrébins dans le cinéma français." In *Les Maghrébins de France*, ed. Mohand Khelil, 111–34. Toulouse: Privat.

——. 2005. "La religion musulmane dans le cinéma *beur* et 'de banlieue.'" In *Perpignan: L'histoire des musulmans dans la ville*, 213–18. Archives communales de Perpignan.

——. 2006a. "La diversité et la place de l'islam en France après 1945." In *Histoire de l'islam et des musulmans en France du Moyen Age à nos jours*, ed. Mohamed Arkoun, 762–83. Paris: Albin Michel.

——. 2006b. "L'islam dans le miroir du cinéma français." In *Histoire de l'islam et des musulmans en France du Moyen Age à nos jours*, ed. Mohamed Arkoun, 1058–75. Paris: Albin Michel.

Frodon, Michel. 1997. *La projection nationale*. Paris: Éditions Odile Jacob.

Geoffroy, Eric. 2006. "L'attraction du soufisme." In *Histoire de l'islam et des musulmans en France du Moyen Age à nos jours*, ed. Mohamed Arkoun, 828–36. Paris: Albin Michel.

Hennebelle, Guy, ed. 1996. "Christianisme et cinéma." *CinémAction* 80.

Latiri, Dora Carpenter. 2003. "Représentations de la femme migrante dans *Inch'Allah dimanche*." *Web Journal of French Media Studies* 6. http://wjfms.ncl.ac.uk/LatiriWJ.htm (accessed September 7, 2008).

Lochon, Christian. 2004. "L'islam des Maghrébins en France." In *Maghrébins de France de 1960 à nos jours: La naissance d'une communauté*, ed. Mohand Khellil, 53–110. Toulouse: Privat.

Tarr, Carrie. 2005. *Reframing Difference:* Beur and Banlieue *Filmmaking in France*. Manchester: Manchester University Press.

Withold de Wenden, Catherine. 2006. "L'intégration des populations musulmanes en France, trente ans d'évolution." In *Histoire de l'islam et des musulmans en France du Moyen Age à nos jours*, ed. Mohamed Arkoun, 800–821. Paris: Albin Michel.

Filmography

Allouache, Merzak, dir. *Salut cousin!*, 1996.

——, dir. *Chouchou*, 2003.

Ameur-Zaïmeche, Rabah, dir. *Wesh wesh, qu'est-ce qui se passe?*, 2002.

——, dir. *Bled number one*, 2006.

——, dir. *Dernier maquis*, 2008.

Arcady, Alexandre, dir. *L'union sacrée*, 1986.

Bahloul, Abdelkrim, dir. *La nuit du destin*, 1999.

Benguigui, Yamina, dir. *Inch'Allah dimanche*, 2001.

Bensalah, Djamel, dir. *Il était une fois dans l'oued*, 2005.

Bouchareb, Rachid, dir. *Baton Rouge*, 1985.

——, dir. *Cheb*, 1991.

Cavalier, Alain, dir. *Thérèse*, 1986.

Charef, Mehdi, dir. *Le thé au harem d'Archimède*, 1985.

——, dir. *Marie-Line*, 2000.

Chibane, Malik, dir. *Hexagone*, 1994.

——, dir. *Douce France*, 1995.

——, dir. *Nés quelque part*, 1997.

——, dir. *Voisins, voisines*, 2005.

Dridi, Karim, dir. *Bye-Bye*, 1995.

Dupeyron, François, dir. *Monsieur Ibrahim et les fleurs du Coran*, 2003.

Faucon, Philippe, dir. *Samia*, 2001.

——, dir. *La trahison*, 2006.

——, dir. *Dans la vie*, 2008.

Ferroukhi, Ismaël, dir. *Le grand voyage*, 2004.

Gatlif, Tony, dir. *Exils*, 2004.

Gilou, Thomas, dir. *Black mic-mac*, 1986.

——, dir. *Raï*, 1995.

——, dir. *La vérité si je mens!*, 1997.

——, dir. *Chili con carne*, 1999.

——, dir. *La vérité si je mens! 2*, 2001.

——, dir. *Michou d'Auber*, 2007.

Jolivet, Pierre, dir. *Zim and co.*, 2005.

Kassovitz, Matthieu, dir. *La haine*, 2005.

Kechiche, Abdellatif, dir. *La faute à Voltaire*, 2001.

——, dir. *L'esquive*, 2004.

——, dir. *La graine et le mulet*, 2007.

Legzouli, Hassan, dir. *Ten'ja*, 2005.

Morel, Gaël, dir. *Les chemins de l'oued*, 2003.

Richet, Jean-François, dir. *Ma 6-T va crack-er*, 1997.
———, dir. *De l'amour*, 2001.
Serreau, Coline, dir. *Chaos*, 2001.
———, dir. *Saint Jacques . . . La Mecque*, 2005.
Sinapi, Jean-Pierre, dir. *Vivre me tue*, 2003.
Volta, Zaïda Ghorab, dir. *Souviens-toi de moi*, 1996.
Zeitoun, Ariel, dir. *Yamakasi, les sept samouraïs des temps modernes*, 2001.
Zemmouri, Mahmoud, dir. *100% Arabica*, 1997.
———, dir. *Beur, blanc, rouge*, 2006.

3

"ET SI ON ALLAIT EN ALGÉRIE?"

Home, Displacement, and the Myth of Return
in Recent Journey Films by Maghrebi-French
and North African Émigré Directors

WILL HIGBEE

Since the late 1990s French cinema has witnessed a reconfiguration
of the representational politics of place and space in Maghrebi-
French and North African émigré filmmaking.[1] Maghrebi-French
protagonists are increasingly shown on screen moving beyond the
banlieue, which has previously functioned as both the locus of
Maghrebi-French identity and an emblematic space of marginality,
criminality, and violence (Higbee 2007, 12). One noticeable trend
within this opening up of the cine-spatial landscape for Maghrebi-
French and North African émigré filmmaking is the increasing
number of road movies or journey narratives that have appeared
since the late 1990s. The journeys depicted are at once physical
(traveling through space and time) and metaphorical (leading
to a greater self-understanding on the part of the protagonist),
and can pose as many problems as they provide answers. They
are not necessarily entered into voluntarily (the destination is
not always a desired location) and are often structured around
seemingly random events within an episodic narrative depicting
a fragmented journey hampered or beset by obstacles.

If we were to compile a basic (but not exhaustive) list of such journey films directed since the late 1990s by Maghrebi-French or North African émigré filmmakers (or films directed by non-Maghrebi directors in which characters of North African origin are the central protagonists) it would include upward of twenty titles and a variety of subcategories: journeys across France that lead to a discovery of identity and place within the nation (*Jeunesse dorée* [Ghorab-Volta 2001]; *Drôle de Félix* [Ducastel and Martineau 2000]); voyages beyond the diasporic axis of France and the Maghreb (*Le grand voyage* [Ferroukhi 2004]); histories of migration from the Maghreb to France (*Inch'Allah dimanche* [Benguigui 2001]; *Vivre au paradis* [Guerdjou 1998]); contemporary journeys to France by illegal North African immigrants (*Salut cousin!* [Allouache 1996], *Adieu* [Arnaud des Pallières 2003]). However, by far the most significant grouping within these journey films are those which focus on the "return" of Maghrebi-French protagonists to North Africa: *L'autre monde* (Allouache 2001), *La fille de Keltoum* (Mehdi Charef 2001), *Exils* (Gatlif 2004), *Ten'ja* (Legzouli 2004), *Il était une fois dans l'oued* (Bensalah 2005), *Bled number one* (Ameur-Zaïmeche 2006).[2] It is this latter group of return narratives that are of particular interest for this chapter, above all for the ways in which they bring into question supposedly fixed notions of the here and there of host and homeland in the diasporic imaginary.

We should not be that surprised to learn that themes of displacement, border crossing, or the journey as a metaphor for the quest for identity are present in such films. Wendy Everett argues more generally for the road movie or journey narrative as a common trope in European and American cinema for articulating and constructing narratives of exile and displacement (2004, 18–19). Elsewhere, Naficy identifies journeys of escape, emigration, exploration, or return as key features of diasporic, exilic, and postcolonial filmmakers working in the West (2001, 222–23). What is noticeable, however, is the increase in return narratives that have appeared in Maghrebi-French and North African émigré filmmaking since the early years of the first decade of the twenty-first century, and the way in which they all engage to various degrees with the possibility of intercultural exchange between France and the Maghreb via the clearly symbolic figure of the Maghrebi-French traveler. (I shall offer some suggestions as to why this may be the case in the final section of this chapter). This approach contrasts with the handful of return narratives produced by Maghrebi-French filmmakers in the 1980s and 1990s (*Le départ du père* [Belghoul 1983], *Cheb* [Bouchareb 1991], *Bye-Bye* [Dridi

1995], *Souviens-toi de moi* [Ghorab-Volta 1996]) where the possibility of "return" for Maghrebi-French youth to a country and culture that they do not really know is fraught with difficulties and ultimately rejected for a future, however uncertain, in France.[3]

The remainder of this chapter will be devoted to an examination of three recent journey films: *Ten'ja*, *Bled number one*, and *Exils*. These three films (released in France between 2004 and 2006) have been chosen since the distinct origins of their respective directors and their relationship to the Maghreb result in three very different responses to the key themes of return, home, and the politics of displacement for the Maghrebi-French subject.[4] They also offer a range of narrative and aesthetic responses to the representation of the myth of return in Maghrebi-French and North African émigré filmmaking.

Ten'ja or the Myth of Return

For North African immigrants who arrived in France as economic migrants during the *Trente Glorieuses* (1945–75), the *mythe du retour* was the commonly held belief that their place in France as economic migrants was temporary and that they, along with their children, would eventually return home to the Maghreb. By investing in this myth of return, many of the immigrants were, unlike their French-born descendants, more accepting of their marginalization within French society.[5] The pull between the "here" of the host country and "there" of the homeland evoked by the myth of return, and its idealization of the ancestral homeland, appears to be one of the defining features of the diasporic experience (Cohen 1997, 184–85). However, if this myth of return is central in the immigrants' understanding of their displacement as a diasporic community and in the deep attachment to their Maghrebi roots, it was not the same for their French-born descendants.

In *Ten'ja* (whose Arabic title literally means the "land is here" or "the land has returned") Hassan Legzouli attempts to reclaim the myth of return that is so roundly rejected in the 1990s by Maghrebi-French directors such as Bouchareb (*Cheb*) and Dridi (*Bye-Bye*). As an émigré filmmaker, even one who has lived in France for over twenty years, Legzouli might be presumed to have a greater emotional investment in the notion of return to the Maghreb than Maghrebi-French filmmakers such as Bouchareb and Dridi who were either born or raised in France, though as shall be discussed in the conclusion to this chapter, we should be wary of applying such a simplistic or essentialized reading of the North African émigré filmmaker's relationship to the Maghreb to these return narratives. What is clear, however, is that *Ten'ja*'s greater investment in the return narrative as a means of reconnection with Maghrebi roots is made possible by the fact that the film focuses on an older Maghrebi-French protagonist (Nordine) who appears economically and socially integrated into French society. Unlike the youthful outsiders of *Cheb* and *Bye-Bye*, Nordine (Roschdy Zem) is a self-employed taxi driver in his midthirties whose rightful place in France is never brought into question.

Legzouli's largely uncritical (re)investment in the myth of return identifies *Ten'ja* as the most conventional of all the return narratives considered in this chapter. It is also the most conventional in terms of narrative structure and film form. The film draws extensively on the established codes and iconography of the road movie genre: the open road, a voyage undertaken by car, the journey as a metaphor for self-discovery. Following the death of his father, Nordine journeys from Nord-pas-de-Calais to the Middle Atlas mountains in southern Morocco to honor his father's last wish that he be returned "home" and buried in Aderj, the village of his birth. Nordine initially views the journey as a burden, though this position changes following various encounters en route to the *bled*. He befriends Mimoun (Abdou El-Mesnaoui), an impoverished porter from the local morgue who dreams of emigrating to Australia to be reunited with his "true love," and Nora (Aure Atika), a graduate from Casablanca who, in spite of a university education, can only provide for her family as the mistress of a rich businessman. Both act as guides for Nordine on the various stages of his journey: intermediaries and interpreters of a country and culture that he is only beginning to understand. It is also worth noting that both Mimoun and Nora are, like Nordine, marginal figures in Moroccan society.

Nordine's dislocation from his Moroccan parents' Arab-Berber heritage is emphasized by the box of his father's possessions that he carries with him: letters, family photographs, a record of his father's favorite song, and a newspaper cutting of his father meeting President Mitterrand while working as an immigrant miner in Sallaumines (Nord-pas-de-Calais). These markers or fragments of a displaced identity bring to mind Begag and Chaouite's observation that the French-born descendants of North African immigrants only inherit selective elements of their parents' culture and religious traditions, fragments of language — constructing a "cultural myth" which is partially absorbed rather than directly lived (1991, 48–50).

For Nordine these objects not only articulate a link to his father's past and Maghrebi heritage, they also enable him to make connections with those he encounters in the here and now of contemporary Moroccan society. On a trip to a local souk, Nordine hears a cassette recording of his father's favorite song, which he asks Nora to translate for him. Nora is initially disinterested, saying that she prefers modern pop music. Eventually, however, she concedes, explaining the song's central theme of honoring a promise of remembrance ("Oh mon Dieu donne-moi la main! Je te fais le serment de ne pas t'oublier" [Oh Lord, give me your hand! I promise not to forget you]). These words carry an obvious significance for Nordine, given the journey he has undertaken. Moreover, by gifting his father's record to Nora toward the end of the film, Nordine strengthens the material, emotional, and cultural bond he has made with both the Morocco of his family's past and the Maghreb of the present (embodied by Nora and Mimoun).

Nordine's return to his North African roots in *Ten'ja* permits the reconfiguration of a fragmented diasporic identity (connecting with the past through memories and material objects) at the same time as it suggests a reconnection with the space and place of "home" in the present. When Nordine finally arrives in the location where Aderj appears on the map, he is told by a man sitting by the roadside that the village no longer exists, as (like Nordine's father) all its occupants have long since departed in search of work. The diasporic imaginary of home constructed by his father is thus fixed in a past that does not correspond to the sociopolitical realities of the present. The central purpose of Nordine's journey, to return his father's body to his village, is denied by this narrative twist: "home" as a physical location is lost. We may well have expected this revelation to prompt an exploration in the final part of the film of the very significance of place and home for the exile or diasporic subject. And yet, the desire to retain the personal and culturally specific link to the imaginary of home common in diasporic or exilic cinema (Morse 1999, 64) is undiminished in the final act of *Ten'ja*. Dressed in traditional costume and carrying the coffin on foot along a narrow mountain, Nordine returns his father to the earth of the ancestral home. These visual markers are accompanied by a diegetic soundtrack of traditional Arab music and further enforced by Nordine's repetition at the graveside of a phrase uttered to him in Arabic by his father following an aborted trip to Morocco when he was a teenager: "Where did this branch come from? From this tree." Through the connections made between landscape, tradition, familial duty, and "roots," *Ten'ja* elides the problematic aspects of return for the Maghrebi-French subject. Instead, the narrative emphasizes the regrounding of Nordine's North African identity from past to present. The act of "coming home" is identified as central to this reconciliation, rendering the myth of return for both first and second generations of the Maghrebi diaspora in France as necessary and enriching.

While *Ten'ja* attracted only modest audiences upon its release in France (just under twenty thousand spectators in a nine-week run), its treatment of the themes of return and reconciliation for the Maghrebi-French protagonist was generally well received by French critics (see, for example, Barlet 2004).[6] In contrast, Moroccan reviewers criticized what they saw as the romanticized portrayal of return in the film, destined for a "European audience in search of exoticism," which glossed over the sociopolitical realities of contemporary Moroccan society: prostitution, drugs, clandestine emigration, the repression of ethnic Amazighs (Bernichi 2006, 42). Elaborating on this critique of the film, we could argue that the SUV Nordine drives through the breathtaking scenery of the Atlas Mountains partially insulates him from these same sociopolitical realities that might destabilize idealized notions of home and return. Similarly, the symbolic act of traversing the waters from France to the Maghreb and crossing the border into Morocco is largely uneventful. The only problem experienced by Nordine concerns irregularities surrounding the paperwork for transporting his dead father's body. Even this is eventually overlooked by sympathetic border guards who regard Nordine as Moroccan (not French) and allow a fellow countryman to pass through customs with his father's body.[7] Nordine affirms their reading of his "true" nationality by stating to the border guards "pour moi aussi, je suis Marocain" [as far as I'm concerned, I'm Moroccan too], eliding in this one utterance the complex negotiation of hybrid identity that takes place in so many other Maghrebi-French films.

In the film's final scenes, which function as something of an epilogue to the burial of the father, Nordine returns to Tangiers to pay off Mimoun's debts to a local people trafficker. They part, addressing one another as "brother," and the film ends with a static shot of Nordine looking back at Mimoun through his rearview mirror. The reconciliation of the Maghrebi-French protagonist with his North African heritage thus appears complete. However, like the family photos that Nordine carries with him, this idyllic image of intercultural reconciliation is fixed in time, isolated from the complex and evolving historical, socioeconomic, and cultural context(s) that surround and inform it. By choosing to end the film in this way, Legzouli diverts the spectator from the fact that Nordine, like his father before him, will make his home in France, while Mimoun, now free from his creditors, is also intent on leaving Morocco for Europe. The ending of *Ten'ja* thus offers a further indication of Legzouli's desire to endorse an integrated and largely unproblematic representation of the myth of return for the Maghrebi-French protagonist.

Bled number one and the Politics of Displacement

If Legzouli downplays the socioeconomic, cultural, and political context of return in *Ten'ja*'s more conventional road movie format, Maghrebi-French director Rabah Ameur-Zaïmeche locates what we might term the politics of displacement for the Maghrebi-French protagonists at the very heart of the return narrative in *Bled number one*. Released in 2006, *Bled number one* was the follow-up to the filmmaker's critically acclaimed debut feature *Wesh wesh, qu'est-ce qui se passe?* (2001). Though set apart by their respective geographical and sociocultural locations — *Wesh wesh* takes place in a rundown housing estate on the outskirts of Paris and *Bled number one* in a rural village in Algeria — the two films are closely linked in a variety of ways. First, through their production methods of (ultra-)low-budget digital video (DV) filmmaking combining a concern for the politics of film form with a quasi-documentary approach (location shooting, episodic narrative, the use of largely nonprofessional actors, including the director's family and friends).[8] Second, *Bled number one* continues Ameur-Zaïmeche's practice of exploring broader sociopolitical issues through a study of local communities and the micropolitics of the family. In this case the enforced return of a Maghrebi-French man to the family home (the *bled* of the film's title) upon his release from prison in France is used to analyze the damaging personal consequences of the *double peine* as well as the specter of Islamic fundamentalism that remains in Algerian society, even after the end of the civil war.[9] Through its focus on the relationship between Kamel (Rabah Ameur-Zaïmeche) and Louisa (Meryem Serbah) — his largely westernized Algerian cousin who is ostracized by her family for seeking to break free from an abusive relationship with her husband — *Bled number one* also addresses the continued inequality, injustice, and often violent repression experienced by women in rigidly conservative and patriarchal Algerian society.

The final link between Ameur-Zaïmeche's two films is the character of Kamel, played by the director himself, who guides us through both narratives. In *Wesh wesh*, having previously been deported to Algeria following his release from prison in France as a victim of the *double peine*, Kamel returns illegally to the only home he knows: the rundown housing estate in the Paris suburbs where he grew up. *Bled number one*, on the other hand, begins with Kamel arriving in the family home in northeastern Algeria. Despite attempts to integrate into the local community, Kamel ultimately experiences a profound sense of alienation in Algeria. By the end of the film he discusses with one of his cousins from the village his desire to escape across the border to Tunisia and then return illegally to France.

The connection between the two narratives is compounded by the ambiguous ending in *Wesh wesh*, where we hear the gunshots fired by the police in pursuit of Kamel but do not see the consequences of this action. It is therefore possible that Kamel is arrested and re-deported to Algeria rather than being killed. In this case, the return narrative of *Bled number one* can be placed either before Kamel's initial return to France at the start of *Wesh wesh* or after his subsequent (re)expulsion to Algeria — an ambiguity that the director himself has encouraged when interviewed (Vassé 2006, 4). Viewing the sequencing of the two films in this way (as an open, uncertain chronology) thus serves to reinforce a reading of Kamel as caught in a perpetual cycle of exclusion from both Maghrebi and French society.

Kamel's journey to the Maghreb is, quite obviously, an enforced return. Ameur-Zaïmeche describes the protagonist as an "exile," but one who "transforms his deportation into a journey of discovery" (Vassé 2006, 6). This internal "journey of identity" involves a mixture of observation and engagement as well as more detached contemplation of Kamel's relationship to his ancestral home (Naficy 2001, 237). His dislocation from the *bled* is primarily articulated through film form and will be repeated throughout *Bled number one*. The film's opening sequence consists of five setups: an extended (detached) tracking shot of the road leading into the *bled*; a much briefer view of the same street from inside the taxi transporting Kamel to the village; a static long shot that contemplates the taxi's arrival from the opposite end of the street; a further tracking shot of a young boy running through the streets alongside the taxi; and finally a long shot of Kamel descending from the taxi to be greeted by his extended family. The opening sequence establishes a blending of documentary with fiction as well as a distanciation of Kamel from his sociocultural environment. As the camera navigates its way into the heart of the community in this opening sequence, many of the villagers in the street, clearly conscious of the camera's presence, meet its gaze. (One man even smoothes his hair back while looking into the camera lens.) And yet, the supposed "objectivity" and distance created by the documentary or ethnographic gaze is destabilized by the variety of perspectives used in this opening sequence — in particular the cut to the shot of the small boy running alongside the taxi that is clearly meant to reflect Kamel's point of view and offer a more intimate connection to the *bled*'s inhabitants.[10]

Distanciation is nonetheless embedded in the aesthetic structure of *Bled number one*. Ameur-Zaïmeche repeatedly films both protagonists and their environment using a combination of long shot and zoom. Spectators therefore observe the *bled* from a position of detachment. They are removed from the physical environment of the *bled* and from moments of intimacy shared by characters on screen, such as Kamel's arrival in the village or his interaction with Louisa on the beach. Moreover, this distanciation is as much aural as it is visual, with spectators frequently being denied access to what the characters are saying during these key and intimate exchanges. The implied cultural distance between Kamel and the villagers is further suggested by the physical barriers (doors, shutters, bodies) that frequently block the path of the camera, preventing the spectators or Kamel from having full and unimpeded access to the cine-spatial environment of the *bled*. The most sinister example of this blocking of the camera comes when Bouzid (Abel Jafri) closes the door from the terrace before administering his savage beating of his sister, Louisa.

The function of this formal strategy in *Bled number one* has as much to do with emphasizing Kamel's profound sense of displacement and disloca- tion as excluding the spectator. While *Bled number one* suggests an initial connection between Kamel and the physical environment of the *bled*, he is ultimately alienated by the strict gender divisions that regulate community interaction. This is well illustrated during the feast of Zerda, where "Kamel la France" (as the villagers call him) oscillates between active involvement in the ceremony (leading the bull from the lorry) and semidetached observer (reduced to a bystander at the moment of slaughter). The use of this nickname presents Kamel as simultaneously accepted and designated as "other" within the *bled* community. He is also visually singled out from the other villagers by the bright orange hat that he wears throughout the film. Elsewhere, Kamel's otherness is alluded to by the fact that he can understand much of the Arab dialect spoken around him but is only able to respond in French or broken Arabic. Similarly, when first sitting on the terrace of the family home, he draws attention to the call to prayer emanating from a nearby mosque but admits that he is not a practicing Muslim.

When initially involved in the social rituals involving the men of the village, such as the dancing on the evening of the feast of Zerda, Kamel appears integrated. His estrangement effectively begins when he laughs off a suggestion by one of the male elders that to eat with the women during the feast is sinful. Kamel's desire to spend time with the women of the village — especially his more liberal and westernized cousin, Louisa — betrays his uncertainty as to his place in *bled* society. Upon learning that Bouzid has beaten Louisa for allegedly "shaming" the family, he confronts his cousin in front of the other menfolk, who disapprove of Kamel's intervention. He is rapidly ostracized by the men in the village and referred to as "Kamel le voleur" (indicating the reason for his deportation from France) rather than "Kamel la France." This unsettling of Kamel's place within the community is reflected by the surreal moments that punctuate the narrative and subvert the docu-realist aesthetic. The morning after his confrontation with Bouzid, Kamel is shown staring pensively across a lake, accompanied by an atmospheric blues guitar soundtrack. The camera then pulls back to reveal the guitarist (journeyman French rock musician Rodolphe Burger) playing on the hillside next to Kamel/Ameur-Zaïmeche, complete with amp and microphones.

In many respects, *Bled number one* is as much about the marginalization of Louisa in a patriarchal society that refuses to acknowledge her right to independence as it is about Kamel's alienation as a hybrid subject who cannot fit in. It is no surprise, then, that the narrative brings these two characters together. And yet, Ameur-Zaïmeche pessimistically denies any possibility for the emergence of a progressive and more liberal Algeria by having Louisa locked away in the psychiatric hospital after a failed suicide attempt. The hospital becomes the only place in which Louisa can truly find her voice and express her "sinful" desire to become the Algerian Billie Holiday without being judged, while the "disturbed" women given refuge from abusive husbands (real patients from the hospital), who are interviewed on camera, express a sense of transnational female solidarity, crying: "Vive l'Algérie, vive la France. La France on t'aime, l'Algérie on t'aime, Chinoises, Allemandes, Américaines" [Long live Algeria, long live France, France we love you, Algeria we love you, Chinese (women), German (women), American (women)]. Surrounded by a barbed-wire fence and located on the outskirts of an unidentified town, the psychiatric hospital becomes (ironically) the only space in *Bled number one* where any optimistic exchange or intercultural dialogue between French (Western) and Algerian culture seems possible.

As in Maghrebi-French films from the 1990s, Ameur-Zaïmeche exposes the myth of return for the Maghrebi-French protagonist as just that: a myth. The *bled* is far from the idealized homeland of North African immigrant parents (Begag and Chaouite 1991, 44). Indeed, as the narrative unfolds, there is an increasingly bitter irony to the chosen title *Bled number one* (which would seem to qualify the *bled* as the ultimate or desirable destination for its Maghrebi-French protagonist). However, unlike earlier films such as *Cheb*, which identified the Maghrebi-French protagonist as an outsider in Algerian society from the outset, *Bled number one* shows that Kamel has tried and failed to initiate an intercultural dialogue between his French and Arab-Berber roots. For Kamel the *bled*, rather than France, becomes the space of exile and displacement: a fact that is graphically illustrated in the film's final scene, which shows Kamel reduced to a darkened silhouette wandering aimlessly on the hillside to the accompaniment of Burger's blues-inflected Arabic melody.

Exils: Encoding "Home," Embodying Exile

Though he is perhaps best known for his Gypsy trilogy (*Latcho drom* [1993], *Mondo* [1995], and *Gadjo dilo* [1997]), Tony Gatlif has directed seventeen films to date. In *Exils*, Gatlif explores the themes of marginality and displacement that characterize much of his work, through the story of two young lovers journeying from the Parisian *banlieue* to Algeria via Spain and Morocco. The film is an intensely personal narrative for Gatlif, who was born in Algiers in 1948 and moved to France at the end of the Algerian War. While the director's (Andalusian) Gypsy origins are well documented in his filmography to date, his connection to the Maghreb is less well known. This fact was acknowledged by Gatlif himself in a speech at Cannes in 2004 (following the award for best direction for *Exils*) where he described the film as "a desire to examine my own scars . . . the land of my childhood: a journey of 7,000 km by train, car, boat, and on foot and 55,000 meters by film" (Marsaud 2004).

Like *Bled number one*, *Exils* displays an acute awareness of the politics of exile and displacement. Although the director's own experience of uprooting is undoubtedly projected onto his protagonists, Gatlif rejected any romanticized notion of return for him as a filmmaker, claiming emphatically that the film was not "about" Algeria, a country that he did not know. Instead, he described *Exils* in more universal terms as "un film sur les enfants d'exilés à la recherche de leurs origines" [a film about children of exile searching for their origins] (Marsaud 2004). The influence of Galtif's own Andalusian Gypsy origins thus means that the "return" journey to the Maghreb undertaken by Zano and Naïma is as much an opportunity for a more general exploration of themes of nomadism, uprooting, and exile in a narrative that travels through France, Spain, Morocco, and Algeria rather than directly from Paris to Algiers.

The "return" of the young lovers to North Africa in *Exils* is quite different from that of *Ten'ja* or *Bled number one*, and not least because Zano (Romain Duris) is the French descendant of pied-noir parents (colonial settlers exiled to France following Algerian independence in 1962) and Naïma (Lubna Azabal) the female French descendant of Algerian immigrant parents. In contrast to *Ten'ja* and *Bled number one*, the journey undertaken by Zano and Naïma is not enforced, nor is it prompted by a sense of familial duty. It is circuitous, impulsive, and at times incomprehensible to those around them. Habib and Leila, the Algerian siblings befriended by Zano and Naïma in Spain, are perplexed as to why they would leave the wealth and comfort of western Europe in order to "return" to Algeria. Compared to the illegal migrants they encounter traveling north from Africa, the young lovers risk nothing in their adventure south to the Maghreb. This fact is emphasized by the scene in which the Spanish police arrest two immigrant workers for deportation, while Zano and Naïma, as holders of French passports, continue their journey uninhibited. Until his arrival at the family home in Algiers, Zano displays a playful (almost childlike) approach to the journey south. The pair engage in a kind of exilic tourism as they return to Algeria, taking a detour to a flamenco festival in Seville and participating in a Sufi trance ritual in Algiers, filmed in its entirety by Gatlif in an intimate documentary style that contrasts with the more stylized approach to form and mise-en-scène found elsewhere in the film.

Despite the privileges enjoyed by Zano and Naïma as the "right kind" of exilic travelers, their journey is nonetheless one of discovery and intercultural dialogue between France and the Maghreb. The presence of Zano as the descendant of pieds-noirs exposes the fact that the movement and exchange of people, culture, and commodities between France and the Maghreb during the colonial period has resulted in the existence in France today of (post) colonial exiles of both European and non-European origin. His presence also complicates any essentialized reading of the journey narrative in Maghrebi-French or North African émigré filmmaking as a simple return to Arab or Berber "roots" (since vestiges of French and pied-noir culture also remain in postcolonial Algeria). And yet, while the film hints at a more complex legacy of France's colonial presence in North Africa through its pairing of Zano and Naïma, it stops short of exploring the potential for symbolic reconciliation between a character of pied-noir descent and another of Algerian origin that their couple could indicate.

In fact, it is Naïma's return to Algeria that prompts the most profound journey of self-discovery in *Exils*. In contrast to Zano's playful energy and self-confidence, Naïma is introspective and uncertain of her place in either France or the Maghreb. In Algiers, she is verbally abused in the street by a complete stranger for dressing immodestly, and later, during a visit to Leila and Habib's family, confesses to feeling "a stranger everywhere" (*je suis une étrangère de partout*). Though of Algerian origin, she is, like Kamel in *Bled number one*, distanced from Maghrebi culture by her inability to speak Arabic. When asked by Habib if her name is Arabic, she simply replies "c'est Naïma, quoi" [it's just Naïma], refusing to define her identity in terms of ethnicity. By presenting Naïma in this way, Gatlif arguably risks perpetuating the stereotype of the damaged Maghrebi-French protagonist trapped between two cultures found in *Beur* cinema (films directed by descendants of North African immigrants born and/or raised in France) of the 1980s and 1990s. And yet, Naïma is not a helpless victim marginalized by her own hybridity. Despite having earlier played down the Arabic origins of her name, when mistaken for a Gypsy by a gitano at the flamenco festival, she vociferously identifies herself (in incorrect Spanish) as an Algerian from France ("soy *Algerina* . . . de Francia") thus endorsing Avtar Brah's understanding of diasporic identity as contingent and shifting, in a process of constant renegotiation (1996, 153–55).

Key to the exploration of a more fluid concept of identity in *Exils* is a cinematic aesthetic structured around displacement and movement. Gatlif displays a preoccupation with displaced framing or fluid and shifting surfaces in the film, which are also projected onto the bodies of the film's exilic subjects. From the opening shot of *Exils* (an extreme close-up of Zano's naked back) the body is identified as a key site of exilic trauma and identity. Later, in the scenes taking place in an abandoned mine in Spain, Zano recounts his grandfather's history in Algeria and the death of his parents in a car crash — formative events that motivate his journey to the Maghreb. His narration is accompanied by an abstracted reflection of his face in a dark pool of water (the reflection itself is placed off center with the majority of the screen in darkness). The reflection (like Zano himself) is in a constant state of movement and transformation. Therefore, in contrast to the final image of Nordine from *Ten'ja*, Gatlif refuses to fix the exilic or postcolonial subject, denying us a clear view of exactly *who* Zano is.

As a diasporic road movie, movement is key to *Exils*'s aesthetic. The film frequently presents point of view shots from inside buses and trains that survey a shifting landscape. Zano and Naïma are also repeatedly depicted as moving against the flow. They fight their way through the mass of oncoming refugees displaced by the earthquake in Algeria and, in one particular scene, move through the streets of Algiers as those around them remain motionless. Such moments function as visual metaphors for their dislocation from the Algerian culture and society that surrounds them, despite their physical presence in the Maghreb.

Arriving at his grandparents' home in Algiers, Zano expects to achieve some kind of reconciliation with his past. Instead, there is only the alienation and the continued grief of exile as Zano weeps uncontrollably before the strangers who now occupy the apartment. Traces of his family are to be found in the material space of the apartment: the decor remains largely unchanged, furniture is still in place, and photos belonging to his family still hang on the walls. However, time has inevitably moved on and these fragments from a lost past are not sufficient to bridge the gap to the present, illustrating just how far removed Zano (and by extension Gatlif) is from contemporary Algeria. In the end, however, both Zano and Naïma achieve some form of reconciliation with and reconnection to the Maghreb. For Naïma this comes from her participation in the Sufi trance ritual, through which she is literally able to exorcize the ghosts of her past. For Zano, partial closure is offered by a visit to his grandfather's grave in Algiers, where he leaves his personal stereo playing on top of the tombstone. This gesture could be read as an attempt to establish a link between a form of expression central to Zano's own sense of self (earlier in the film he comments that "music is my religion") and his ancestral heritage from the Maghreb. However, the fact that *Exils* ends with the couple walking away from the grave, recommencing their journey with no indication of where they will go next, identifies them as symbolic (and to an extent romanticized) nomads. Above all, Zano and Naïma's return to Algeria is evidence of a loss of belief in a fixed sense of either home or identity.

The three films analyzed in this chapter are representative of an increasing number of return narratives found in Maghrebi-French and North African émigré filmmaking since the early years of the first decade of the current century. How then might we account for this recent development? We could point to the fact that conditions in Algeria (the ultimate destination in many of these films) were simply too dangerous to contemplate shooting in for much of the previous decade due to the civil war that ravaged the country between 1992 and 1998.[11] In this respect, a film such as *Bled number one* not only articulates a politics of displacement for its Maghrebi-French protagonist, it also documents how Algerian society, even at the micro-level of the *bled*, is still dealing with the aftermath of the civil war and the specter of Islamic fundamentalism. And yet, as *Ten'ja* shows, such return narratives do not need to be set exclusively in Algeria. Equally plausible is the suggestion that by the first decade of the twenty-first century, the French-born descendants of Maghrebi immigrants are, by and large, more integrated than in the 1980s and 1990s, when *Beurs* were the focus of a series of broader debates around citizenship and national identity in a postcolonial, multicultural France.[12] In the political climate of the 1980s and 1990s, most *Beur* filmmakers and political activists were, for obvious reasons, more concerned with arguing for the rightful place of Maghrebi-French youth in France than they were in investing the possibilities of opening up an intercultural dialogue with their North African heritage by journeying to the *bled*. Nevertheless, it should be noted that *Ten'ja*, *Bled number one*, and *Exils* are all films produced on extremely small budgets of between 1 and 3 million U.S. dollars, attracting modest audiences in France of 19,750, 6,8010, and 310,046 spectators, respectively.[13] Even if such journey films can be seen as indicative of a greater confidence on the part of Maghrebi-French youth as to their place within contemporary French society, they are not attracting the interest of mainstream producers nor are they engaging with sizable crossover audiences in France.

We might reasonably assume that the differing relationship of these three directors to the Maghreb itself affects how the act of return is articulated in each film. Thus Legzouli's status as a Moroccan émigré arguably helps to explain the more unproblematic reconnection with North African "roots" in

Ten'ja, whereas the impossibility of reconciliation and breakdown of cross-cultural Franco-Algerian dialogue in *Bled number one* could be interpreted as a consequence of Ameur-Zaïmeche's own position as Maghrebi-French: born in Algeria but raised in France from a young age and somewhat ambivalent to the emotional and cultural pull exacted by the diasporic "homeland." We should, however, be cautious of imposing such an essentialized reading onto films that are, precisely, dealing with the potential transformation of diasporic identities, achieved through intercultural exchange and taking place in narratives predicated on mobility and journeys of self-discovery. While the three films examined in this chapter may adopt quite distinct approaches in relation to the "myth of return," they all present identity as contingent, unstable, and in a process of becoming in a way that is clearly not predicated on a closed or final return to the Maghreb (or indeed wholesale rejection of the potential benefits of this act of return). *Exils* ends on a point of (uncertain) departure for Zano and Naïma, *Bled number one* depicts an alienated Kamel contemplating his prospects for "escape" to France via Tunisia, while *Ten'ja* endorses reconciliation with Maghrebi roots but leaves Nordine on the point of return to France. Similarly, all three films, in their different ways and to varying degrees, reground the identity of their protagonists in the context of the contemporary Maghrebi society. In so doing they reexamine the place and significance of "home" within the diasporic imaginary. Perhaps most curious of all, though, is that all three directors, regardless of their origins or relationship to the Maghreb, choose to explore the myth of return through Maghrebi-French protagonists, rather than North African immigrants whose connection as exilic or diasporic subjects to the Maghreb is more immediate. In French cinema of the first decade of the twenty-first century, then, it would appear that Maghrebi-French protagonists remain, due to their perceived interstitiality, the symbolic focus of the complex and continuing cultural, historical, and sociopolitical exchange between France and the Maghreb.

Notes

1. I am using these terms to distinguish between French filmmakers of North African origin (Maghrebi-French) and those émigré directors who, for a variety of reasons, reside and work in France but were born and raised in the Maghreb. I prefer the term "Maghrebi-French" to *Beur*, as the latter is largely identified with the second generation (and not subsequent generations) of North African immigrants and has, in the past, been rejected by many of those it presumes to describe (Begag 2007; Durmelat 1998).

2. If we were to incorporate return narratives by filmmakers of non-Maghrebi origin,

we would also add *Un aller simple* (Heyneman 2001) and *Les chemins de l'oued* (Gaël Morel 2002).

3. A similar point is made by Carrie Tarr in her analysis of these films: "Even if the establishment of their identity in France continues to be problematic, the prospect of crossing the border to Algeria or other countries of the Maghreb presents a threat to the beur's westernized identity" (2005, 189).

4. Legzouli was born and raised in Morocco and has resided in France and Belgium since emigrating to Europe as a student in the mid-1980s; Ameur-Zaïmeche was born in Algeria but arrived in France at a very young age and was raised in the Parisian *banlieue* where he has lived ever since; Gatlif, of Andalusian Gypsy origins, was born in colonial Algeria in 1948 and was effectively exiled to France as a teenager at the end of the Algerian War in 1962.

5. For more details, see different accounts of the myth of return documented in Benguigui's *Mémoires d'immigrés* (1997).

6. The source for audience numbers is CBO Box Office (2009).

7. This could not be further from the experience of Merwan, the young Maghrebi-French protagonist in *Cheb* (Bouchareb 1991), who upon his arrival in Algeria is labeled by hostile border guards as "immigrant," "foreigner," and "delinquent."

8. *Wesh wesh* was shot for a miniscule 230,000 euros; *Bled number one* for 1.04 million euros (CBO Box Office 2009).

9. The term *double peine* refers to legislation introduced in 1945 that permits the expulsion of any foreign national following release from prison in France. While it supposedly targets "foreigners," the legislation makes no distinction between foreigners arrested of a crime while on French soil and those who have resided in France for a number of years or since a young age (as is the case for Kamel in *Wesh wesh* and *Bled number one*). While they may not have full French citizenship, they are to all intents and purposes "French," having been raised and educated in France. The legislation referring to the *double peine* was banned by the socialists in 1981 but then temporarily reinstated by the right-wing government between 1986 and 1988 (Hargreaves 1995, 189–92). Although the *double peine* was abolished in November 2003 (with the exception of cases involving terrorism or "threats to national security"), accusations remain that the process of expulsion is still being practiced in France (Geraud 2009).

10. I hesitate to use the term "ethnographic" here, conscious of its obvious and often negative connotations in relation to colonial documentary filmmaking (Bloom 2008, 159–60). However, the deliberate use of the camera in *Bled number one* to observe and document life in the Algerian village by an outsider (Maghrebi-French) filmmaker is arguably ethnographic or anthropological filmmaking.

11. Following the overturning of democratic elections in 1992, the secular military government brutally repressed opposition with death squads and mass detentions while the militant Islamic opposition responded with suicide bombings, assassinations, and death threats in an attempt to destabilize the nation. It is estimated that more than 150,000 Algerians (many of them innocent civilians) lost their lives in the political violence that dominated between 1992 and 1998 when the nation was effectively in a state of civil war (Bonner, Reif, and Tessler 2005, 3).

12. While it is clear that significant advances have been made since the early 1980s, I am not suggesting that political and economic integration has been achieved across the board for the Maghrebi-French population in France. Alongside the increasing social mobility enjoyed by the "beurgeoisie," sections of the Maghrebi-French population — described by Begag (2007) as *rouilleurs* (literally "rusters") — remain excluded due to socioeconomic inequalities, continued ethnic discrimination, and decades of political neglect in the deprived areas of the *banlieue*.

13. All figures are from CBO Box Office (2009).

References

Barlet, Olivier. 2004. Review of *Ten'ja*. http://www.africultures.com/php/index .php?nav=article&no=3580 (accessed February 12, 2009).

Begag, Azouz. 2007. *Ethnicity: France in the Balance*. Trans. Alec G. Hargreaves. Lincoln: University of Nebraska Press.

Begag, Azouz, and Abdellatif Chaouite. 1991. *Écarts d'identité*. Paris: Seuil.

Bernichi, Loubna. 2006. "Legzouli fait les yeux doux aux Français." *Maroc Hebdo International* 693 (7–13) (April): 42.

Bloom, Peter J. 2008. *French Colonial Documentary: Mythologies of Humanitarianism*. Minneapolis: University of Minnesota Press.

Bonner, Michael D., Mega Reif, and Mark A. Tessler, eds. 2005. *Islam, Democracy, and the State in Algeria: Lessons for the Western Mediterranean and Beyond*. Oxford: Routledge.

Brah, Avtar. 1996. *Cartographies of Diaspora: Contesting Identities*. London: Routledge.

CBO Box Office. 2009. http://www.cbo-boxoffice.com (accessed September 2, 2009).

Cohen, Robert. 1997. *Global Diasporas: An Introduction*. London: UCL Press.

Durmelat, Sylvie. 1998. "Petite histoire du mot beur ou comment prendre la parole quand on vous la prête." *French Cultural Studies* 9 (2): 191–208.

Everett, Wendy. 2004. "Leaving Home: Exile and Displacement in Contemporary European Cinema." In *Cultures of Exile, Images of Displacement*, ed. Wendy Everett and Peter Wagstaff, 17–32. New York: Berghahn Books.

Geraud, Alice. 2009. "La double peine n'est toujours pas totalement abolie." *Libération* [database online]. http://www.libelyon.fr/info/2009/01/la-double-peine.html (accessed February 12, 2009).

Hargreaves, Alec G. 1995. *Immigration, "Race," and Ethnicity in Contemporary France*. London: Routledge.

Higbee, Will. 2007. "Re-Presenting the Urban Periphery: Maghrebi-French Filmmaking and the Banlieue Film." In "Beur Is Beautiful: A Retrospective of Maghrebi-French Filmmaking," supplement, *Cineaste* 33 (1) (November): 8–13.

Marsaud, Olivia. 2004. "Retour d'exils en Algérie: Le film de Tony Gatlif enfin dans les salles en France." http://www.afrik.com/article7578.html (accessed January 21, 2009).

Morse, Margaret. 1999. "Home: Smell, Taste, Posture, Gleam." In *Home, Exile, Homeland: Film, Media, and the Politics of Place*, ed. Hamid Naficy, 63–74. London: Routledge.

Naficy, Hamid. 2001. *An Accented Cinema: Exilic and Diasporic Filmmaking*. Princeton: Princeton University Press.

Tarr, Carrie. 2005. *Reframing Difference:* Beur *and* Banlieue *Filmmaking in France*. Manchester: Manchester University Press.

Vassé, Claire. 2006. Interview with Rabah Ameur-Zaïmeche. In *Press dossier for* Bled number one, 4–11. N.p: Why Not Productions.

Filmography

Allouache, Merzak, dir. *Salut cousin!*, 1996.

———, dir. *L'autre monde*, 2001.

Ameur-Zaïmeche, Rabah, dir. *Wesh wesh, qu'est-ce qui se passe?*, 2001.

———, dir. *Bled number one*, 2006.

Belghoul, Farida, dir. *Le départ du père*, 1983.

Benguigui, Yamina, dir. *Mémoires d'immigrés: L'héritage maghrébin*, 1997.

———, dir. *Inch'Allah dimanche*, 2001.

Bensalah, Djamel, dir. *Il était une fois dans l'oued*, 2005.

Bouchareb, Rachid, dir. *Cheb*, 1991.

Charef, Mehdi, dir. *La fille de Keltoum*, 2001.

des Pallières, Arnaud, dir. *Adieu*, 2003.

Dridi, Karim, dir. *Bye-Bye*, 1995.

Ducastel, Olivier, and Jacques Martineau, dirs. *Drôle de Félix*, 2000.

Ferroukhi, Ismaël, dir. *Le grand voyage*, 2004.

Gatlif, Tony, dir. *Latcho drom*, 1993.

———, dir. *Mondo*, 1995.

———, dir. *Gadjo dilo*, 1997.

———, dir. *Exils*, 2004.

Ghorab-Volta, Zaïda, dir. *Souviens-toi de moi*, 1996.

———, dir. *Jeunesse dorée*, 2001.

Guerdjou, Bourlem, dir. *Vivre au paradis*, 1998.

Heyneman, Laurent, dir. *Un aller simple,* 2001.

Legzouli, Hassan, dir. *Ten'ja*, 2004.

Morel, Gaël, dir. *Les chemins de l'oued*, 2002.

4

TURNING INTEGRATION INSIDE OUT

How Johnny the Frenchman Became Abdel Bachir
the Arab Grocer in *Il était une fois dans l'oued*

HAKIM ABDERREZAK

Il était une fois dans l'oued (2005) is the third feature film of French
director of Algerian ancestry Djamel Bensalah. Bensalah's previous
films, *Le ciel, les oiseaux et . . . ta mère!* (1999) and *Le raïd* (2002),
each attracted over 1 million spectators.[1] Featuring Julien Courbey,
a talented actor who was instrumental in turning Bensalah's films
into major hits, *Il était une fois* clearly belongs to the category of
highly successful commercial films.

Il était une fois is a comedy that centers on Johnny Leclerc
(Julien Courbey), born in Porte de Clichy to white working-class
parents (a Norman mother and an Alsatian father) and raised in
the *cité* Paul Éluard in a Parisian *banlieue*. Johnny desperately
wants to be regarded as an Algerian, an Arab, and a Muslim. As
a result, the film elicits laughter from the audience through the
use of an abundance of stereotypes, from Johnny's overzealous
observance of Islam to his passage as a stowaway on an Algeria-
bound ferry, his settling in Oran, and his adoption of the invented
name "Abdel Bachir." Yet, as I will argue, the director's playful
inversion of typical accounts of migration makes *Il était une fois*

dans l'oued a site for original and provocative reversals of commonly held identificatory perceptions. Bensalah invites his audience to consider the figure of the "first" Franco-French clandestine migrant to Algeria by transposing the stereotypical figure of the Arab grocer in France onto the "first" Franco-French "Arab" grocer in Algeria. Bensalah's use of stereotypes and parodies thus becomes instrumental in this filmic experiment in which characters switch typecast cultural roles in order to audition, rehearse, and perform new postcolonial migratory situations. This essay will therefore present Djamel Bensalah's road trip southward as a roadmap for the implementation of an experimental identity and a model for the reversal of common societal and cinematographic migration narratives.

While praising the originality of *Le ciel, les oiseaux et . . . ta mère!* for its alternative representations of *banlieue* youth, Carrie Tarr convincingly argues that Bensalah's previous two films are characterized by thematic and structural crudeness. *Le raïd*, for instance, has "a ludicrous . . . plot." In spite of "a budget of about £12 million" it is filled with "(not very impressive) visual gags and special effects, a surreal plotline . . . and obsessive toilet humor" (2005, 171). Similarly, *Il était une fois dans l'oued* features a tortuous storyline and a cascade of misadventures, as well as a muddle of ethnic jokes. At best, *Il était une fois* will entertain an audience aware of the film's ironical and satirical import. At worst, the film risks fueling firmly seated prejudices due to the very invocation of these prejudices.

The film's carnivalesque structure, however, enables it to perform multiple unexpected displacements and transformations. Johnny/Abdel Bachir's metamorphosis is literally set in motion when he invites himself into a new geographic and familial space.[2] He hides in the trailer of his best friend's parents and travels to Algeria along with his best friend, Yacine (David Saracino), Yacine's younger brother, Medy (Medy Kerouani), their father, Si Mohammed (Sid Ahmed Agoumi), and Moroccan stepmother, Khiera (Amina Annabi). On the ferry, he befriends two other travelers, Nadège (Marilou Berry) and Nadia (Karina Testa). In an Almodóvaresque conflation of intertwined subplots, Johnny ends up marrying Nadège, and Yacine ties the knot with Nadia, who happens to be the young lady with whom his father had meant to arrange his marriage.

From the outset, we are taken aback by Johnny's astounding claims to be an Algerian, a Muslim, and an Arab. Franco-French Johnny fits the stereotypical image of white French *banlieusards* who, along with their disillusioned *Beur* neighbors in the *banlieues* of Paris and Lyon, have converted to Islam in "réislamisation" movements since 1985 (Kepel 1987, 353, 376). Interestingly, blond-haired Johnny also adopts a *"Beur* look" and claims to be an Algerian.[3] By introducing Johnny as a prototype, that of a perplexing French-*Beur*-Algerian allegorical figure, Bensalah deconstructs all these institutionally recognized identities. Johnny is a hybrid, not in the sense of ethnic *métissage*, but rather, he performs hybridity in his own peculiar way. Ostensibly of northern French ancestry, he is a religious convert (a Muslim), culturally *Beur* and affectively Algerian.

Johnny's idea of his "original" identity and cultural destiny is presented as a parody of *Beur*ness. It is founded on a patchwork of excesses and approximations. A case in point is his unruly multifacetedness, which shows the dizzying range of possible identities between and within "French" and "Algerian." Johnny vaguely recalls being from "un petit bled entre Alger et Oran" [a small village between Algiers and Oran],[4] but the Algerianness, Arabness, and Islamness he covets originates possibly from secondhand objects (e.g., a drawing of "his village" purchased in a flea market), culturally reified linguistic usage (rudimentary Arabic words roughly interjected into French), and a Muslim education learned in situ, as is the case for many French converts.[5]

Still, it is not certain what Johnny's conception of Algerianness really is, and the viewer wonders if Johnny himself even knows, since he never really explains what it entails, uttering instead simplistic statements ("Je suis un Djazaïri" [I am an Algerian]). Johnny's strong nationalist feelings makes him condemn any association with France, as is illustrated by the following words he shouts at Medy on the soccer field: "J'suis sûr que t'as parié pour la France, p'tit con" [I'm sure you bet on France, little bastard] — a position that entices Mr. Sabri to warn him: "Attention, Johnny, tu deviens raciste" [Be careful, Johnny, you're becoming a racist].

Another revealing example of Johnny's ironic and troubling adoption of "racist" terms is when Mrs. Sabri, worried that Johnny might damage his skin on the beach from covering himself with cooking oil, advises the young man to be careful, to which Johnny replies, "Vous inquiétez pas Mme. Sabri, du vrai cuir d'Arabe ça, ça craint pas l'soleil" [Don't worry, Mrs. Sabri, this is genuine Arab hide, it don't fear the sun]. The scene mocks the prejudices of the sunburned Johnny, who equates machismo with natural toughness against inclement weather, and his belief that because he thinks he is an Arab, his physical body will follow suit. Johnny's statement of hiding under Arab hide — so to speak — is disconcerting since its comic aspect relies on his sincere yet ironic identification with a racist reification of the Arab body as having a "hide" like a (dead) animal, a hunted and traded object. He seems to be unaware of the disparaging nature of such conjectures, as if they were inscribed in his acquired cultural and linguistic baggage. Meanwhile, Johnny's adventure has something uncannily neocolonial about it. The film does not really problematize the fantasy that a French oddball would be welcomed like an Algerian hero. Johnny's smuggling into Algeria in the Trojan Sabri car and his taking root in a "deep-settler colony" may reanimate French colonial nostalgia.[6] However, Johnny's emotional identification with Algeria also facilitates what may be deemed, in the postcolonial era, a subversive proposition: Algeria as a desirable *colonie de vacances* (summer camp).

Johnny piggybacks on the ritual summer trip that many families of Maghrebi heritage make from their European dwellings to North Africa. The Sabris' journey includes driving to the south of Algeria to visit relatives, whom Johnny informs that his own village is "quelque part dans l'ouest" [somewhere in the west]. Untraceable to the familiar West (Occident) or the American "Far West," Johnny's village is "lost," as in the French expression *être à l'ouest*. *Il était une fois* shatters the sense of direction on which its title seems to play. The western West of *Once Upon a Time in the West* (1968) is replaced with the Maghreb (the Arab "ouest"). Besides, where we expected "west" in the title, we read "oued" [river]. However, instead of filming a story set on the banks of a *oued*, Bensalah's camera follows the characters driving to the *bled*: from the French housing projects to a ferry on the Mediterranean Sea, Algiers, the desert, and then back north to Algiers, Oran, and Algiers again. The "oued" of the title is lost in the narrative. Using a false metonymic indication, Bensalah's substitution of the cardinal point in the title with a phonetically close location *dis*orients the viewer. By dislocating words and places, Bensalah destabilizes easy generic categorizations of his film and revisits notions of identity, territory, and migration, leaving them in a different place than where he found them.

The film's subversion of the characters' sense of direction and the meaning attached to the return "home" also invokes the political history shared by France and Algeria. In a comical scene in which Johnny's parents get lost in Algiers while visiting him, the camera zooms in on the parents puzzling over a street sign that used to bear the name of a famous French writer, Anatole France. Following independence, it was renamed "Anatole Algérie" and translated into Arabic as "Anatole el-Djazaïr" [Anatole Algeria]. This scene points both to the blindness of postindependence Arabization politics as well as the nostalgic myopia of contemporary French travelers to Algeria rendered by Mr. Leclerc's exclamation: "Anatole Algérie, ça n'existe pas!" [Anatole Algeria, there is no such thing!] Indeed, the Leclercs, who may be connected to colonial Algeria, miss the crossed-out former street name that appears on the adjoining wall, next to the one they are looking at. Lost, they are *à l'ouest* and literally *à côté de la plaque* as the French slang has it, in that they are standing next to the street sign (*plaque*). The street sign is a metaphor for unique postcolonial creations — French-Algerian Djamel Bensalah's Johnny being one of them.

As is the case of *Big City* (2007) — Bensalah's fourth feature set in the American West of 1880 — *Il était une fois* can be described as a "couscous western." Its camp character is an obvious homage to Sergio Leone's "spaghetti westerns," which enables Bensalah to overlay serious moments of postcolonial Algerian history with farce to advance seemingly far-fetched scenarios in his contemporary Algerian Far West.[7] *Il était une fois* uses a playful western-style duel scene that parodies the western genre with the extra-diegetic clicking sound of guns and close-up shots that frame the characters' eyes. This duel follows the scene when Nadia refuses to comply with her male cousin's demand that she leave the male space of the coffee shop. When Yacine asks Nadia's cousin to treat her with respect, her relative angrily retorts: "Fais gaffe à ta bouche, le Françaoui. Ici, t'es pas chez toi. Ici, t'es qu'un émigré" [Watch your mouth, Frenchie. Here you're not home. Here you're just an emigrant]. Unlike westerns, however, Bensalah's story is not set on a physical frontier but a symbolic one. It spans an imagined *bled* buttressed by the unknown, against which characters define who they are and identify their "others." In this light, the "duel" illuminates existing perceptions about the supposed incompatibility of "dual" identities, in this case French/Algerian. It also relegates the interlocutors into two firmly marked camps, with "authentic" Algerian constituents on one side and *pas chez toi* visitors (outsiders) on the other.[8] While inclusion in national identity is refused to Yacine, Johnny is spared, signaling the film's unconventional handling of the spectators' expectations.

The arena of sports has become the theater where issues of citizenship, and of social and national inclusion, are played out. In the film, Nadia, Nadège, Yacine, and Johnny are playing table football, which prompts Johnny to resort to identitarian binaries. Indeed, when his teammate Nadège urges him not to "faire des passes à l'arrière" [pass the ball off to the back], Johnny proclaims himself the embodiment of "Laldjéria" [Algeria] and immediately reacts by accusing Nadège of playing like "une Bretonne qui a perdu ses papiers" [a Breton chick who lost her papers]. Ironically, it is he who is undocumented. He will also prove to play soccer poorly in a later scene. In the first soccer game between Algeria and France since the independence of Algeria, which took place on October 6, 2001, at the Stade de France, the predicted "friendly" nature of the event was unhinged by *Beur* fans, who viewed the dual event in "duelistic" terms. Fans booed at the playing of the French anthem and interrupted the match by intruding onto the (battle)field.[9] Bensalah's 2005 film, which takes place at the end of the 1980s, stages an anachronistic parodic "coda" to the historic soccer match in which Johnny is eager to participate by playing for the Algerian team.[10]

In the "rematch" staged this time on the field, the flabbergasted on-site Algerian commentator denounces Johnny, who wears the Algerian jersey, as a traitor for kicking the ball with his head into the net behind him, thus mistakenly scoring a point against his own team and making the Algerians lose against the French. Had the commentator spoken in the local language, he could have used the heavily loaded *harki*, thereby acknowledging Johnny's "original" Algerianness by the very same act of denigrating it.[11] Sensitive to Johnny's crying over his soccer failure, his Algerian hosts express sympathy. Their empathy is a subtle commentary on ongoing calls from various binational sources in favor of political acts of forgiveness, including for *harkis*.

Bypassing Johnny by Passing as Abdel Bachir

Annoyed by half-Alsatian Johnny and his infatuation with his story about being from Algeria, Yacine objects loudly: "À la rigueur, tu peux être un peu allemand mais tu seras jamais arabe de ta vie" [You could perhaps be a bit German but you will never in your life be an Arab]. Yacine's bitterness may come from the experience of not being able to "pass" as French in France nor as Arab in Algeria, where he is refused entry to a nightclub because of his inability to speak Arabic. Johnny, however, is admitted without question because he happens to know the bouncer "Jean-Michel Tahar la Rochefoucauld," who we learn was expelled from France.[12] The inflated but incomplete Frenchness of the bouncer's invented name echoes the parodied Arabness of "Abdel Bachir." Jean-Michel and Johnny's complicity enables the latter to become the star of the disco and perform in an "Arabian Nights" atmosphere. Yacine's stepmother's response to Yacine — "Mais qu'est-ce que ça peut te faire? On est du pays où on se sent le mieux" [Why do you care? One is from the country where one feels the best] — moves the question of national identity beyond the clear delineation between *jus soli* and *jus sanguinis* and proposes a third route to citizenship, one that transforms a potential *pas chez toi* into a *chez soi*.[13]

To assemble his Arabness, Julien Courbey's character has to pass as someone else. He adopts the compound first name Abdel Bachir. The first element of his name starts with an *A* and the second with a *B*. Probably following the Roman alphabet, "Abdel Bachir" is not possible in any linguistically authentic or appropriate form because "Abd el" (the servant/slave of) ought to precede "Allah" or any of God's ninety-nine other names, but "Bachir" is not one of them. Johnny's approach to choosing his "Arab" name makes the viewer wonder had he chosen a third element, if it would have started with a *C* such as Cherif.[14] Johnny's perfunctory self-"translation" highlights his naïve belief that de-identification from Frenchness and passing as an Arab is as simple as *abc*.

Bensalah both highlights and challenges the importance of naming in facilitating social and ethnic belonging and an integrated sense of identity. Before his migration to Algeria, Johnny feels overwhelmed with his "Françaoui" heritage. He is devastated to hear his mother's racist remark after she calls his *hbaya* a "costume de Chabbat" [Shabbat outfit]: "C'est pareil, c'est des fêtes de bougnoules" [It's the same, they're both raghead's holidays].[15] Johnny is also humiliated in front of his *Beur* friends by his father's insistence that he return home to eat sauerkraut, to which he responds: "J'suis un *Muslim*, j'vais pas casser mon jeûne avec du porc" [I'm a Muslim, I ain't gonna break my fast with pork]. Johnny's suffering conforms to Charles Taylor's statement that "our identity is partly shaped by recognition or its absence, often by the *mis*recognition of others. . . . Non-recognition or misrecognition can inflict harm, can be a form of oppression, imprisoning someone in a false, distorted, and reduced mode of being" (1992, 25). In Taylor's terms, Johnny's anxiety to free himself from the "*mis*recognition of others" in the *banlieue* pushes him to flee the national confines of his "imprisonment."

Algeria will become Johnny's escape from the French *banlieue*, a "wild" space of fractures of various kinds including familial and social. In order to be grafted back on to his imagined — in the Andersonian sense — but nonetheless real Algerianness, Johnny embarks on a ferryboat that transports him to Algeria. There, he uses a botanical metaphor to suggest that he has been cultivating the dream of a *jus soli* and the "return" to his "roots." Like an uprooted plant, Johnny's parents are accused of cutting him off from his stock: "J'ai été recueilli par des Français. Y connaissent rien à l'Algérie. Depuis tout petit, ils ont tout fait pour me couper de mes racines" [I was taken in ("picked up") by French people. They don't know nothing about Algeria. Since I was a child, they did everything to cut me off from my roots]. In *Il était une fois*, where no scenario can be dismissed, "picked up" Johnny could be making everything up, or he could be living a fairy-tale dream of being a "changeling."

Johnny insists that his parents did more than deprive him of his Algerian roots; they inflicted upon him a degrading identity in France through their choice of name: "Ils m'ont donné un prénom de beauf" [They gave me the name of a loser]. Indeed, in the French popular vernacular, *beauf* and *Johnny* are synonyms and they both mean "loser" when used as a common noun. But rather than playing the role of the *beauf* in France, Johnny conforms to the image of the social type of the farcical "buffoon." In *banlieue* slang, *bouffon* is an insult. This figure of the outcast is a victim of ridicule, as is the case of Johnny. For instance, in the opening scene, Johnny's *Beur* friends laugh at him when his mother threatens that should he not obey her, he will "lose" more of his self: "j'te fais bouffer tes chicots" [I'll make you eat your teeth]. In an interesting twist on the botanical metaphor of being "uprooted," the slang term *chicot* designates a stump (*souche*), which in French refers to a person's dominant ethnic ancestry.[16] Whether intended or not, Mrs. Leclerc's double entendre conveys the idea that she could separate Johnny from his root(stock) by removing, along with his teeth, his ability to claim his otherness. Johnny's mother's intimidation seems to confirm the possibility of a hidden Algerian connection that the mother is eager to silence, as her complaint to her husband betrays: "Eh, daron, il a encore traité notre race" [Hey, Pop, he just insulted our race again], to which the husband responds, "Fils de con" [You son of a bastard].

For Johnny's future wife, Nadège, Johnny's Johnny*ness* makes him all the more attractive: "T'es un seigneur décalé mais t'es un seigneur quand même" [You're an out-of-place prince but you're a prince nonetheless]. Nadège's comment about liking Johnny for being "out of place," in other words *à l'ouest*, seems to confirm the notion that *décalage* (offset) is a particularly privileged modus operandi in Bensalah's work.[17] The originality of *Il était une fois* resides in its treatment of identity and emigration/immigration between France and Algeria. Bensalah questions normative accounts of emigration from south to north by reversing the direction of Johnny's clandestine migration. Upon discovering that Johnny had tagged along and embarked on the trip with neither passport nor ferry boarding pass, Mr. Sabri is outraged and afraid that his family might spend their month of vacation in jail. When the Algerian customs officer orders that Mr. Sabri's car be searched, the latter cries out: "Mais qu'est-ce que tu cherches? Un passager clandestin, c'est ça? Hein? Mais qui va venir dans ce pays à part nous?" [But what are you looking for? A clandestine migrant, right? Eh? But who would think of coming to Algeria, except for us?] To win over the customs officer, the father desperately resorts to the rhetoric of the stereotypical perception of the northward flow of clandestine migrants institutionalized by mainstream mass media. He bets on the belief that entering Algeria illegally ought not to make sense.

The presentation of this belief is problematic since it does little to contest the Eurocentric view of Algeria as essentially an undesirable place. Mr. Sabri's trick works: the officer has "nothing to declare" to Mr. Sabri — so to speak — for the former trusts that *hrig* originates strictly south of the Mediterranean.[18] This verbal duel is short-lived, and Johnny is not deported in spite of his missing passport, thus becoming a *French* clandestine passenger. Bensalah therefore humorously introduces both the fact of the "first" Frenchman crossing into Algeria without identity papers, and the novel idea that he would want to do it.[19] Johnny's groundbreaking immigration is facilitated by a joke at Algeria's expense. Yet such jokes allow Bensalah's characters the mobility to change, challenging essentialist discourse on national and cultural hierarchies. Ultimately, the customs officer — whose normative thinking is his downfall — is revealed to be far more foolish than Johnny.

Il était une fois proposes further reconfigurations, including those of gender power relations. In order to engage Yacine to Nadia, Mr. Sabri sets up a plot to prank his son into accompanying him to Algeria to escape a fictitious prosecutor. After being lured into Algeria, Yacine tries to recover his passport from his father at night, with the help of his younger brother. This subplot restages *Beur* narratives featuring female characters sequestered in Algeria by their families in order to sever the young women from a love or sexual relationship as is the case in Aïcha Benaïssa's *Née en France*, where the female narrator is sent to Algeria and her French passport is confiscated, or to force them to marry there as in Jamila Aït-Abbas's *La Fatiha*. However, in Bensalah's male version of "forced" marriage, the engagement and wedding of Nadia and Yacine are officialized with the consent of both characters. This outcome challenges negative Orientalist assumptions about union practice in the Maghreb. However, one possible criticism of this parodic subplot is that it is not pushed further than its comical value, comfortably reenacting the tradition of arranged marriage by representing it, in Hollywood fashion, as an essentially consensual "happy ending." The reversal remains mere social comedy, mockery without critique.

"Remakes" of Arab Grocers, "Authentic" Stews, and "Licit" Beers

In addition to flirting with social commentary, Bensalah's reversal of the typical migration patterns and of the identity of the *sans-papiers* (undocumented migrants) contradicts assumptions prevalent in Western mass media coverage of Maghrebis, including those who have settled in France. The figure of the Arab grocer is a common French stereotype of the Maghrebi migrant who has "made it" in the local community by setting up a small business in France. The expression *aller chez l'Arabe*, which is firmly grounded in the French imaginary, has come to mean a visit to the local convenience store, usually open late at night. In the last scene of the film, Johnny Leclerc has become the owner of a small grocery store. Turning widely held French stereotypes on their head, Bensalah transforms the French national Johnny "Leclerc" into "l'Arabe du coin," and in so doing, reduces the French chain of supermarkets Leclerc to a single corner shop. Even more startlingly, this Franco-French *épicier arabe* is located not in Paris, Marseilles, or any other French city or *banlieue*, but rather in an Algerian metropolis.

The film's use of cultural stereotypes is uncomfortable, yet Bensalah's position remains ambiguous since such clichés are revealed through the buffoonish figure of Johnny. Johnny's relationship to *chorba*, which he elevates to gastronomic symbol of Algeria, is an illustrative example. When Johnny breaks fast with the Sabris back in France, he laments he was served a Moroccan soup: "Ummm, elle est bonne votre *harira*, Mme Sabri. Moi je suis algérien, j'aurais préféré une *chorba* [Your *harira* is good, Mrs. Sabri. But *I* am an Algerian, and I would have preferred a *chorba*]. Though it is consumed in Morocco, too, Johnny associates the *chorba* (a thick stew) with Algeria, making it an arbitrary symbol of "authentic" national identity. Johnny's parochial comment leaves Mrs. Sabri smiling at his naïveté. This scene embodies the film's ambiguous posture, for Johnny is at once a prototype that disorients usual identificatory categories and a character whose search for authenticity reasserts stereotypical associations (*chorba* with Algeria).

In another scene at an Algerian restaurant in Algeria, Johnny explodes and comes to blows with the cooks when he finds the chef's *chorba* to be flavorless. To his great consternation, Johnny had been made to eat an industrial *chorba* that came from a packet of the multinational Maggi brand for sale in chains of supermarkets such as Leclerc. The chef's substitution of what Johnny considers to be the essence of Algeria with a cheap imitation of the rich national dish inspires Johnny a hyperbolic statement: "C'est la honte de l'Algérie" [This is the shame of Algeria]. Johnny had tasted other *chorbas* before, none of which had lived up to his expectations. Rather than the stew's flavor, what aggrieves the character is the realization that longing for a stronger tie with an origin conceived as "authentic" is never quite satisfying because it is as unattainable as the perfect *chorba*. Wanting to renationalize the recipe, Johnny energetically shows the local chef how to make an "authentic" *chorba*. Nevertheless, the personalized rendering of the stew boils down to an overly fixed, and finally alienating, identitarian quest since the instructions he gives the chef are for a *chorba* à la Johnny.

The treatment of culinary identity is contiguous with the film's questioning of notions of authenticity, belief, and truth. Significantly, the viewer is left wondering as to the authenticity of Johnny's claim to be an Algerian. Yacine discarded Johnny's assertion as mere mythomania, alleging that Johnny's native Algeria is imaginary, inspired by a purchased drawing. Yet on the way to Oran, the car has a flat tire and Johnny comes across the very village from which he claims to hail. There, Yacine and Johnny meet an old man with disheveled hair who states that he knew an Abdel Bachir, whom he identifies as Bachir el Moussaoui and Johnny's father. One is suspicious from the start since the name "Abdel Bachir" cannot exist. Johnny, the new convert, agrees to buy the old man a beer in exchange for directions to his father's tomb but protests that the drink is "hram" [illicit]. The old man circumvents Johnny's interpretation of Islam by misreading the label "Heineken Lager Beer" as

"Heineken Ajar Kbir," which the old man explains as meaning "Ici, il y a quelque chose de très grand" [Here lies something very big], and which in fact translates literally as "Heineken Tremendous Reward in the Afterlife." He also reads the Arabic inscription on the tombstone as "Abdel Bachir el Moussaoui, dit le clown" [Abdel Bachir el Moussaoui a.k.a. the clown] when it actually reads "Qbar majhoul" ["Grave of a stranger" as is indicated in the French subtitles]. With this example, Bensalah playfully suggests that identity is not — so to speak — written in stone.

Majhoul also means "anonymous." Its trilateral root *ja-hi-la* — Arabic being root based — contains the additional notion of "foolishness," which introduces the idea that Johnny's quest could be linked not to a physical father but a clan of fools. When the young men leave the mining ghost town, the old man puts on a clown's nose found on the tomb as if to tell us that he has just fooled the two visitors and the audience by the same token. Although the old man's story seems nothing more than a tissue of lies, it does not completely eliminate the plausibility of Johnny's story. In encouraging Johnny to be an Abdel Bachir (i.e., a clown?), the old man enhances the farce, hails Johnny as a Harlequin, as well as complicates the material reality of the stories at play. Did he overhear Johnny's loud recounting of his childhood as the two young men walked through the ruins of the village? Or could Johnny be standing at the grave of his deceased biological father? This scene manages to unsettle the viewer's certainties (as well as Yacine's — who functions as a surrogate spectator within the scene) about Johnny's true heritage. Is the deceased clown a colonial, and Johnny, in Bhabha's terms, a mimic — but in reverse? In other words, is Johnny not quite white but not quite Algerian-Arab-Muslim either? (After all, Johnny's idiosyncratic identity is ultimately an effective model of mimicry: in the end, he achieves his aim of integration.) Even the tombstone, a traditional site of closure, leaves the identity of the "majhoul" who lies there open to speculation. No matter who is right, the cemetery becomes a place of free trade where the exchange of a "bière" [coffin] for a "bière" [beer] benefits all parties.

As Taylor explains, "inwardly derived, personal, original identity doesn't enjoy . . . recognition a priori. It has to win it through exchange" (1992, 35). Therefore, the telling of stories is primordial for Johnny. When dining with the Sabris' relatives, Johnny imposes his favorite joke, that of a soccer game between Morocco and Brazil involving a *djinn* (genie), which triggers delayed laughter. Perplexed, the grandfather of Mr. Sabri's future daughter-in-law qualifies the storyteller as "intelligent," a "jenn" [sly], and a "mahboul" [fool]. Embarrassed, Mr. Sabri tells his interlocutor that Johnny is not a "mahboul"; however, they agree that he is "ness ness" [half-half]. Contrary to his misleading French last name Leclerc (a homonym of Le Clair, "the Clear One"), it is not at all clear who Johnny is. Johnny is *Moha le fou, Moha le sage*, half a madman, half a wise storyteller, "dépositaire de voix multiples" [endowed with multiple voices] (Urbani 2008, 40). Johnny-Moha, a wise fool, is bequeathed multiple facets, for he is altogether Joha (the Arab iconic buffoon), a jenn, a djinn, and a genie.

Il était une fois . . . The End

Johnny *qua* Abdel Bachir takes his performance of self very seriously, while Bensalah's cinematographic tale suggests that all identity is to some extent a repeated parodic performance. This holds true for personal identity as well as for the film genre: *Il était une fois dans l'oued*—both the film and the title—are parodies of *Il était une fois dans l'ouest* and of the western genre. Meanwhile, the excessive use of parody leaves us wondering where it ends. It also points to the unsettling uncertainties regarding origin, nationality, and the relationship between the two, which are at the core of the film, as well as the repetition of stereotypes (even if inverted) on which they rely.

Yet the excesses and the distance between illusion and reality in *Il était une fois* could be seen as the film's strengths because they allow the director to turn upside down a number of commonly held perceptions pertaining to migration and identity. Some of the many reversals in the film are difficult to celebrate because the changeable nature of the figure of the clandestine in the region is hardly conceivable. Yet *Il était une fois* merits praise for its new perspective on the myth of the return "home." The comic register of the film, along with its open-endedness (announced by the title), allows Bensalah to create an integrated Algerian utopia. His resorting to the comedy genre stands out in respect to other *Beur* filmmaking, which tends to use "social realist" modes. It helps us think through issues of identity construction by appealing to our imagination. Characters play out futuristic individualities and experiment with new ways of assessing their relationship to France and Algeria. As for Johnny, he reproaches France for his identity crisis in order to better approach his Algerianness. In emigrating to Algeria, he simultaneously abandons his French *cité* and his *Francité* (Frenchness).

The promise of this far-out narrative derives precisely from the fact that it overlooks unsolved problems such as the illegality of Johnny's status in Algeria. Of course, we do not know if Johnny will remain Algerian during the civil war of the 1990s — for such a possibility is foreclosed by the chronological limits of the film's narrative — or if he will rediscover his Frenchness and go back to his "first" *bled*. Another question that the film leads the viewer to ask is what kind of *Beur* this postcolonial "Algerian" born somewhere between Porte de Clichy and a village in the Algerian west is. Focusing on promising premises, *Rebeu* or *Rabza* director Djamel Bensalah has turned his satirical lens back onto both Algeria and France in order to propose a unique way of viewing migrational identities. By returning to the decade (the 1980s) in which *Beur*ness was first being explored in France, and making Johnny the representative of an ingenious and unexpected prototype, *Il était une fois dans l'oued* reflects on the future of emigration, immigration, and integration, as well as tangentially contributes to the ongoing questioning of the act of naming, and misnomers such as *Beur*. In this film, Djamel Bensalah offers innovative takes on clandestine migration at a time when an increasing number of Maghrebi youths relentlessly dream of reaching the other side of the Mediterranean.

Notes

I would like to thank the editors, Greta Bliss, Sarah B. Buchanan, Judith E. Preckshot, Nasrin Qader, Mireille Rosello, Eileen B. Sivert, Corbin Treacy, and Christopher Wagner for their insightful comments.

1. Of these, over 870,000 spectators were in France alone.

2. For the sake of clarity, I will use "Johnny" except when I discuss the implications of his assumed name, "Abdel Bachir."

3. "Chaussé . . . d'Adidas, vêtu . . . d'un blue-jean délavé et évasé à la mode de cette année-là, d'un tee-shirt . . . et du gel dans les cheveux . . . scandant ses propos de formules rituelles dans un arabe tout neuf" [Wearing Adidas sneakers, prewashed boot-cut jeans in line with the fashion of the time, a T-shirt . . . and gel in the hair . . . accentuating his speech with ritual formulae in a brand-new Arabic language] (Kepel 1987, 371). The color of Johnny's hair could be the result of a common practice in the *banlieues* in the 1990s of dyeing one's hair blond.

4. *Bled* used both in French and Arabic can be translated as "location," "village," or "country of origin."

5. As Kepel (1987) explains, the "réislamisation" of *banlieues* in the mid-1980s brought forward the practice of an Islam different from that of the Maghrebi immigrant community.

6. McClintock identifies various types of colonies such as "settler colonies" and "deep-settler colonies." The latter includes Algeria, "where colonial powers clung on with particular brutality" (1992, 88–89).

7. The film was made in 2005 but conveniently takes place at the end of the 1980s just before the Algerian civil war raged in the 1990s. Antedating his film allows Bensalah to avoid incorporating tragedy into his comedy.

8. I have coined the expressions *chez toi/soi* (insider) and *pas chez toi/soi* (outsiders) to refer to the characters' identificatory battles. One notes that the *pas chez toi* replica, traditionally uttered by French people, is used here by an Algerian national and directed to a *Beur*.

9. See Rosello (2005) and Durmelat (2008) for compelling analyses of the 2001 game.

10. The 2001 soccer game is also central to Mahmoud Zemmouri's 2006 film *Beur, blanc, rouge* in which Julien Courbey also plays a leading role as a working-class soccer fan. In Zemmouri's comedy, Courbey's character supports the French team but attends the match wearing a jersey and a scarf printed with the Algerian colors, which interrogates the fixity of national identity even in a high-stakes situation. Thematic similarities of Zemmouri's film with Bensalah's include the presence of an *épicier arabe*, a road trip to the Algerian south (undertaken in the form of a daydream), and the administrative complications that Algeria-bound characters face at customs.

11. *Harkis* (*harka* is the plural in Arabic) are Muslim Algerians who fought on the side of the French during the Algerian War of Independence. See Hargreaves (1997) and Rosello (2010) for a thorough discussion of *harkis*.

12. This name, modeled on famous seventeenth-century moralist François de la Rochefoucauld, points to a continuum between France and Algeria that Johnny rejects by refusing his French name entirely.

13. From the Latin, *jus soli* (right of the soil) is the principle by which one can claim citizenship. "Article 23 of the [French] Nationality Code stipulates that the child born of foreign parents at least one of whom was born in France is French at birth (known as 'the double jus soli')" (Silverman 1992, 142). Conversely, Algerian citizenship works on the principle of *jus sanguinis*, literally, right of blood, or genetic inheritance of citizenship. Consequently, Johnny has to have Algerian parents to become Algerian, hence his insistence that his parents are not French.

14. This burlesques the belief, inherited from colonial times, that naming in the Maghreb consists of a variably long list of names.

15. A *hbaya* is a light robe-like garment worn by a man.

16. *Français de souche* signifies "Franco-French."

17. The other meaning of the expression contains the idea of being *à côté de la plaque* (to be completely mistaken), a sign that the director is joking with us and invites us to play along to better displace linguistic, identitarian, and geographic constructions of various types.

18. The Arabic *hrig* (to burn) designates clandestine emigration. The related term *harraga* (those who "burn," that is, clandestine migrants) is used both in Maghrebi and French media. For a discussion of *hrig*, see Abderrezak (2009) and (2010).

19. The DVD cover reads "le premier passager clandestin pour l'Algérie" [the first clandestine passenger to Algeria].

References

Abderrezak, Hakim. 2009. "'Burning the Sea': Clandestine Migration across the Strait of Gibraltar in Francophone Moroccan 'Illiterature.'" *Contemporary French and Francophone Studies: Sites* 13 (4) (September): 461–69.

———. 2010. "Entretien avec Boualem Sansal." *Contemporary French and Francophone Studies: Sites* 14 (4) (September): 339–47.

Aït-Abbas, Jamila. 2003. *La Fatiha: Née en France, mariée de force en Algérie*. Paris: Michel Lafont.

Benaïssa, Aïcha, and Sophie Ponchelet. 1990. *Née en France: Histoire d'une jeune beur*. Paris: Payot.

Durmelat, Sylvie. 2008. *Fictions de l'intégration: Du mot beur à la politique de la mémoire*. Paris: L'Harmattan.

Hargreaves, Alec. 1997. *Immigration and Identity in Beur Fiction: Voices from the North African Community in France*. 2nd ed. Oxford: Berg.

Kepel, Gilles. 1987. *Les banlieues de l'islam*. Paris: Seuil.

McClintock, Anne. 1992. "The Angel of Progress: Pitfalls of the Term 'postcolonial.'" *Social Text* 31–32:84–98.

Rosello, Mireille. 2005. *France and the Maghreb: Performative Encounters*. Gainesville: University Press of Florida.

———. 2010. *The Reparative in Narratives: Work of Mourning in Progress*. Liverpool: Liverpool University Press.

Silverman, Maxim. 1992. *Deconstructing the Nation: Immigration, Racism, and Citizenship in Modern France*. New York: Routledge.

Tarr, Carrie. 2005. *Reframing Difference: Beur and Banlieue Filmmaking in France*. Manchester: Manchester University Press.

Taylor, Charles. 1992. *Multiculturalism and "the Politics of Recognition."* Princeton NJ: Princeton University Press.

Urbani, Bernard. 2008. "Entre humour et dérision: *Moha le fou Moha le sage* de Tahar Ben Jelloun." *Expressions Maghrébines* 7 (2) (Winter): 37–49.

Filmography

Bensalah, Djamel, dir. *Le ciel, les oiseaux et . . . ta mère!*, 1999.

———, dir. *Le raïd*, 2002.

———, dir. *Il était une fois dans l'oued*, 2005.

———, dir. *Big City*, 2007.

Leone, Sergio, dir. *Once Upon a Time in the West (C'era una volta il West)*, 1968.

Zemmouri, Mahmoud, dir. *Beur, blanc, rouge*, 2006.

5

RE-VISIONS OF THE ALGERIAN WAR OF INDEPENDENCE

Writing the Memories of Algerian Immigrants into French Cinema

SYLVIE DURMELAT

In the fiction films produced by the French descendants of Algerian immigrants, the war of independence (1954–62), while not absent, has rarely taken center stage. A few notable exceptions — *Sous les pieds des femmes* (Rachida Krim 1997), *Vivre au paradis* (Bourlem Guerdjou 1998), and *Cartouches gauloises* (Mehdi Charef 2007) — have proposed historical reenactments of the war, while other films have touched on the subject in subtle, if meaningful, ways. The overall discreet presence of the war in these films contrasts with the renewed public interest in the conflict since the 1990s, which historians Mohammed Harbi and Benjamin Stora have termed "the end of amnesia" (2004). In this chapter, I propose to put this relative absence into perspective by exploring the specific challenges filmmakers of Algerian descent face in producing cinematic re-visions of the war. By inviting viewers to re-envision their relationship to a contested past through popular understandings of history that foreground the role played by Algerian immigrants in France, these filmmakers have not only compensated for the overall paucity of representations of the war on the French domestic front (Branche 2008, 112), they have also interrogated the way national genealogies are constructed. Such cinematic revisions of the role of immigrants in France go beyond building a "retrospective sense of historical continuity"—which endows the descendants of immigrants with legitimacy, thus fostering integration in France in the present (Tarr 2005, 126)—to question the building of national commemorative narratives and explore the possibility of writing a transnational, French-Algerian history of the war, one that is still being shaped on and off the silver screen.[1]

Writing the War of Algerian Immigrants into National Genealogies

At first glance, filmmaking by the descendants of immigrants does not seem to significantly differ from French cinema as a whole, with respect to the relative lack of references and reenactments of the war, on which it has become customary to comment, if not to lament (Branche 2008, 107). Cinema critic Jean-Michel Frodon corrects this view somewhat: Algeria is present in a significant number of the most beautiful films of the 1960s ("*Le petit soldat, Muriel, Le combat dans l'île, Cléo de 5 à 7, Adieu Philippine, Les parapluies de Cherbourg, Le joli mai*")—albeit in fragmented, roundabout, and distant ways. French cinema, he suggests, recorded the Algerian War of Independence as such because the colonial empire had in fact been written off, and out of the national genealogy (2004, 75): "Cette histoire-là n'est jamais entrée dans la mémoire collective française, elle n'est pas refoulée (à l'intérieur) mais reste exclue (à l'extérieur)" [This history has never made its way into French collective memory; it is not repressed (inside) but remains excluded (outside)] (2004, 76). To be sure, state censorship, and the self-censorship it induced, played an active role in keeping images and references to the war off the silver screen (Stora 1997, 111–25; Jeancolas 2007, 14).[2] However, lack of interest and indifference on the part of both directors and the public (Stora 1997, 193; Branche 2008, 109) also ensured that the war—as well as the larger history of colonial migrations to the metropole, and colonial history—remained peripheral and hardly integrated into the core of French society (Stora 2005, 58–59). In fact, the very coinage of the word "decolonization" in the 1960s helped to convey the fallacious impression that colonization could actually be wished away, thus adding to the mystification that the latter not only happened elsewhere but was also a thing of the past (Shepard 2006, 269–72).

Writing the war into, rather than off, what has been hastily constructed as two separate French and Algerian national historical legacies becomes the aesthetic, political, and personal challenge of those who, whether they are of Algerian descent or not, deem that colonization still shapes the former metropole, despite independence. For these filmmakers, Frodon's distinction — between repression and exclusion, between an inside and an outside — does not hold. In re(en)visioning the war, their works invite viewers to account for the unacknowledged and complex ways in which France and Algeria inhabit and are inhabited by each other, thus confirming what Étienne Balibar brilliantly articulated: when added together, France and Algeria, although they are two states, more likely amount to one and a half nations (1998, 78).[3]

The crucial role played by the Algerian diaspora during the war of independence defines one such uneasy zone of interpenetration and makes it impossible to consider the conflict as a clean line of separation. However, with "decolonization," the immigrants' participation in the conflict was not only excluded from French collective self-representations but was also neglected in official commemorations in Algeria, and often repressed within family memorial transmissions. The Algerian state barely acknowledged the immigrants' voluntary and forced contributions to the FLN (Front de Libération Nationale) which financed the war effort (Colin-Jeanvoine and Derozier 2008; Thénault 2005, 225). Their absence from a national territory sanctified by war contradicted the postwar promotion of national unity, and their continued presence in France characterized an embarrassing neocolonial situation, nonetheless tolerated, when it was not promoted, by the FLN state for economic reasons (House 2006). Furthermore, even if Algerian nationalism took shape in the metropole — where the connection could be made between Algerian "political" émigrés and the masses of Algerian immigrants (peasants turned into urban proletariat) — before being re-exported to the colony and then back again (Sayad 1999, 155), this French history of Algerian nationalism, along with the internecine war between rival nationalist factions for the control of Algerian immigrants, was conveniently left out of the national genealogy rewritten by the newly founded Algerian FLN state in 1962.[4]

Within immigrant families, the transmission of parents' experiences of the war to their descendants remained fragmented, due to the very nature of war trauma, the widely held belief that they would all soon return "home" to an independent Algeria, and the marginal place accorded to immigration within the French national imagination (Noiriel 1995).[5] Furthermore, because North African immigrants were considered as traitors, or potential double agents at best, during the war — which, far from stopping immigration from

Algeria caused it to double from 1952 to 1964 (Stora 1995, 40) — it is only when their descendants publicly claimed their French citizenship that this contentious past could begin to be addressed.

In the 1990s the renewed public interest and media hypermnesia about the Algerian War have been attributed in part to the emergence of the French children of Algerian immigrants as a new group of "memory carriers" (Stora 2004, 506; Rousso 2004, 133–34, 139–40).[6] However, if their memorial activism is often invoked, it would be more accurate to qualify their involvement. For instance, historian Claude Liauzu (2004, 166) and cinema critic Jean-Pierre Jeancolas (2007, 15) have deplored the ignorance of descendants of Algerian immigrants in regard to the war. Furthermore, historian Sylvie Thénault stresses that despite the combined efforts of associations like "Au nom de la mémoire" and the network of antiracist groups largely responsible for the eventual unveiling in 2001 of an official plaque commemorating the massacre of October 17, 1961, in Paris, the memory of the event remains that of activists and only engages a portion of French society (1998, 99).[7] These nuances attest to internal differentiations within what is hastily, and at times problematically, constructed as a second generation, and to the difficulties of disseminating memories within, as well as across, groups. Indeed, the memories of this war remained private, generated and maintained within families, rather than shared and elaborated in the public sphere (Stora 1994, 132, 137).

Through film technology, however, memories of the war can be commodified into cultural artifacts and become part of "the common public domain" (Landsberg 2004, 11). By circulating images that foster the acquisition of memories that are not necessarily one's own, cinema and mass media contribute to reconfiguring the collective past of a nation. Thus, as the films by directors of Maghrebi origin become mainstream — and as passing references to the war give way to higher-budget historical dramas — viewers are not only encouraged to reexperience the past but also to rethink it. Through the manipulation of (dis)identificatory techniques, and the "somatic intensity of the cinematic experience" (Burgoyne 2007, 553), reenactments of the past make room for a (potentially critical) reassessment of the present, for they intervene in the transmissions operated and controlled by family, school, and mainstream media. In this capacity, cinematic production can encourage the construction of "new political alliances" (Landsberg 2004, 155). Indeed, films that reconstruct the war or portray the parents' generation in the past

1. Balou (Charly Chemouny) struggles to spell *théorème* in *Le thé au harem d'Archimède* (1985).

2. Slimane (Jalil Naceri) flirts with an ANPE employee while trying to obtain a job in *Hexagone* (1994).

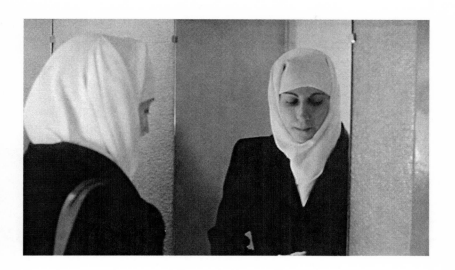

3. Farida (Fadila Belkebla) begins to reassess her choice to wear a headscarf in *Douce France* (1995).

PARIS, 17 OCTOBRE 1961

4. Algerian victim of October 17, 1961, framed in *Vivre au paradis* (1999).

5. Nina (Fanny Ardant) recognizes a cross-dressed Sami
(Roschdy Zem) in *Change-moi ma vie* (2001).

6. Alloune (Sotigui Kouyaté) arriving in Harlem on a
genealogical quest in *Little Senegal* (2001).

7. Zouina (Fejria Deliba) listening to a popular French radio program in *Inch'Allah dimanche* (2001).

8. Angela (Alexandra Laflandre) with friend Gwénaëlle
(Alexandra Jeudon), documenting suburban life in *Jeunesse
dorée* (2002).

9. Frida (Sabrina Ouazani), Lydia (Sarah Forestier), and
Rachid (Rachid Hami) during a classroom performance of
Marivaux's play in *L'esquive* (2004).

10. Nordine (Roschdy Zem) and his newfound friend,
Mimoun (Abdou El-Mesnaoui), in *Ten'ja* (2004).

11. Reda (Nicolas Cazalé) and his father (Mohamed Majd) on their way to Mecca in *Le grand voyage* (2004).

12. Selim (Mohamed Hicham) and his father (Hammou
Graïa) share a meal in *Un fils* (2004).

13. Johnny's parents (Frankie Pain and Max Morel) decipher renamed streets in *Il était une fois dans l'oued* (2005).

14. Expelled from France, Kamel (Rabah Ameur-Zaïmeche) connects with his extended Algerian family in *Bled number one* (2006).

15. Abdelkader (Sami Bouajila) mourns the loss of his
comrades in *Indigènes* (2006).

16. At the picnic, soon after Manu (Johann Libéreau) is
introduced to Mehdi (Sami Bouajila) and Sarah (Emanuelle
Béart) by Adrien (Michel Blanc), in *Les témoins* (2007).

17. Ali (Mohamed Faouzi Ali Cherif), the omnipresent
witness of the Algerian War of Independence, in *Cartouches
gauloises* (2007).

18. Halima (Zohra Mouffok) joins in prayer at the local mosque in *Dans la vie* (2008).

19. Esmeralda (Esmeralda Ouertani) challenges her teacher,
Monsieur Marin (François Bégaudeau), in *Entre les murs*
(2008).

20. Transforming the workplace into a place of worship in
Dernier maquis (2008).

21. Sonia Bergerac (Isabelle Adjani) holding her students hostage in *La journée de la jupe* (2009).

have also made possible, in the present, a shift from France to Algeria, both in the diegesis and for shooting locations. This move, recently facilitated by Algerian authorities for a number of films, underscores the need for a transnational French-Algerian history of the war, one that accounts for the two nations' (post)colonial entanglement, as the memory of this war involves more than just the French (Re)public.[8]

It is therefore telling that *Les sacrifiés* (1983), made in France by Algerian émigré filmmaker Okacha Touita with the contribution of Mohammed Harbi, an FLN leader turned political exile and historian in France, was one of the first feature films to depict the life of simple immigrants turned nationalist fighters.[9] Set in 1955, a time of hardship for the FLN, this low-budget film focuses on Mahmoud (Miloud Khetib). Freshly arrived from Algeria, he settles down as a hairdresser and becomes an FLN fund collector in the Nanterre *bidonville* (shantytown) near Paris. The film documents the brutal management of FLN leaders, the bloody feud between political rivals from the MNA (Mouvement National Algérien) and FLN, treason from within the Algerian immigrant community, and the merciless repression by Parisian police. Its gritty style eschews the glossy characteristics of heritage films: the romance between Mahmoud and a gypsy girl is barely developed, there is no extra-diegetic music, and the choppy montage conveys Mahmoud's confusion and the uncertainty of the struggle to the viewers. Mahmoud survives all this only to end up in an internment camp with his fellow FLN combatants. Crushed by historical events, but loyal to the nationalist cause until the end, this ordinary hero loses his mind by the time independence is announced at the end of the film. Not unlike other Algerian immigrants, as the film's title — *Les sacrifiés*, in the plural — may figuratively suggest, Mahmoud cannot enjoy the independence for which he fought, which makes for a bleak, sober, and unromanticized representation of the war on the French front. Yet in highlighting the sacrifices of the Algerian diaspora, and by addressing the brutality exercised by nationalist factions, this film by an Algerian director working in France provides a corrective to both Algerian and French national histories of the war. Although *Les sacrifiés* initiated a historical vein to which the reenactments of the late 1990s, released fifteen years later, could be affiliated (Cadé 2004, 123), it has remained obscure, due perhaps to its harsh portrayal of the nationalist struggle, as well as to its refusal to give in to victimization and commemoration.[10]

Malik Chibane: Passing References to the War

Malik Chibane's *Hexagone* (1994) and *Douce France* (1995) hint at the war through understated references, but they are among the few in "*Beur* and *banlieue* filmmaking" (Tarr 2005) that even attempt to do so. As they touch ever so briefly on the war, his films focus on how it lingers on and affects the lives of young people of Algerian origin. In *Hexagone*, a noisy nightclub scene features a discussion about integration between Ali (Karim Chakir) — a college student and community activist — and a friend, played by Chibane himself. His cameo appearance helps to draw attention to this otherwise unremarkable scene in which Ali argues, and convinces his friend, that as the children of disenfranchised immigrants, they face a socioeconomic handicap that is compounded by the invisible legacy of colonization — and notably the Algerian War. It is not innocent that Ali — a character presented as a gentle satire of the educated and upwardly mobile *beurgeois* — is the one who brings up the Algerian War to theorize its invisible yet marked impact, in a rhetorical exercise destined to persuade his friend and the public. It speaks to the different levels of involvement in memorial activism within the same generation, as discussed earlier, and suggests that such activism accompanies — rather than deters — socioeconomic integration.

It is easy, however, to overlook this dialogue: the music in the nightclub is loud and the characters are interrupted, then blocked from view, by a friend who comes by to say hello. Yet this scene concludes a larger narrative sequence in which three of the main protagonists, including Ali, experience exclusion. When denied entry to a party in downtown Paris — ironically organized by a member of SOS Racisme, the famous antiracist association — they end up, along with other youth of Maghrebi descent from the surrounding suburbs, in the same suburban nightclub as usual, where this peripheral conversation takes place. Here, Chibane avoids didactic devices. Rather, he opts for a gentle, nonconfrontational, and dialectical way of posing the question of the link between integration issues and colonial legacy, while running the risk of remaining, literally and figuratively, unheard.

Douce France, Chibane's second feature, is the first film by a director of Algerian descent to focus on the son of a *harki* soldier, Moussa. But his portrayal of the old *harki* father downplays the drama and tragedy of history to highlight the integration of his son. Moussa strikes it rich when he finds the loot that a jewelry store thief had hidden in a trash bin. With his friend Jean-Luc, he buys a traditional North African café and turns it into a law office by day for Jean-Luc and a gaming parlor by night. When Moussa's father finds out, he flies into a rage and gives him a beating, as best he can, with his cane — a reference to the father's physical disability, his helplessness, and his compromised authority. As the father beats his son, his cane breaks the glass in a frame hanging on the wall. The camera zooms in on it just long enough for viewers to identify the father's name on an official document recognizing him for services rendered in the French military. Even though the father's military past is proudly displayed on the walls throughout the house, as shown by the camera's panning shots, the film itself does not explicitly comment on it. In linking the cane and the broken frame, the film may suggest, by metonymy, that Moussa's father uses the cane to compensate for a combat wound. But more importantly, Moussa's actions are the trigger that literally and figuratively break the glass between his father and his military past, to foreground his engagement as a *harki*. In Chibane's comedy, the *harki* figure is both faithfully patriotic — the camera lingers on de Gaulle's portrait prominently featured in the house — and resolutely attached to Algeria — the father explains to Moussa that his umbilical cord is buried in Algeria. But his fiction about an all too "douce" France offers no further explorations of the father's past actions in the military, no claims for a political rehabilitation of the *harki*, no virulent critique of France's abandonment of its *harki* troops, and no denunciation of the FLN regime's repression and stigmatization of the *harki* — just the portrait of a family that both celebrates Christmas and yearns to keep its connection to Algeria. To heal his father's old wounds and reconcile him with the *bled*, Moussa is even ready to sacrifice his budding love for Farida, a young French woman of Maghrebi descent, and accept an arranged marriage with a distant Algerian cousin. In this sense, Moussa offers to become a prosthetic umbilical cord between his father and his native land, and make up for the loss and estrangement experienced by the *harkis*. Likewise, Chibane's films highlight the central role descendants of immigrants play in the reinvention and rebirth of their parents' past. Yet his conciliatory approach signals some of the challenges faced by filmmakers of Maghrebi descent who "have tended to reconstruct a potentially contentious past through personal rather than directly political stories, presumably in order not to antagonize majority audiences" (Tarr 2007, 5).

Reconstructing the Past in Historical Dramas

In the late 1990s, filmmakers of Maghrebi descent turned to the depiction of their parents' aging generation and reconstructed their past experiences in historical reenactments made possible by better access to financing in the film industry: *Sous les pieds des femmes* and *Vivre au paradis* were the first films since *Les sacrifiés* to reenact immigrants' previously neglected participation in Algerian independence. Two films in the same historical vein sidestepped the war — the commercially successful *Le gone du Chaâba* (Christophe Ruggia 1998; 826,765 box office entries) and the critically well-received *Inch'Allah dimanche* (Yamina Benguigui 2001). Taking place in 1965 and 1974, respectively, they reconstruct the past in more "uncontentious, even nostalgic" stories (Tarr 2005, 127).[11] Yet both films mention the war in key places. The Algerian national anthem accompanies the opening credits and first scene in *Le gone du Chaâba*, a film based on the popular autobiographical novel by Azouz Begag. The recent history of the war is acknowledged from the start, tenuously yet persistently, as Bouzid (Mohamed Fellag), the young protagonist's immigrant father, listens intently to an Algerian radio broadcast celebrating the third anniversary of independence. The radio fades out as the father and other men from the shantytown leave for work. It is then ironically contrasted and replaced with the self-introduction of ten-year-old Omar (Bouzid Negnoug): "My name is Omar. I am nine and I was born in France. I am French." Likewise, in *Inch'Allah dimanche*, the soundtrack conjures up the war discreetly. A song in Berber about the torture inflicted by the French military plays as Zouina (Fejria Deliba), recently arrived from Algeria, gazes over pictures of Mme Manant (Marie-France Pisier)'s husband, a colonel who disappeared in Algeria during combat operations. Subtitled in French for the majority audience, the song hints at the thoughts going through Zouina's mind. However, the two women's budding friendship suggests an optimistic sorority between France and Algeria whose symbolic reconciliation calls for the (re)mediation and intervention of Algerian immigrants and their children.[12]

In contrast, *Sous les pieds des femmes* and *Vivre au paradis* embody the war through the love stories of ordinary characters and couples.[13] They also provide a corrective to official historiographies by foregrounding the contributions of immigrant Algerian women to the nationalist cause: female characters temporarily leave the traditional domestic realm to collect money for the FLN, deliver messages and luggage, and even carry out the execution of a police officer. Both films deliver pointed critiques of the FLN, as well as denounce French police violence. In *Vivre au paradis*, Lakhdar (Roschdy Zem) — who dreams to escape the wretched *bidonville* for the comfort of an apartment, even at the expense of his fellow immigrants — vociferously denounces the pressures of the FLN, while his wife, Nora (Fadila Belkebla), embraces the nationalist cause and the community of the *bidonville*. Shortly after independence, the couple's conflicting aspirations — an image of the diaspora? — remain unfulfilled. A final didactic intertitle explains that Algerian immigrants, abandoned by the newly independent Algeria, had to wait until 1973 to be moved to temporary housing in France. The final scene shows the reunited family, isolated in a courtyard and at first hidden from view by a floating white sheet that fills the screen. This visual and narrative caesura signals that a new blank page opens up with independence. Yet despite the sunny decor that contrasts with the preceding dominance of dark gray images, not much has changed for the family.

In *Sous les pieds des femmes*, Aya (Claudia Cardinale) reminisces about her experiences as an FLN activist and her adulterous love for FLN cell leader Amin (Mohammed Bakri). Although he goes back to Algeria after the war, Aya remains in France after she realizes Amin's and the new Algerian state's unwillingness to address questions of gender equality in what she hoped could be a transformative liberation struggle for all. Through the constant back and forth between past and present, the film clearly traces the origins of the civil war in contemporary Algeria, which Amin escapes briefly for a visit to Aya and her family, to the shortcomings of the War of Independence. This critical device precludes slippage into stilted commemoration and nostalgia, yet *Sous les pieds des femmes* does not probe as keenly Aya's position and relationship to a contemporary French society in which her daughter and granddaughter's integration is shown as unproblematic. This stern critique of the FLN state does not call into question the contributions of the parents' generation to the independence cause, but rather it shows that the younger generation is comfortable enough with its status as French citizens to formulate criticisms that their parents could not have uttered in the public sphere for fear of being considered traitors, or worse, losers having fought a war for naught.

Guerdjou's is the first fiction film to reenact the racist attacks of October 17, 1961.[14] This date has now taken its rightful place in the chronology of the war (Thénault 1998, 99) and is even "the most frequently evoked episode in the history of colonial migration" (Hargreaves 2006, 217). The legacy of October 17, 1961, with its cover-up for twenty years until a new generation came of age in the early eighties, plays a pivotal role in the reconstruction of the history of Algerian immigrants, for they became political subjects in France as they supported an independent Algeria. Yet as Thénault explains, despite the numerous materials now available on the subject, the transmission of this memory to the French general public still runs up against "des mécanismes d'indifférence plus profonds" [deeply entrenched mechanisms of indifference] (1998, 98).

In this context, *Vivre au paradis*, produced in 1997, devotes six minutes to the on-screen reenactment of the attacks, six years after the association "Au nom de la mémoire" first unveiled an informal plaque commemorating the massacre in 1991, and four years before an official plaque took its place in 2001. In this sequence, anonymous demonstrators are filmed at eye level and spectators are thrown *in medias res* as people scramble for their life during the attacks. The police's faces remain hidden behind their helmets, thus encouraging viewers to identify with the demonstrators. Although Lakhdar is the only one shown to oppose the demonstration imposed by the FLN, he eventually joins in and gets beaten up, taking the police blows to protect his family. The focus on the figure of a reluctant peaceful patriot underscores the blindness of the assault and makes police violence even more unbearable, further encouraging viewers' identification with the Algerians. At the end of this sequence, the camera lingers over the dead body of an anonymous protester in a suspended long shot. A sober non-diegetic intertitle superimposed on the body reads: "Paris, 17 Octobre, 1961." While the intertitle could have been placed at the beginning to announce the sequence, the strategic placement of this simple date summarizes the event for the audience and gives it a heightened iconic value. This edifying filmic device highlights the new centrality of this date, not only in the film but also in the recollection of the war. Following the intertitle, the characters make no intra-diegetic references to the event in the rest of the film. What may be an allusion to the active repression of the memory of the attacks by institutional forces, as well as by the immigrant victims themselves, also contributes to isolate the sequence, turning it into a cinematic plaque of sorts. So much so that the film was screened during commemorations of the event in 2001.

By inviting viewers to side with the demonstrators and see themselves in the faces of Algerian immigrants, the film explores two contradictory yet possible readings of the event. The first one, inspired by Anderson's interpretation of Renan, suggests that a sense of belonging to a nation is achieved through "the reassurance of fratricide" (Anderson 1991, 199) — that is, being constantly reminded of past conflicts that one had to forget, in ways that make them seem to be well-known pieces of family lore. Can October 17, 1961, ever be retold as fratricide and find its place in the French historical pantheon, when mainstream audiences remain indifferent to it in the first place? Recounting the events of October 17, 1961, as a civil war of sorts, that is, as a war between brothers, could indeed retrospectively endow Algerian immigrants with the quality of citizens. Yet, because the French Republic was also a colonial empire whose colonial subjects were at once theoretical equals and subjugated natives with limited rights, Algerian immigrants are not remembered as brothers or sisters, and their children struggle to be accepted into the nation-as-family.

On the other hand, when majority viewers are invited to empathize with Algerian immigrants on screen, to take into account "the cause of the Other" (Rancière 2004, 202–20) and thus partake in memories that are and are not their own, they are also asked to disidentify from an oppressive national community. This self-reflective critique allows for ways of belonging to the nation that go beyond the conjuring trick of "the reassurance of fratricide," to permit the emergence of political subjects through disidentification with official definitions of the national self (Rancière 2004, 212). Thus, by retrospectively embodying the experiences of colonial immigrants and including them in the "national projection" (Frodon 1998), the filmic medium invites viewers to take into consideration the uncounted and unaccounted for, those who are not quite brothers or sisters but not foreigners either.

These two films have not just evoked but have reenacted on screen the parents' war. While their focus remains metropolitan France, their frank critique of the FLN points to Algeria. For if decolonization is less achievable than ever without the examination of France's inner Algeria (Balibar 1998, 78), it calls in turn for the recognition that Algeria's inner France remains to be screened.

Indigènes: A Second World War Epic as Screen for the Algerian War

Rachid Bouchareb's blockbuster war epic tells of the sacrifice of four heroic infantrymen, three Algerians and one Moroccan, conscripted in the French colonies to fight with the Allies in Europe. However, when watching *Indigènes* (2006), the Algerian War immediately comes to mind — even though the film deals with the Second World War and barely refers to Algeria, and even though the scenes set in Algeria were actually shot in Morocco. As Tarr suggests, *Indigènes* "displac[es] antagonistic memories of the Algerian War of Independence while at the same time suggesting why it was inevitable" (2007, 6). As producer of *Vivre au paradis*, Bouchareb had already played a major role in the recent reexamination of the Algerian War in French cinema. Furthermore, as stated in interviews for the release of *Indigènes*, the film was designed as the first part of a larger historical diptych that was to include the period from the Sétif massacre on May 8, 1945, to the end of the war. So, if *Indigènes* seems strikingly conciliatory—maneuvering between appeasement and indignation, through the portrayal of loyal, sacrificial heroes who are mostly uncritical of French colonization—it may have been to prepare viewers for a subsequent epic on the more controversial subject of the Algerian War of Independence.[15]

Indeed, even as *Indigènes* points to the racism and humiliations endured by the heroes in the French army, it shows them as being pro-French throughout without the slightest inclination toward independence. For instance, Saïd (Jamel Debbouze), in a silent and Chaplinesque scene, uses German tracts inciting colonial troops to rebel against the French to fill a hole in his shoe, literally stepping on the idea of independence. Messaoud (Roschdy Zem) falls in love with a French woman, a Marseillaise (an allusion to the national anthem?) with whom he experiences for the first time a sense of equality and dignity. Initially reluctant, Yacir (Sami Naceri), who enlisted alongside his brother to pay for the latter's wedding, ends up not only burying his cherished sibling in French soil but also dying a selfless hero for France. The righteous Abdelkader (Sami Bouajila), whose name reminds us of the great spiritual and political leader of the Algerian resistance to the French conquest, obeys his superiors dutifully until the end, locked in a desperate quest for recognition that he will never get.

The situation in colonial Algeria is addressed indirectly through the symbolic couple formed by Saïd and Sergeant Martinez (Bernard Blancan), the Pied-Noir officer he serves and whose mother, he finds out by accident, is Algerian. When Saïd suggests to Martinez that their respective mothers look just like sisters, Martinez violently rejects this narrative of brotherhood based on a shared ethnicity. Saïd and Sergeant Martinez nevertheless die embracing each other, as Saïd, loyal to the end, tries to help Martinez escape his room under German gunfire. Only in the theater of war, and in death, can the two men become, both literally and figuratively, brothers in arms. The camera lingers on their bodies lying side by side, suggesting that the fates of Algeria and France are inextricably linked. Such images celebrate the sacrifice of patriotic heroes locked within the "horizontal comradeship" of the nation (Anderson 1991, 7). This is further reinforced by a striking prolepsis — a leap of sixty years forward to 2006 — that blatantly erases, more so than it displaces, the Algerian War of Independence, to focus on an aging and socially disenfranchised Abdelkader as he visits the graves of his forgotten comrades.

Bouchareb's powerful epic verges on consensual hagiography with its emphasis on the characters' unshakable loyalty. Capitalizing on sacrifice, *Indigènes* hesitates between claims for rehabilitation and recognition, and political denunciation. By paying homage to colonial troops, the film deliberately promotes a sense of collective identity and retrospective pride that foster the integration of "succeeding generations" by giving them "a legitimate wedge into French society" (Baum 2007). It also validates Bouchareb's republican credentials before launching a film on the war of independence — a potentially more divisive subject.

Cartouches gauloises: Reconciling Colonial Nostalgia and Independence

Mehdi Charef's *Cartouches gauloises* (2007) is the first film on the war by a French director of Algerian immigrant origin to be shot in Algeria, as well as the first one filmed from the semi-autobiographical perspective of a child. It was released ten years after the war experiences of the parents' generation were brought to the screen, in the late 1990s, along with Thomas Gilou's *Michou d'Auber* (2007), the story of a young Algerian boy placed in a French rural foster home by his father during the war, in a plot reminiscent of *Le vieil homme et l'enfant* (Claude Berri 1967). Charef explains that he kept postponing this semi-autobiographical project — although it was close to his heart — for fear of accusations that he was out to settle a score. Both films indicate that the war experiences of children, although they were late in coming in French cinema, promote reconciliation. Indeed, despite Charef's fears, the presence of children as main protagonists signal the emergence of a somewhat appeased perspective on the war. Following Ali (Mohamed Faouzi Ali Cherif), a schoolboy who delivers newspapers, the camera introduces the viewers to a comprehensive and somewhat didactic panorama of all the groups that made up French colonial Algeria (from FLN fighters and supporters to Europeans of various origins). Ali is a ubiquitous arch-witness of sorts who records every war-related event in town: the grim living conditions of Algerians regrouped in camps; the atrocities committed by the French army as well as its humanitarian outreach campaign; the terrorist attacks by Algerian nationalists and the torture to which they are subjected; the easy life of some Europeans and the collective tragedy of the Pieds-Noirs; and so on.

Cartouches strives to provide a compassionate and balanced view of each group, to recreate the multicultural fabric of colonial Algeria, at the risk of producing a somewhat flattening and unrealistic succession of vignettes. Violent scenes follow lighter anecdotes, all seen through the eyes of Ali as demonstrated by repeated close-ups of his face. This fragmentation may help convey the confusion inherent in the breakdown of French Algeria, embodied on screen by the explosion of a bust of Marianne, a symbol of the French republic. It also conveys the incomplete yet insightful perspective of a child, since Ali is the one and only element of cohesion between scenes. Yet no interpretation of the war emerges clearly, and the film seems to shy away from taking a stance by hiding behind Ali's recording gaze.

On the one hand, through Ali's innocent eyes, the film's collage establishes a truce between rival memorial factions — all represented — thus allowing Charef to fend off the potential accusation that he is out to get revenge. On the other hand, nostalgia sometimes fills the screen: Ali feels abandoned when his European friends, his brothers of sorts, leave one after the other, making him the sole and lonely owner of the hut they built together (an obvious symbol for Algeria); Rachel, the Jewish lady, even has to remind him to go celebrate "his independence" with everyone else. The Pieds-Noirs, the former villains, are rehabilitated as victims whose crime is to love Algeria too much. Charef's compassionate depiction of the demise of colonial Algeria in 1962 is tinged with his nostalgia for his childhood, so much so that in his cinematic semi-autobiography, he chooses not to include his departure for France, soon after independence, to join his immigrant father. Charef prefers to end on the celebration of independence and on the reunion between Ali and his father, an FLN fighter, in a move that pushes immigration aside. As Charef's film revisits the breakdown of multicultural colonial Algeria, it suggests, like Balibar, that the separation is incomplete, as France lives on in Algeria, albeit in the mind of Ali and his absent friends.

Despite, or perhaps because of, their overall limited success at the box office (with the exception of *Indigènes*), these films pose enduring questions about the place of immigration and (de)colonization within national collective understandings of the past. Although the war made a somewhat late appearance in the films by and about descendants of Algerian immigrants, these films usually revise official national histories by reconstructing the overlooked experiences of immigrants and their descendants. Filmmakers have documented the racist violence of French police, the participation of Algerian women in the struggle, and resistance to the hegemony of the FLN (Guerdjou, Krim, Touita); they have accounted for the memory of the *harkis* (Chibane) and described warring factions vying for control over the Algerian community in France (Touita, Krim), thus putting into question the legitimacy of the FLN.

Such films and their directors are uniquely positioned to reexamine both French and Algerian official commemorative rhetoric. They weave complex narratives that oscillate between two conflicting performances of belonging and opposite modes of identification. On the one hand, a potential interpretation of the Algerian War of Independence as civil war — one that mobilizes such tropes as the "reassurance of fratricide" and the male-centered rhetoric of "horizontal brotherhood" (Anderson 1991) — suggests that Algerian immigrants could be French brothers and citizens. On the other hand, the acknowledgment that Algerian immigrants — who contributed to Algerian independence from metropolitan France — cannot readily be assimilated into the French national imagination compels the political redefinition of what it means to be French and Algerian and allows viewers to retrospectively question what nations do in their name.

Notes

1. In this respect, Rachid Bouchareb's *Hors-la-loi* (2010) is the first film on the Algerian War of Independence whose story line and shooting locations straddle Algeria and France.

2. Michel Cadé disagrees somewhat with Frodon's interpretation to propose that far from ignoring the war, French filmmakers chose to record its traces by showing the subtle ways in which this distant conflict affected the lives of regular French people (1997, 56).

3. For Balibar, to the ideological fallacy of an indivisible entity uniting metropolitan France and "Algérie française" as one Republic, decolonization substituted the illusion of a separation between two distinct states, when in fact, he proposes, Algeria and France overlap in complex ways. For instance, do Algerian immigrants in France count as French

citizens (at the cost of erasing their Algerian allegiance), as citizens of both Algeria and France (hence as double citizens), or as one and a half (given their uneven participation in both countries and the fact that they cannot inhabit both countries at the same time)?

4. The first Algerian nationalist organization, the Étoile nord-africaine (North African Star), was founded in Paris in 1926 by Messali Hadj.

5. For a synthetic overview of the factors that precluded the expression and production of immigrant memories during and after the colonial period, see Alec Hargreaves (2006, 220–21).

6. This translates the French expression *porteurs de mémoire*, used by Benjamin Stora to designate the groups defined during colonization and by the war: the 1 million European settlers — who left Algeria — and their descendants in the French metropole; the 2 million draftees; the French ultras of the Organisation Armée Secrète; the *harkis*, Algerian soldiers who fought in the French army for a variety of reasons; the French supporters of Algerian independence; and finally, Algerian immigrants, squeezed and silenced between two nation states after independence. According to Stora, 6 to 7 million people, roughly 10 percent of the French population, have a direct connection to the war (2005, 58). Notwithstanding this impressive number, the war, he adds, remains peripheral in contemporary French society.

7. On October 17, 1961, between twenty thousand and thirty thousand Algerians, led by the FLN, marched through the streets of the capital in peaceful pro-independence demonstrations. They were protesting the discriminatory measures and the curfew imposed by police chief Maurice Papon to curtail FLN activities. A series of police killings by the FLN further exacerbated the anti-Algerian sentiment in the security forces; encouraged by Papon, they killed, at the very least, fifty Algerian demonstrators that night, and over the following days, in detention centers. At least eleven thousand were arrested and about a thousand were injured. The memory of this event, actively suppressed by state authorities (the exact number of deaths on that very night is still being debated), did not resurface until the early 1980s (Thénault 1998; House 2006).

8. In *Vivre au paradis* (Bourlem Guerdjou 1997), the scenes depicting the immigrant hero's family in an Algerian oasis were shot in Tunisia. Less than ten years later, the civil war being mostly over, Algerian authorities have made it possible to shoot on location. *La trahison* (Philippe Faucon 2006), *Mon colonel* (Laurent Herbiet 2007), and *Cartouches gauloises* (Mehdi Charef 2007) were all shot in part in Algeria, and indicate that the filmic representation of the war has entered a new phase that may encourage the inclusion of the memories and oral testimonies of Algerians themselves, not just that of their faces as extras. Bouchareb's *Hors-la-loi* — shot in Algeria, France, and Belgium and financed by French, European, and to a lesser extent, Algerian funds — confirms such an incipient cooperation.

9. A previous film, *Élise ou la vraie vie* (Michel Drach 1969) — the love story between French factory worker Elise (Marie-José Nat) and her Algerian coworker, Areski (Mohamed Chouikh) — was the first to focus on a North African immigrant hero and FLN activist (Cadé 2004, 120). In this film, Areski is shown as a responsible political leader, yet the war takes a back seat to romance and social content.

10. In Paris *Les sacrifiés* attracted 4,858 spectators according to Cadé (2004, 123). National admission figures are unavailable. As of this writing, the film is no longer available on VHS and has not been reissued in DVD format.

11. Tarr contrasts the reception of *Vivre au paradis* (62,828 entries) and *Sous les pieds des femmes* (9,882 in 1998) to the success of *Le gone du Chaâba* (826,765) — and, one could add, of *Inch'Allah dimanche* (126,846) — to suggest that cinematic depictions of the Algerian War remain unpalatable to mainstream audiences (2005, 127).

12. For a detailed analysis of the film, see Latiri (2003) and Rosello (2005, 143–51).

13. See Carrie Tarr's chapter "Memories of Immigration: *Sous les pieds des femmes* and *Vivre au paradis*" (2005, 124–35) for a compelling analysis of these films.

14. Since *Vivre au paradis*, the television film *Nuit noire, 17 octobre 1961* (Alain Tasma 2005) reenacted the event. Also, although *Caché* (Michael Haneke 2005) does not represent the attacks, its manipulative plot powerfully revolves around the haunting concealment rather than the (re)presentation of October 17, 1961.

15. Bouchareb's *Hors-la-loi* (2010) — the story of three Algerian immigrant brothers involved in the war of independence on the French front — did indeed stir the passions. It picks up where *Indigènes* ended in 1945, and features the same cast of popular actors, which fosters a sense of historical continuity between the two films despite discrepancies in their plots. This did not benefit *Hors-la-loi*, however (381,106 admissions according to www.allociné.fr at the time of this writing). European settlers' lobbies and associations mobilized against the film before it even came out, under the pretext that its reenactment of the 1945 Sétif massacre — a cinematic first according to Stora (Venaille 2010) — was misleading. On the other hand, Bouchareb's film competed as an Algerian film at the 2010 Cannes Film Festival, and despite its critical stance on the wartime actions of the FLN, not unlike the films by Rachida Krim and Bourlem Guerdjou studied in this chapter, the Algerian Culture Ministry continued to support the film (Sotinel 2010). So although *Hors-la-loi*'s box office performance (especially when compared to *Indigènes*'s 3 million viewers) confirms the French public's lack of appetite, to say the least, for films on the Algerian War of Independence, it points again to the central role played by directors of Algerian immigrant descent in the continued construction of a shared cinematic memory of the war.

References

Anderson, Benedict. 1991. *Imagined Communities*. London: Verso.

Balibar, Étienne. 1998. *Droit de cité: Culture et politique en démocratie*. La Tour d'Aigues: Éditions de l'Aube.

Baum, Géraldine. 2007. "France's Forgotten Liberators: 'Days of Glory' Recalls the Heroics of Colonial Subjects Who Fought and Then Were Swept Aside." *Los Angeles Times*, February 27, Calendar, E6.

Branche, Rapahëlle. 2008. "Une impression d'absence: L'Algérie et la guerre d'Algérie au cinéma et à la télévision française depuis 1962." In *L'Algérie dépassionnée: Au-delà du tumulte des mémoires*, ed. Eric Savarèse, 107–15. Paris: Syllepse.

Burgoyne, Robert. 2007. "The Balcony of History." *Rethinking History* 11 (4): 547–54.

Cadé, Michel. 1997. "Les films des années 60: D'abord les effets sur les Français." In "La guerre d'Algérie à l'écran," ed. Guy Hennebelle. *CinémAction* 85:48–56.

————. 2004. "Une représentation en éclats: Les Maghrébins dans le cinéma français." In *Maghrébins de France*, ed. Mohand Khelil, 111–34. Toulouse: Privat.

Colin-Jeanvoine, Emmanuelle, and Stéphanie Derozier. 2008. *Le financement du FLN pendant la guerre d'Algérie 1954–1962*. Paris: Éditions Bouchène.

Frodon, Jean-Michel. 1998. *La projection nationale*. Paris: Odile Jacob.

————. 2004. "Le film de guerre n'existe pas: De l'Algérie au Vietnam." *Cahiers du cinéma* 593 (September): 74–76.

Harbi, Mohammed, and Benjamin Stora, eds. 2004. *La guerre d'Algérie 1954–2004: La fin de l'amnésie*. Paris: Robert Laffont.

Hargreaves, Alec G. 2006. "Generating Migrant Memories." In *Algeria and France, 1800–2000: Identity, Memory, Nostalgia*, ed. Patricia M. E. Lorcin, 217–27. Syracuse NY: Syracuse University Press.

House, Jim. 2006. "The Colonial and Post-Colonial Dimensions of Algerian Migration to France." *History in Focus* (Autumn). Institute for Historical Research, University of London. http://www.history.ac.uk/ihr/Focus/Migration/articles/house.html (accessed August 5, 2009).

Jeancolas, Jean-Pierre. 2007. "French Cinema and the Algerian War: Fifty Years Later." *Cineaste* 33 (1): 44–46.

Landsberg, Alison. 2004. *Prosthetic Memory: The Transformation of American Remembrance in the Age of Mass Culture*. New York: Columbia University Press.

Latiri, Dora Carpenter. 2003. "Représentations de la femme migrante dans *Inch'Allah dimanche*." *Web Journal of French Media Studies* 6. http://wjfms.ncl.ac.uk/LatiriWJ .htm (accessed August 5, 2009).

Liauzu, Claude. 2004. "Mémoires croisées de la guerre d'Algérie." In *La guerre d'Algérie dans la mémoire et l'imaginaire*, ed. Anny Dayan Rosenman and Lucette Valensi, 161–80. Paris: Éditions Bouchène.

Noiriel, Gérard. 1995. "Immigration: Amnesia and Memory." *French Historical Studies* 19 (2): 367–80.

Rancière, Jacques. 2004. *Aux bords du politique*. Paris: Gallimard.

Rosello, Mireille. 2005. *France and the Maghreb: Performative Encounters*. Gainesville: University Press of Florida.

Rousso, Henry. 2004. "Les raisins verts de la guerre d'Algérie." In *La guerre d'Algérie (1954–1962)*, ed. Henry Rousso, 127–51. Paris: Odile Jacob.

Sayad, Abdelmalek. 1999. *La double absence*. Paris: Seuil.

Shepard, Todd. 2006. *The Invention of Decolonization: The Algerian War and the Remaking of France*. Ithaca NY: Cornell University Press.

Sotinel, Thomas. 2010. "*Hors la loi* et ceux qui ne changent jamais d'avis." *Le Monde*, May 21. http://sotinel.blog.lemonde.fr/2010/05/21/hors-la-loi-ceux-qui-ne-changent -jamais-davis/ (accessed May 22, 2010).

Stora, Benjamin. 1994. "La guerre d'Algérie quarante ans après: Connaissances et reconnaissance." *Modern and Contemporary France* 2:131–39.

———. 1995. *Histoire de la guerre d'Algérie (1954–1962)*. Paris: La Découverte.

———. 1997. *Imaginaires de guerre, Algérie–Viêt Nam en France et aux Etats-Unis*. Paris: La Découverte.

———. 2004. "1999–2003, guerre d'Algérie, les accélérations de la mémoire." In *La guerre d'Algérie 1954–2004: La fin de l'amnésie*, ed. Mohammed Harbi and Benjamin Stora, 501–14. Paris: Robert Laffont.

———. 2005. "Quand une mémoire (de guerre) peut en cacher une autre (coloniale)?" In *La fracture coloniale*, ed. Pascal Blanchard, Nicolas Bancel, and Sandrine Lemaire, 57–65. Paris: La Découverte.

Tarr, Carrie. 2005. *Reframing Difference:* Beur *and* Banlieue *Filmmaking in France*. Manchester: Manchester University Press.

———. 2007. "Maghrebi-French (Beur) Filmmaking in Context." *Cineaste* 33 (1): 2–7.

Thénault, Sylvie. 1998. *Histoire de la guerre d'indépendance algérienne*. Paris: Flammarion.

———. 2005. "Le 17 octobre 1961 en question." *Cahiers Jean Jaurès* 148:89–104.

Venaille, Caroline. 2010. "En France, 'certains n'ont toujours pas accepté la décolonisation.'" *Le Monde*, May 21. http://www.lemonde.fr/festival-de-cannes/article/2010 (accessed May 21, 2010).

Filmography

Benguigui, Yamina, dir. *Inch'Allah dimanche*, 2001.

Berri, Claude, dir. *Le vieil homme et l'enfant*, 1967.

Bouchareb, Rachid, dir. *Indigènes*, 2006.

———, dir. *Hors-la-loi*, 2010.

Charef, Mehdi, dir. *Cartouches gauloises*, 2007.

Chibane, Malik, dir. *Hexagone*, 1994.

———. *Douce France*, 1995.

Drach, Michel, dir. *Élise ou la vraie vie*, 1969.

Faucon, Philippe, dir. *La trahison*, 2006.

Gilou, Thomas, dir. *Michou d'Auber*, 2007.

Guerdjou, Bourlem, dir. *Vivre au paradis*, 1999.

Haneke, Michael, dir. *Caché*, 2005.

Herbiet, Laurent, dir. *Mon colonel*, 2007.

Krim, Rachida, dir. *Sous les pieds des femmes*, 1997.

Ruggia, Christophe, dir. *Le gone du Chaâba*, 1998.

Tasma, Alain, dir. *Nuit noire, 17 octobre 1961*, 2005.

Touita, Okacha, dir. *Les sacrifiés*, 1983.

6

RACHID BOUCHAREB'S *INDIGÈNES*

Political or Ethical Event of Memory?

MIREILLE ROSELLO

The film that will serve as my point of departure was directed
by Rachid Bouchareb and distributed in France in 2006. I suppose that I could say that this film is about France's colonial past
(and especially about the role of colonized North African subjects enrolled in the French military during the Second World
War), but the idea that a film is "about" the past is precisely what
quickly became problematic when I started watching *Indigènes*
(*Days of Glory*).

In this chapter I first examine the relationship between *Indigènes*
and what we call history, that is, a discipline that sometimes tells
stories. It is impossible, however, to assume that there is a clean
distinction between the film and "history" since the movie both
narrates historical events but also becomes part of French contemporary history: the film appears at a specific moment when
France is struggling with its colonial past, with the ways in which
it is possible to memorialize it, and it contributes to that debate. To
some extent, the film belongs to history too because it constitutes
a memorial narrative that invites us to legitimize it. *Indigènes* both

talks about how we practice history and, at the same time, is itself a historical event. In the second part of the chapter, I look for a theoretical definition of such a type of cultural historical event and ask what such interventions may be expected to achieve. I suggest that *Indigènes* is not "about" memory but constitutes what I will call an event of memory.

Indigènes as a Political Event of Memory

Indigènes fictionalizes what the spectator is expected to discover as having been repressed and to remember as what should not have been forgotten. The message is that the French should already know about what is depicted (the role played by colonial troops in the liberation of France during the Second World War). It is not a film that interrogates the way in which the story is told and the limits of its own storytelling.

Indigènes was a most successful cultural and political intervention. The film focuses not only on a forgotten past but also on the impact that remembering that past should have on our immediate present. The narrative is set in the past and follows the tragic destinies of four North African soldiers who are portrayed as the victims of history. *Indigènes* is interested in documenting a long and complex adventure that starts in the villages where the soldiers were recruited and ends with the last surviving character visiting the graves of his friends in a French cemetery. The film's thesis is that these men who defended France against the Germans were not recognized as war heroes and so must carry out their own lonely ritual of commemoration in the midst of general indifference. Their heroic deeds were never recorded as part of France's history; their courage and abnegation were forgotten. Were it not for the film, we, the public, would not know about these men. From a formal point of view, *Indigènes* is relatively traditional, relying on the conventions of realism and linearity. Both Alec Hargreaves and Colin MacCabe admit that they were not particularly impressed by the aesthetic qualities of the film. Hargreaves writes that "while well written and skillfully photographed and edited with strong acting performances, *Indigènes* breaks no new ground artistically" (Hargreaves 2007, 205), and MacCabe states that at the Cannes festival, "the one French film that did touch both audience and jurors, Rachid Bouchareb's *Indigènes* (*Days of Glory*)[,] was not an art film but an exercise in an all but historic American genre" (2006, 107). For both critics, the interest of the film does not lie in its artistic merit but in its ability to move its audience and to influence history by changing public opinion.

The story counts on our suspension of disbelief precisely to make us believe in the extra-diegetic existence of the heroes. The point is that national memory is guilty of not telling their story. In other words, there is a remarkable coincidence or performative power in such a film: the process of storytelling constitutes the historiographic intervention itself. Summarizing the plot of the movie leads to the revelation of something that was, until now, unfairly ignored and forgotten. These men were heroes, and the failure to reiterate or celebrate their actions is, in itself, injurious. It produces an effect of truth that spectators are invited to receive as the truth and not as fiction. Generic French spectators can now be expected to share the same narrative about the role played by North African colonial troops during the Second World War, whether or not their ancestors have been French nationals for one, two, or twenty generations. The history lesson is not restricted to any given community: it wishes to reach the *banlieues* as well as urban centers, it is meant for the unknown neighbor or the imaginary national.

Indigènes gambles that the individuals who watch it will agree to a number of mental steps. We are expected to treat the four North African heroes as representatives of a whole group that has, until now, remained invisible. We are expected to agree that the whole group has suffered from historical discrimination and to recognize that if we knew nothing about colonial troops, it is because the national narrative that French citizens share was flawed. In other words, the film hopes to revise one of the chapters of national history books by shocking spectators out of their indifference or comfortable sense of historical knowledge.

Indigènes treats national memory as the sum of individual memories: once the incorrect narrative that forgot the role played by colonial troops is revised, then the group as a whole has solved the problem of forgetfulness. A better historical truth has replaced the inaccurate version. The story relies on an implicit notion of historical progress, and even if this stage is perceived as provisional, there is no question that it thinks of itself as an improvement.[1]

Indigènes would clearly not count as "history" if history is narrowly defined as an academic discipline whose legitimate representatives are professional historians. Moreover, Bouchareb claimed that he "also wanted to have the freedom not to remain faithful to history" (Lermercier 2006). Yet at the same time, he clearly wanted to intervene beyond the cultural realm, and thus might be seen as intervening in the historical domain. Furthermore, the film is not only credited with providing us with a counternarrative, it is also perceived to have had immediate and remarkable political and economic effects. Commentators in France and abroad suggest that this work of fiction was the cause, or at least the catalyst, for the resolution of a forty-year-long dispute over African veterans' pensions. The type of narrative historical intervention exemplified by *Indigènes* could thus be described as political to the extent that it has a clear vision of what it wants to achieve: the goal is to reveal a long-hidden truth and to repair the symbolic injustice that such silences constitute.

Spectators who knew nothing about this controversial issue discover, at the end of the film, a text superimposed over the images of the military cemetery. The frame tells us about the fact that the pensions owed to African veterans had been frozen at the end of the 1950s. Since 1959, soldiers who, like the protagonists, had served in the French army were receiving a fraction of the sum paid to French veterans. Many protested the injustice that made individuals the victims of historic decolonizing processes. For decades, nothing was done. In 2001 the situation improved somewhat (for those veterans who were still alive). Their pensions were adjusted. But Africans were still penalized because the increase was aligned with the cost of living in their own country rather than with the prevalent rate for French pensions.

And finally, in what may appear as a rather extraordinary and theatrical turn of events, *Indigènes*, a story made of moving images and sounds, a work of art, changed all that. As Emma Wilson puts it: "The film's significant historical achievement, rightly vaunted, has been in triggering Jacques Chirac in 2006 to bring the level of the pensions still paid to citizens of these nations in line with those paid to the French" (Wilson 2007, 21).

What is curious, however, is the way in which the film is supposed to have produced its political effect or, more accurately, the way in which its influence was described in the media. The film was a commercial success, it reached a very large audience, and we may assume that the public would have been ready to mobilize and to put pressure on the government.[2] Instead, when the film was released, it was already too late for citizens to decide whether or not to organize: Chirac had already intervened and, apparently, single-handedly solved the problem. In other words, when the spectators discovered the superimposed text about frozen pensions, the denunciation was obsolete. Pensions were going to be recalculated.

While there is every reason to celebrate the end of an injustice, it may be just as important to wonder about the strange journalistic myth that presented the political change as a result of a "private screening" organized for President Jacques Chirac and his wife before the film was launched. If the screening was indeed a "private" affair, then isn't it the case that Jacques and Bernadette Chirac were there as ordinary French citizens rather than as president elect and first lady? And if a decision was actually made at the end of the show, and on the basis of a film, how can we describe such a process? Does Chirac's apparently unilateral decision have a place within a democratic regime or does this look more like a sovereign's largesse? The story of how the Chiracs reacted to *Indigènes* quickly circulated and does not seem to have generated any public outcry or even questions about the seemingly direct connection between a private screening and a matter of public policy. It was also insinuated that Bernadette's (feminine) emotional reaction had influenced her husband, which contributes to paint an alarmingly individualized and vaguely sexist picture of the whole episode. Here is how an article published in *Libération* describes the scene:

> "Jacques, il faut faire quelque chose!" L'émotion de Bernadette Chirac après la projection privée du film *Indigènes*, le 5 septembre, en présence de Jamel Debbouze et Rachid Bouchareb, a convaincu le président de la République qu'il fallait "aller plus loin" pour améliorer la situation des anciens combattants coloniaux. ["Jacques, something must be done!" Bernadette Chirac's emotion, following the private screening of the film *Indigènes*, on September 5th, in the presence of Jamel Debbouze and Rachid Bouchareb, convinced the president of the Republic that he must "go further" to improve the situation of colonial veterans.] (Merchet 2006)

For "Bernadette Chirac," the "president of the Republic" is "Jacques." But for African veterans, Jacques is the individual who has the power, once moved by his wife and by a film, to change their fate. What is perhaps so disturbing about this historical fairy tale is the serendipitous aspect of the cluster of events that led to the new policy. Had Bernadette not been moved, had the film not been privately shown, had Jacques not listened to his wife, what would have remained of the so-called political impact of *Indigènes*? Is it not a most depoliticized reading of the event to suggest that the fate of veterans depended on the president's wife's visceral appreciation of what critics described as a not so good film? What is presented as the political consequence of this film can only be applauded, but is it not precisely a strange depoliticizing process to describe the link between the new policy and the film as what happened in a nonpublic, privatized space where the audience was individualized and personalized? Is this the kind of political power that history in general and progressive history in particular wishes to have? If a political decision is indeed the direct result of a head of state's exposure to a film, then we must assume that the opposite result could also have been brought about by a different narrative. Another movie might have been read as a strong argument in favor of a more conservative position and still have as much influence on powerful viewers.

The strange mixture of political satisfaction and deep malaise that I kept trying to dismiss in order to enjoy what seemed like a clear moment of successful resistance simply did not go away, which made me aware that the discomfort should be treated seriously as part of my theoretical reaction to what had happened. Maybe the discomfort was the manifestation of a site of conflict that could never be resolved. I have learned to suspect that this often vague sense that something is amiss, messy, and theoretically unpleasant is precisely a moment where what Rancière calls "le politique" is emerging (Rancière 1995). In his model, politics is not the type of negotiation that is supposed to lead to a consensus among already well-recognized parties but the moment when parts of the community get reorganized and when new voices that, up until then, did not count as voices, are heard. Often, the moment when the parts of the community are redistributed or when the "uncounted" are finally heard is a messy moment that Rancière associates with what he calls "mésentente" [dispute and misunderstanding, dissent and mishearing], a moment when people talk to each other but are not on the same plane, cannot hear each other as equals, and mistake each other's language for a sort of noise. In the case of *Indigènes*, the "mésentente" is obviously not between Chirac and the film, but between several types of what I propose to call "events of memory," that is, events that constitute not only historical events during which history is changed but also historical events that force us to self-reflexively ask questions about the difference between an ethics and a politics of history. I suggest that what the film frames is the invisible and repressed dispute between those irreconcilable and yet equally indispensable imperatives.

Indigènes implicitly relies on the notion of the political power of historical progress (and expects us to believe in that invisible grand narrative too) without being able to found the notion of progress in an ethically tenable definition of progress: we don't know how we move, democratically, from the circulating of a narrative of progress to a progressive policy. *Indigènes* presents itself as a deliberate attempt to correct the past, to write a better, more accurate version of something that was neither told nor told properly. And the dispute has to do with the fact that I do not know, as a theorist, how to construct a useful working definition of what I would be willing to recognize as historical progress, given that even teleology is suspect, that progress sounds tainted with Eurocentrism and modernity, and that it seems impossible to talk about progress without at least some notion of shared values or ideological bias. I am not ready to completely give up on the idea of progressive history, but at the same time I am no longer sure that progress exists, let alone that it is something we should celebrate.

Indigènes, then, is a political intervention that makes me realize that an ethics of history is both inseparable from and irreconcilable with a politics of history. A politics of history warns me that history may be what always sides with the powerful and the dominant, with the masculine or even the West, whereas an ethics of history warns me that it would certainly be naïve to assume that whenever history is forced to change in the presence of discursive pressures applied by the forgotten of history, the new narrative will necessary constitute some sort of universal or universally accepted improvement. If history itself can make us aware of its own canonical limitations and can successfully relay voices that were previously excluded from our textbooks (women, the subaltern, the voiceless), it is obviously capable of doing exactly the opposite. Ethically, it is necessary to revise; but I have no guarantee that revisions will serve the political agenda that I define as progressive or even that revisions will have any political impact. And when a revision is politically effective, it may have escaped the ethical. I suggest that this is exactly what *Indigènes* did: by proposing a new narrative that we are invited to accept as a new (even provisional) truth, the film changes a historical canon rather than our relationship to historical truth.

This film can therefore be described as the site of a dispute that forces me to ask a different question about rewriting the past: which kind of reading strategies could help us look at moments of historical rewritings from a perspective that would be neither ethically paranoid (each successive revision is a different type of exclusionary process) nor politically angelic (each revision corrects the past and finally does justice to the victims, repairs the community from the trauma of silence)?

From that point of view, *Indigènes* participates in the much larger debate that is currently going on in contemporary France about whether or not one should reexamine the role of the colonial past, and especially of the war of Algeria, within French history. This cultural conversation sometimes deteriorates into a war of positions where there seems to be only two sides, two options. Some fulminate against what President Sarkozy has called the "detestable fad of repentance" (Sarkozy 2007). Anti-repentance voices refuse what they perceive as being stuck in the past, being bogged down in a debate about whether the nation or the state is accountable. According to them, such a process is divisive and contributes to the social or colonial "fracture" (Bancel, Blanchard, and Lemaire 2005). At the opposite end of that spectrum are those who demand that the past be interrogated either because they feel that their own history has been unfairly ignored or because they are moved by a sense of historical injustice. It is clear, I suppose, from the way in which I describe both "camps" that if it were, or that when it is, a question of choosing camps, I know which one I will not choose. But after watching *Indigènes*, I came to the conclusion that it is probably precious to dwell on the discomfort that is created by the opposition that pretends to split ethics and politics.

Moments of Memory: Political and Ethical Events of Memory

In order to articulate the distinction that I find it necessary to make between the political and the ethical in historical narratives, I propose to add to Pierre Nora's classic *lieu de mémoire* an element of temporality that enables us to account for continuities and discontinuities in the processes of anamnesis or forgetfulness.[3] We know that a *lieu de mémoire* does not have to be a real space (although it can be a monument or a city or a plaque). But I suggest that it is also worth thinking in terms of *moments* of memory. A film like *Indigènes* is not *a* moment of memory but one of the manifestations of a moment of memory.[4]

To be more explicit, the film is a political *event* of memory which is part of a specific moment of memory, that is, a provisionally stable period during which the paradigms that we accept as what is historical discourse and what we consider to be just noise are relatively set. A moment of memory functions like a literary genre, enabling and constraining the range of what constitutes acceptable discourse about a historical event. It organizes the politics of verisimilitude, that is, the narrative or cluster of narratives that sounds so true that it discourages the meta-question of the access to what is recognized as the truth. For example, the moment of memory that I am identifying here makes the war between France and Algeria a highly controversial but legitimate object of study. The war is not denied or forgotten, it is debated, and that is legitimate. Whether or not we can explain why it is now legitimate is relatively irrelevant. The moment of memory is not reducible to one version of any given event but it opens up a scene of production and reception, it delineates the contours of a specific public during a specific time and place. It also produces effects of truth in the realm of what readers accept as relevant or irrelevant to an event, as connected or disconnected, and as significant, either individually or collectively. They make us realize that even a *lieu de mémoire* can only be seen if it has been validated by a "moment of memory." Even if *lieux de mémoire* are instable (statues of leaders are erected and then pulled down, names of streets and cities change, reflecting ideological tidal waves), this instability temporarily solidifies as the manifestation of a moment of memory during which a public imagined as historically educated encounters a narrative canonized by the naturalization of a certain verisimilitude. A moment of memory is thus not only inseparable from a public and from a collective narrative but also from a third crucial element: a system of representation that constitutes a relatively hegemonic means of symbolic circulation. Not every story is capable of contributing to a moment of memory.

Indigènes has successfully organized (or performatively imagined) a public that shares, not so much the same memory of a certain event, but the same moment of memory. Although a moment of memory obviously has to do with temporality, each moment does not necessarily correspond to a given period. A moment of history does not necessarily include all the books or testimonies published at a given moment, since what characterizes each moment of memory is its ability to hear or ignore certain paradigms. In retrospect, we can describe specific moments of history by analyzing what was left out of history in a given period. The books and testimonies that denounced the use of torture in Algeria and that were published in the 1960s belong to the moment of memory that started in the 1990s. This seems paradoxical only if we do not distinguish between a historical period and a moment of memory. Similarly, the moment of memory that makes a film like *Indigènes* legible may or may not include other genres, other forms of testimonies or analyses. It may be that the definitive history book about the role played by colonized soldiers during the Second World War has already been written or is about to be written without participating in the moment of memory.

That is, for example, what happened when intellectuals were denouncing the use of torture. Or we may want to think about what is currently, right now, being edited out of our moment of memory. *Indigènes* presents itself, convincingly, as the first attempt to tell that story. It does not really matter whether its political power comes from the fact that it really is the first of its kind or if its revelatory power comes from its popularity. As Hargreaves points out, there are precedents that can be read as comparable attempts. Not only are there intertextual links between *Indigènes* and the American tradition of recent war films (such as Steven Spielberg's 1998 *Saving Private Ryan*), but Bouchareb's work is also indebted to other historical filmic rewritings.

Hargreaves suggests that *Indigènes* was not

> as the hullabaloo surrounding the movie led many to believe, the first feature film to depict colonial troops mobilized in the service of France. Almost twenty years earlier, in *Le Camp de Thiaroye* (1987), Ousmane Sembene had highlighted grave injustices meted out to West African soldiers at the end of World War II. Pierre Javaux's *Les Enfants du pays*, depicting a unit of *tirailleurs sénégalais* (West African colonial soldiers) in the Ardennes during the fall of France in 1940, preceded by five months the French release of *Indigènes* in the fall of 2006 but attracted little publicity. (Hargreaves 2007, 206)

Thinking in terms of a moment of memory accounts for the acceptability of a "for the first time" rhetoric. *Indigènes* is the conduit of what we recognize as facts, in the absence of evidence to the contrary. A moment of memory may be as short-lived as the time during which a film remains visible or lasts as long as the period during which a hegemonic regime controls historical discourse (colonialism as a "mission civilisatrice" for example). What cultural critics may contribute to an analysis of such moments is a study of which conditions must be present before something changes within the national *lieu de mémoire*. Each moment of memory will change the shape of the community's or the nation's preexisting *lieux de mémoire*. Moments of memory provide readers, viewers, and the public in general with a set of norms that they will then be able to decline across disciplines but also according to what they imagine to be the point of their story.

What I am calling an *event* of memory, however, is slightly different: an event of memory is what modifies the whole paradigm and what makes us see that we were blind to the borders set by the hegemonic moment of memory.

Each event of memory troubles the norms that govern the moment, and each will deal in its own political and/or ethical way with such norms and will contribute to shaping and reshaping the current ensemble of *lieux de mémoire*. The specific manner in which the *lieu de mémoire* will be changed helps us distinguish between the ethical and political status of the event of memory or endure the discomfort of not being able to distinguish. There is, however, nothing predictable about whether or not any event of memory will have any kind of performative power. Just as realist art movements wish to give the illusion of representing reality and make us forget that they are constructing it, moments of memory have a revelatory ambition and they address a public that they are in the process of creating.

As critical analysts, then, how can we assess the contribution that *Indigènes* makes to the debate about the place of France's colonial past? At a very elementary level, those of us who are relieved to see that contemporary history no longer embraces a triumphant colonial mentality, or that Western countries are prepared to debate the impact of the colonial enterprise, are probably quite aware that different forms of negationism have not disappeared and will probably never disappear even if they are made illegal.[5] Moreover, without analyzing very carefully what exactly we would be willing to recognize as "progress," we may end up adopting whatever contemporary values are implicitly deployed in our new and improved stories, without realizing that we are now embracing a version of the "civilizing mission" that we will, in a few generations, mock as obsolete and hypocritical. So, what is the equivalent today of the "civilizing mission" paradigm and how would we recognize it? Would a hegemonic paradigm not be, by definition, a cultural blind spot?

If we ask such questions of a film like *Indigènes*, what interpretive parameters can we use when we judge fictionalized historical narratives from a political and ethical point of view? Is there a difference between a historical fiction that enables political changes and one that forces us to consider the ethics of history in general? A historical fiction that enables political changes would be a story that has a direct impact on the law that determines how veterans' pensions are calculated (this would be a political change resulting from a new version of an historical event, and that is exactly what happened with *Indigènes*). A story that forces us to consider the ethics of history in general may not have such a direct impact, but it would make us read other histories and other historical versions — that is, other historical events — as infamous lies, irresponsible omissions, or desirable rewritings.[6]

How do we even select a narrative that we agree constitutes a progressive rewriting but that we wish to analyze for hidden political or ethical agendas? The film unfolds against a structuring background of exacerbated manifestations of class and economic and racial discrimination that link the (un)forgotten past to a still traumatized present.[7] It is therefore plausible to wonder if the only possible reading of this film is not that it confirms the worst about contemporary Europe: for all its talk about its colonial history, it is not recovering from it, mourning it, or finding ways of formulating its accountability. Instead, as Étienne Balibar puts it, Europe is involved in a process of recolonization that the incessant debate about repentance conveniently masks.[8]

When the film came out in France, the debate had already shifted from a demand for recognition of what happened to a discussion about which memorial events are appropriate where and when.[9] The film participates in this quest or questioning of what constitutes an appropriate way to remember such a tragic event in the public space, especially at a moment when the nation is forced to take into account the impact of a colonial past upon its uncertain present. The questions that the film has helped us formulate have to do with a very specific aspect of this search for a proper form of national and public remembrance: is there a difference between the politics and the ethics of collective and individual forms of memory and commemoration? Do we ask the same questions and provide the same answers if we analyze the political or ethical consequence of those acts of memory, which, as they accumulate, end up changing the shape of a community's memory? The answers to such question will not be found if we watch *Indigènes* without interrogating the place of such films as events of memory within a given moment of memory, and only after such an analysis does it become possible to suggest that the relationship between fictional historical rewritings and historical progress is always the site of an ethical dispute.

Notes

1. See, for example, the interview that Bouchareb granted to Fabien Lemercier: he talks about his desire to "open chapters" within French history (Lemercier 2006). Ayo Coly even suggests that *Indigènes* was welcomed by the French public because it was read "as a corrective to omissions from the official French history of the war" (Coly 2008, 154).

2. I am not even talking here about the fact that the film was a box office hit (according to the Council of Europe database, http://lumière.obs.coe.int, there were 2,995,992 entries in 2006 in France alone). For remarks on the director's ambitions in terms of

popular success, see Alec Hargreaves (2007, 210). Coly points out, however, that "the overwhelming positive reception of this film in France was not echoed in Algeria" because it does not "offer a counter, Algerian, memory of the event. Algerian critics point to the magnitude of the glaring omission in Bouchareb's film: the forced and often violent mobilization of colonial African troops" (2008, 154).

3. The international visibility of Nora's work is such that his coinage "lieu de mémoire" has passed into everyday speech. The volumes published between 1984 and 1992, but also the critiques that highlighted the limits of the historian's project in the Algerian context (Derderian 2002; Apter 1999, 2), have helped to forge a complex concept-tool that enables us to analyze the memorial mechanisms exhibited by any "significant entity, whether material or non-material in nature" (Nora 1996, xvii), whether archive or museum, commemorative plaque or more abstract form of collective memory.

4. Scholars interested in performativity might want to say that it is the iteration of such a moment, by which I mean that the film is both made possible by the moment of memory but also contributes to it, due to the spiraling rather than static nature of such moments.

5. A government may choose to draft laws that will protect the victims of genocides (and the general public) against narratives that would deny their existence. In France, the law of June 30, 1990, makes it a crime to deny the existence of crimes against humanity (and it is used against negationists). In 1999 the French government also officially modified the national record that still talked about the Algerian "events" and finally accepted that a "war" had taken place. A few years later, the law of January 29, 2001, officially recognized the existence of the Armenian genocide. But this is obviously a double-edged sword since it is the same principle that in 2005 allowed Parliament to vote in favor of a law whose flavor was distinctly nostalgic: the law of February 23, 2005, scandalized many historians who had noticed that one of its original articles made it mandatory for history teachers to teach the colonial period without forgetting its positive aspects. It is not surprising that historians, regardless of their ideological and political opinions, tend to insist that the government should stay out of their field and refrain from policing history. Pierre Vidal-Naquet, who spent his life fighting against "les Assassins de la mémoire," declared in an interview granted to *Libération*: "Je vomis les négationnistes. Mais j'ai toujours été contre la loi Gayssot. Ce n'est pas à l'Etat de dire comment on enseigne l'histoire" [Negationists make me throw up. But I have always been against the Gayssot Law. The State should not tell us how to teach history] (2005).

6. I suggest elsewhere that Michael Haneke's *Caché* (2005) would be worth exploring as an event of memory. In that film, the memory of what happened in October 1961 in Paris is represented not as the "new chapter" of history that we should now all know about and that should have been taught a long time ago but as what is repressed and deliberately forgotten by the hero. No clear narrative emerges of what we should remember as spectators. The film questions the ways in which we access, process, and welcome or reject bits and pieces of information that may or may not solidify into a memorial narrative. See *The Reparative in Narratives: Works of Mourning in Progress* (Rosello 2010).

7. The North African soldiers suffer from discrimination: they are not as well equipped as their metropolitan counterparts, and sometimes they do not have access to the same

food (the heroes are ready to rebel when they discover that they are the only ones who will not be given tomatoes). Climbing up the hierarchical ladder proves impossible for one of the North African soldiers. Even attempts at entertaining the men divide the military into incompatible communities, the officers enjoying a high culture performance while the men gradually leave the room.

8. In chapter titled "*Droit de cité* or Apartheid," Balibar suggests that the colonial heritage is responsible for carving the space of the stranger-insider within Europe. They can only be integrated as a fake citizen whose contractual relationship with the state they may never negotiate for themselves (Balibar 2004, 40). This "recolonization" process affects, I would argue, not only immigrants but all the subjects who are treated as such (whether their parents or grandparents were immigrants or whether their bodies are misread as evidence that they are from elsewhere).

9. A significant turning point becomes noticeable if we compare the current debate over "memorial laws" to the silence that shrouded the war between France and Algeria until the beginning of the 1990s. While it is not until 1999 that Parliament changed the text of several articles of law to include the word "war" in reference to the conflict between France and Algeria, since the beginning of the twenty-first century the debate has been reconfigured as indicated by a proliferation of controversial new laws. Each of the so-called memorial laws not only recognizes the existence of historical events (the Shoah, Algeria, the slave trade, France's "overseas presence," and the Armenian genocide) but also recommends specific ways of memorializing them.

References

Apter, Emily. 1999. *Continental Drift: From National Character to Virtual Subjects*. Chicago: University of Chicago Press.

Balibar, Étienne. 2004. "*Droit de cité* or Apartheid?" In *We, the People of Europe? Reflections on Transnational Citizenship*, trans. James Swenson, 31–50. Princeton NJ: Princeton University Press.

Bancel, Nicolas, Pascal Blanchard, and Sandrine Lemaire, eds. 2005. *La fracture coloniale: La société française au prisme de l'héritage colonial*. Paris: La Découverte.

Coly, Ayo. 2008. "Memory, History, Forgetting." *Transition* 98:150–55.

Derderian, Richard. 2002. "Algeria as a *lieu de mémoire*: Ethnic Minority Memory and National Identity in Contemporary France." *Radical History Review* 83 (Spring): 28–43.

Hargreaves, Alec. 2007. "*Indigènes*: A sign of the times." *Research in African Literatures* 38 (4) (Winter): 204–16.

Lemercier, Fabien. 2006. "Interview with Rachid Bouchareb: Opening Chapters in History." *CineEuropa* (May). http://cineuropa.org/interview.aspx?documentID=64764 (accessed February 2009).

MacCabe, Colin. 2006. "Film: Cannes 2006." *Critical Quarterly* 48 (3): 105–9.

Merchet, Jean-Dominique. 2006. "*Indigènes* fait craquer Chirac." *Libération*, September 25. http://www.liberation.fr (accessed January 2009).

Nora, Pierre. 1996. *Realms of Memory: Rethinking the French Past*, trans. Arthur Goldhammer. New York: Columbia University Press.

Rancière, Jacques. 1995. *La mésentente: Politique et philosophie*. Paris: Galilée.

Rosello, Mireille. 2010. *The Reparative in Narratives: Works of Mourning in Progress*. Liverpool: Liverpool University Press.

Sarkozy, Nicolas. 2007. Speech delivered in Caen, March 9. http://www.u-m-p.org/site/index.php/s_informer/discours/nicolas_sarkozy_a_caen (accessed May 31, 2008).

Vidal-Naquet, Pierre. 2005. "Interview with Hervé Nathan: L'Etat n'a pas à dire comment enseigner l'histoire." *Libération*, April 14. http://www.liberation.fr (accessed January 2009).

Wilson, Emma. 2007. "*Days of Glory/Flanders*: Emma Wilson on Two Prize-Winning, Politically Ambitious French War Films." *Film Quarterly* 61 (1) (Fall): 16–22.

Filmography

Bouchareb, Rachid, dir. *Indigènes*, 2006.

Haneke, Michael, dir. *Caché*, 2005.

Spielberg, Steven, dir. *Saving Private Ryan*, 1998.

7

CLASS ACTS

Education, Gender, and Integration
in Recent French Cinema

CARRIE TARR

In 2008 Laurent Cantet's *Entre les murs* was the surprise winner
of the Palme d'Or at Cannes for its riveting, low-budget representation of the day-to-day life of a multiethnic secondary school
in the twentieth arrondissement of Paris. Two other relatively
successful films released a few years before *Entre les murs* have
foregrounded secondary education in the multiethnic Parisian
banlieue: Abdellatif Kechiche's award-winning *L'esquive* (2004)
and Eric Rochant's comedy *L'ecole pour tous* (2006).[1] This cluster of films builds on a series of representations of the school in
French cinema that engage with contemporary anxieties about the
problematic role of the French education system and its ability
to deliver equality, and by extension integration, in a postcolonial, multicultural France.[2] For if the state school has been "a
very visible, if contested, site of nation-building in France since
the Third Republic (1871–1940)" (Swamy 2007, 64), it is widely
perceived to be failing to achieve its goals. Statistics demonstrating the high levels of school failure and unemployment among
ethnic minority youths, and events such as the nationwide riots

of October–November 2005, in which schools were frequently the targets of violence, have underscored the existence of an underclass of alienated teenagers of immigrant origin who are more likely to have experienced the French education system as a place of exclusion or repression than hospitality and learning (Ott 2006). In his critique of France's ruling republican elite and its "hatred of democracy," philosopher Jacques Rancière goes so far as to say that it is "autour de la question de l'éducation que le sens de quelques mots — république, démocratie, égalité, société — a basculé" [around the question of education that the meaning of certain words — republic, democracy, equality, society — has given way] (Rancière 2005, 37).

The representation of the state school needs to be seen in the light of the ideals of French republican universalism, according to which France's supposedly secular education system is expected to integrate the nation through the universal forms of human knowledge and values exemplified by French language and culture. As Pierre Bourdieu (1979) and others have demonstrated, however, the system serves rather to reproduce the dominant culture, one that requires those who wish to be French citizens to distance themselves from the language and culture of their country of origin. The Eurocentric attitudes of the ruling elite toward the culture of those originating in France's former colonies were exposed in 2005 by the introduction of a law on final financial reparations to be paid to French "repatriated" from Algeria, article 4 of which controversially required secondary school teachers and textbooks to "acknowledge and recognize in particular the positive role of the French presence abroad, especially in North Africa."[3] Though President Chirac subsequently repealed the article due to public and international protest, the teaching of history in French schools is typically informed by a republican narrative that conventionally ignores the ways in which the French empire's "civilizing mission" violated republican principles through its denial of equal rights and its exploitation of colonized lands and peoples.[4] As Valérie Esclangon-Morin (2003) points out, history teachers need to be trained to interrogate dominant histories and construct a more complex, inclusive narrative of nation and national identity if pupils from France's former colonies are to achieve integration.[5]

Problems of integration and equality in the classroom are raised not just by the limitations of the curriculum but also by the ways in which the descendants of postcolonial immigrants — the "new French" — are perceived.[6] In *La république mise à nu par son immigration* (2006), sociologist Nacira Guénif-Souilamas analyzes the pervasiveness of negative racialized and sexist stereotyping in the French imaginary. She argues that *le garçon arabe*, the young Arab male, is perceived to incarnate a violent, delinquent form of masculinity which is attributed to his uncivilized and uncivilizable nature rather than to his need to create a valid masculine identity in a society in which he has no paternal role model and no legitimate place. In contrast, *la fille voilée*, the young veiled Arab female, is presumed to incarnate a submissive, alienated femininity, attributed to her inability to free herself from patriarchal traditions rather than her desire to create a different feminine identity in a society that devalues her existence. Although other more acceptable figures — the (sexy or studious) *Beurette* and the "lay" Muslim — may indicate successful integration as a possibility, or at least conformity to the abstract universalist rhetoric regarding integration (Guénif-Souilamas 2006, 111), they do not take account of the reality of the complex, multiple, often contradictory, identities that characterize contemporary society. Those they designate, including pupils in the secular French classroom, may still find themselves the objects of racist discrimination rather than subjects of their own existence.

For Laurent Cantet, director of *Entre les murs*, the state school is "comme une caisse de résonance, un lieu traversé par les turbulences du monde, un microcosme où se jouent très concrètement les questions d'égalité ou d'inégalité des chances, de travail et de pouvoir, d'intégration culturelle et sociale, d'exclusion" [like an echo chamber, a space traversed by the turbulences of the world, a microcosm where questions of equality or inequality, work and power, and social and cultural integration or exclusion get played out in a very concrete fashion] (Mangeot 2008, 6). If the inequalities he identifies are to be addressed, however, the French education system needs to reconsider how best to achieve its goals. Article 121 of the Education Code stipulates that it should provide not only "une formation à la connaissance et au respect des droits de la personne" [an education that fosters knowledge of and respect for human rights] but also "la compréhension des situations concrètes qui y portent atteinte" [an understanding of the concrete situations that threaten them] (Code de l'éducation 2007). Arguably, a more integrated, egalitarian society can only be achieved through an acceptance of a more plural form of culture that values the contribution to French society made by people of postcolonial immigrant origin, which it has conventionally excluded. This cultural plurality needs to feature within, and be transformative of, the education system if the school is to be meaningful for those it is meant to serve.

An analysis of representations of the school in French cinema, then, raises a number of questions. Do these representations align themselves with dominant discourses on republican education, or do they provide a critique of its "indifference to difference"? Do they construct negative, gendered stereotypes of France's ethnically diverse population, or do they acknowledge the complexities of the identities negotiated by "the new French"? Are staff and pupils of ethnic minority origin allowed to be the subjects rather than the objects of the narrative and the cinematic gaze? A brief survey of films ranging from Mehdi Charef's *Le thé au harem d'Archimède* (1985) through to Coline Serreau's *Chaos* (2001) will provide a context in which to assess the originality of the ways in which *L'esquive*, *L'ecole pour tous*, and *Entre les murs* address these questions.[7]

Critiques of the French School System

Le thé au harem d'Archimède, the first feature film by a director of Maghrebi origin and also one of the first films to address the topic of unemployed youth in the multiethnic *banlieue*, actually derives its title from a key sequence that foregrounds the multiethnic classroom. The sequence is focalized by Pat, one of the film's main protagonists, as he remembers a moment at school when Balou, one of the Maghrebi-French boys in his class, is singled out by an aggressive, alcoholic teacher to put the term *théorème d'Archimède* up on the blackboard. His memory of that moment is motivated by Balou's surprise appearance back in the Paris *banlieue* housing estate at the wheel of a car, wearing a dinner jacket and smoking a cigar, a blond-haired prostitute draped over the back seat and five-hundred-franc notes plastered over the windows. Balou clearly incarnates the negative stereotype of the *garçon arabe*, but the film's editing directly links his behavior with the way he was treated at school. Because of his Maghrebi origins, the boy confuses the word *théorème* with the phrase *thé au harem* (which he can at least write, even if he cannot spell correctly). Slapped by the teacher and further humiliated by being made to parade around the classroom with a dunce's sign on his back, he finally rebels and runs off, disappearing across the field outside.

The sequence is privileged within the diegesis as the only flashback, a discrete film within the film, shot in black and white, and accompanied by the sound of a whirring projector. Though enacted comically, it suggests a causal relationship between failure at school and the adoption of an aggressive, sexist performance of masculinity (one which is criticized by the only girl in the film's *banlieue* gang). Significantly, Balou, the humiliated boy, becomes a wealthy pimp, his academic failure in direct proportion to his success in the criminal underworld. The film, then, demonstrates how the school functions to prepare Balou for his future exclusion.

Over a decade later, Jean-François Richet's cult film, *Ma 6-T va crack-er* (1997), provides an almost equally brief but even more extreme vision of the school's failure to integrate its ethnic others. Its title sequence of images of revolutionary struggle cuts directly to an establishing shot of a school, followed by a violent drug-related fight between groups of youths inside the building. This invasion of the school by the worst aspects of *banlieue* culture precedes a scene in which, ignored by most of the class, an English teacher embarks on a discussion of the significance of July 4, 1776, in American history (the date of the Declaration of Independence), a topic that links to republican discourses on the significance of freedom and equality in the history of France. Three of her pupils, one white, two of Maghrebi origin, are subsequently expelled from school for a week without any investigation to prove their responsibility for the fight (which they did not actively initiate). The action of the white French head teacher thus unwittingly confirms the irrelevance of discourses on the rights of man for the youths in question, particularly those perceived as stereotypical *garçons arabes*. The rest of the narrative, which coincides with the period of their exclusion, then shows the wider consequences of the school's (and society's) failure to achieve integration. The three banned pupils get swept up in a wave of violence unleashed by gangs of older youths on the estate, and one of them is shot dead by the police over a torched car. The film's final, climactic confrontation with the police registers the extent of the gap between those excluded by the system and those who defend it.[8]

A further criticism of the school system is to be found in Philippe Faucon's *Samia* (2001), which also opens with a scene set in a classroom. Feisty young Samia is being interviewed about her career prospects by a teacher who is trying to orient her toward acceptance of a future role as a cleaner (euphemistically described as "un employé de collectivité"). Samia's protest at the way her life is being written off offers a critical view of a system that must bear some responsibility for the future marginalization of its pupils. If *Le thé au harem* and *Ma 6-T* show how the school contributes to the production of young male delinquents, *Samia* demonstrates how it relegates young women of immigrant origin, however resilient, to the bottom of the social ladder.[9]

Ethnic Stereotyping

In contrast to films that incorporate a critique of the school system and its failure to accommodate difference, other *banlieue* films attribute failure at school either to the intrinsically disruptive behavior of young people of ethnic minority origin or to the influence of their dysfunctional families. For example, in *Pierre et Djemila* (1987) by white French director Gérard Blain, the relationship between a studious *Beurette* schoolgirl and a white French youth is opposed by the girl's older brother, a stereotypical *garçon arabe* who ends up stabbing Pierre, the boy, leaving Djemila to commit suicide. The film's Eurocentric scenario makes it clear that the schoolgirl needs to be "saved" by someone representing majority French culture from the violent, primitive values of her culture of origin. Its demonization of the *garçon arabe* is echoed in *La squale* (2000), directed, worryingly, by former French teacher Fabrice Génestal, which suggests that the failure at school of young people of both Maghrebi and sub-Saharan African origin is largely due to their dysfunctional single-parent families (Tarr 2005, 117–22). Its dramatization of the need for the studious *Beurette* to be "saved" from her negatively stereotyped Maghrebi family is replayed in Coline Serreau's *Chaos* (2001), where a schoolgirl is rescued by her westernized elder sister and her sister's white French friend from an unwelcome arranged marriage back in the *bled*, after her family has removed her from school to prevent her taking her exams.

The combination of Eurocentric rescue narrative and demonization of the ethnic other is most clearly played out in the troubling comedy *Le plus beau métier du monde* (1996) by white French director Gérard Lauzier, a box office success (2,266,511 entries in France alone) in which the multiethnic school is a structuring location (as in the films of the mid-2000s). Made a year after Mathieu Kassovitz's *La haine*, *Le plus beau métier* stars Gérard Depardieu, the embodiment of white "Frenchness," as Laurent Monier, a teacher at a lycée in Annecy who moves to the Parisian *banlieue* to be near his estranged wife and children and finds himself teaching *4ème techno* (eighth grade at vocational school in the United States), the class of no-hopers, in the Collège Serge Gainsbourg. Depardieu's role, combined with that of the neurotic head teacher and his chief administrator, reasserts a reassuring, if embattled, white adult perspective on the *banlieue*, which gestures toward cultural difference and racial tolerance (Monier embarks on a romance with Radia, his Maghrebi-French teaching colleague, distances himself from his violent white racist neighbor, and appeals to his pupils by describing Arab numerals as "des chiffres rebeus"), but is actually heavily dependent on negative stereotyping.

The main narrative strand concerns Monier's attempts to be a good, caring teacher despite a series of traumatic events involving local youths of immigrant origin, including some in his class. These events make it increasingly difficult for him to do his job, from the stealing of tires from his car outside the block of flats to the trashing of his flat and classroom, and the attack on bright little Malou, a black version of the studious *Beurette* whom he has allowed to study in his flat to escape her large, noisy, fatherless, immigrant African family. Monier eventually manages to save Malou, bring about the arrest of the most violent *banlieue* youths, and enable several of his pupils, including Malou, to achieve unprecedented academic success. The film's feel-good ending shows him returning to the *banlieue* school the following year rather than taking up a post at a lycée in Paris. Its ideological message, then, is that the dedicated white French teacher can "save" at least some of his underprivileged *banlieue* pupils (particularly loyal little black girls), thus demonstrating the validity of republican universalist ideals.

Nevertheless, the film's message gets undermined in a number of ways. For example, Monier enthusiastically endorses the notion of France as the country of the "rights of man," telling his pupils that "c'était dans notre pays que, pour la première fois, un immense, irrésistible désir de justice, de liberté et de respect des autres, quelle que soit leur couleur, leur race ou leur religion, s'est manifesté" [it was in our country that, for the first time, an immense, irresistible desire for justice, freedom, and respect for others, whatever their color, race, or religion, was made manifest]. However, this lesson on the values of French republicanism is given only to a select group of pupils invited back to his flat, the others being punished for their tacit support for Aziz, the demonized *garçon arabe* of the class. Furthermore, Monier does not address the contradictions between this affirmation and the way people of immigrant origin are treated in France, including in the school itself. Despite the school's apparent commitment to cultural plurality, evident in its celebration of Christmas with North African music, dance, and food, three girls wearing Islamic headscarves are expelled without being given the opportunity to express their points of view, their behavior implicitly attributed to "les barbus," the supposed Islamic fundamentalists waiting at the school gates.[10]

In the course of the film, it becomes evident that Monier does not have the skills to address Aziz and his older brother Ahmed without condescension or recourse to threats and violence. He is uninterested in the causes of their escalating violence, which is thus construed as a manifestation of their innate, unassimilable, violent nature, but justifies his own escalating violence because it is provoked by his attackers. His final destruction of his own classroom, shards of glass filling the screen, graphically illustrates his frustration at the contradictions and limitations of the system. Nevertheless, by giving Monier a hero's welcome on his return from the mental hospital (and consolidating the "rescue" and romance narratives), the film papers over the cracks, refusing to acknowledge links between the unacceptable behavior of the now absent *garçons arabes* and *filles voilées* and the school's own discriminatory practices and inability to engage fundamentally with the need for equality, respect, and change.

L'esquive

L'esquive, written and directed by Abdellatif Kechiche (who is of Tunisian origin and grew up in the *banlieue* of Nice), provides a strong contrast with *Le plus beau métier du monde* in that it sets out to challenge ethnic minority stereotyping and dominant media misconceptions of the *banlieue* as the site of violence and aggression (Mélinard 2004). It focuses not on the teaching staff, but rather on the adolescent pupils of a multiethnic *banlieue* school, a group of whom are preparing an end-of-year performance. The play in question, Marivaux's *Le jeu de l'amour et du hasard*, a classic of eighteenth-century French literature, is based on the delicately negotiated love interest between two aristocrats and their two servants in disguise, and would seem to have little immediate interest for a group of *banlieue* pupils of primarily immigrant origin. Nevertheless, the two extroverted leading female characters, white French Lydia and Maghrebi-French Frida, enthusiastically rehearse their roles as servant and mistress, while shy male Krimo, who is also of Maghrebi origin, "purchases" the role of Arlequin from fellow pupil Rachid as a disguise for wooing Lydia, since he cannot find the way to do so in his own words. The unusual foregrounding of lively, active female characters and of the play (and disguise) of feelings (as in the Marivaux play) transforms the way the *banlieue* is represented (Tarr 2007). The film culminates in the successful performance of the play for an audience of teachers, parents, and pupils, following an equally successful presentation of a fantasy tale set to music by a class of smaller children, bringing the multiethnic *banlieue* community together in an act of shared cultural appreciation in what appears to be a local community center. It thereby suggests that the education system is working well, and that ethnic minority *banlieue* adolescents can achieve integration, particularly through their understanding and mastery of the French classics.

However, the limitations of this education are signaled in a key classroom scene in which the anonymous (white, female) French teacher explains the meaning of the Marivaux text to her charges, who are arguing about the nuances of Frida's performance as the mistress disguised as a servant. She points out that in Marivaux's universe there is no such thing as chance: despite their disguises, servants and masters recognize each other because they are, and will remain, "prisoners of their origins." Kechiche's panning shots of her unnaturally quiet pupils, most of whom are of immigrant origin (Maghrebi, sub-Saharan African, Southeast Asian, Portuguese), invite the spectator to question whether, despite their ability to switch language codes and inhabit other roles, these *banlieue* adolescents are prisoners of both their class and their ethnic origins. The fact that the otherwise sympathetic teacher does not question — and therefore appears to endorse — the notion of a society of irreducible difference is potentially shocking, and runs counter to her own obvious belief in her mission to help her students better themselves through an appreciation of classical French culture (and its presumed universal values).[11] Yet the teacher does not pick up on the contradiction or invite reflections and debate on the Marivaux model from her pupils. Indeed, she makes no attempt to capitalize on the creative energies arising from their cultural differences, evident elsewhere throughout *L'esquive* in their exuberant use of *banlieue* slang. Her acceptance of the one-way, top-down cultural traffic imposed by a curriculum that has little or no interest in bringing into play her pupils' cultures of origin constitutes a clear sign of the limits of the school as the site of integration (though it is up to the spectator to perceive this, rather than it being spelled out within the film).

At the same time, Kechiche's choice of the Marivaux text is peculiarly apt in demonstrating that class and other differences are not to be willed away. In another key scene, which directly precedes the end-of-year performance, Krimo, Lydia, and friends are stopped and searched by the police, who treat even a textbook as a possible hiding-place for drugs. The police violence demonstrates that whatever their educational prowess, these young people continue to be contained by the gaze of those representing the power of the state. Their potential exclusion is even more evident in the fate of Krimo. Goaded by the teacher's demand that he put more energy into his lifeless, uncomprehending performance of Arlequin, a humiliated Krimo walks out of the class (recalling Balou's exit in *Le thé au harem*), but he is subsequently seen gazing wistfully at the final performance from outside the community center windows and does not respond to Lydia when she eventually comes to call. The film shows that the system may allow some to succeed — those who can master the language of Marivaux, for example — but not others; and it is not mere coincidence that, of the central couple, it is Lydia, the blond, white French girl, who succeeds, and Krimo, the sympathetic Maghrebi-French "lay Muslim" whose father is in prison, who does not, and whose future remains in suspense. *L'esquive* thus makes spectators aware of the ambiguities and contradictions of a system that does not produce education or integration for all.

L'ecole pour tous

The theme of education for all is taken up in *L'ecole pour tous*, a comedy of mistaken identity, which draws on the traditions of French farce to explore the place not of the pupils, nor of the white teacher, but of the teacher of immigrant origin in the multiethnic classroom. It centers on the amiable character of Jahwad (Arié Elmaleh), a *garçon arabe* on the run from the police, whose academic qualifications amount to "le bac moins huit" [eight years short of a high school diploma]. By chance, Jahwad finds himself in a position to assume the role of a new French teacher at a *banlieue* school when the "real" highly qualified teacher (who is approaching his new post with some trepidation) is hospitalized after a car accident. Thanks to his charm, various comic misunderstandings, and the desire of his new colleagues to demonstrate their political correctness, Jahwad is accepted without question and, as in *Le plus beau métier*, given the multiethnic *4ème* class of no-hopers. When his pupils discover that he has nothing to teach them, however, they paradoxically become motivated to apply themselves, learning Molière's *Le médecin malgré lui* (*A Doctor in Spite of Himself*) by heart in order to make fun of him. In a comic reversal of roles, they subject him to questioning and penalize his errors, making him strip to his underwear and moon dance outside the head teacher's open door. Jahwad's abdication of an authoritative teacherly presence thus has certain unexpectedly positive results, and when the "real" teacher recovers and Jahwad's true identity is revealed, the beleaguered white French head teacher allows him to stay in post. The happy ending is further underlined by Jahwad's romance with one of his white French colleagues.

L'ecole pour tous, primarily a star vehicle for Elmaleh, has the merit of suggesting both that pupils might respond well to a nonauthoritarian teacher from a background similar to their own, and that the delinquent, unemployed *banlieue* male can still make a success of his life. Despite its humorous reversal of classroom dynamics and its (limited) acknowledgment of pupil power, however, the film does not signal the need for a new approach to the traditional diet of French language and literature in the multiethnic classroom. Rather, Jahwad's buffoonery can itself be likened to a role in a Molière farce. And the film's comic premise that a man with no qualifications, no training, no classroom skills, and no ideas about education can unproblematically become a teacher is singularly unhelpful in thinking through the ways in which the French education system might adjust to the needs of a multiethnic society.

Entre les murs

Le plus beau métier and *L'ecole pour tous* are comedies that offer contrasting models of teaching in the multiethnic classroom, one authoritative, the other submissive. In *Entre les murs*, Laurent Cantet, himself the son of a teacher, opts for a more nuanced approach to the ongoing, fraught relationship between teacher and class. The film draws on an impressive multiethnic, amateur cast of pupils, teachers, and parents (from the Collège Françoise Dolto in Belleville) who participated in extended preparatory workshops. It centers, however, on François Bégaudeau, author of the semiautobiographical novel on which the film is loosely based, as white French teacher François Marin (Bégaudeau 2006). Structured around the school year, starting with a shaky, handheld close-up of Marin at "la rentrée" and ending with shots of an empty classroom in the summer, the action, such as it is, takes place primarily within the *huis clos* of the classroom, punctuated by staff-room scenes or more formal meetings with staff, parents, and/or pupils. Occasional high-angled surveillance-type shots of pupils during recreation in the outside courtyard underline the centrality of the teacher's point of view (unlike *L'esquive*, where the teacher's role is secondary).

The film follows the tensions and contradictions in Marin's day-to-day performances as a French teacher as he attempts to expand his pupils' knowledge of standard French, from vocabulary exercises to the problematic use of the imperfect subjective. Unusually, compared with other French cinematic representations of teachers and teaching, he tries to enter into a relatively informal dialogue with his pupils and provide them with tasks relevant to their situations. Thus, the production of a self-portrait allows them to introduce elements of their own language and culture into the classroom; the opportunity to speak in front of the class on topics of their choice encourages their self-expression, and *Le journal d'Anne Frank*, written by an adolescent victim of prejudice and intolerance, appears to be a more appropriate choice of text for study than Voltaire's *Candide*, the eighteenth-century French classic suggested by the history teacher. To conduct his class, however, Marin exercises discipline in a conventional manner and punishes those who break the rules, impressing on his pupils the need to remove their hoods, raise their hand before speaking, and speak politely and "correctly." Rather than obtaining positive responses to his initiatives at dialogue, then, each micro-teaching situation constitutes a struggle for authority, reflected in the constant shifts of camera position and editing. Thus, a recalcitrant pupil, Souleymane, only grudgingly produces a portrait of his immigrant Malian family; the boys of Moroccan and French Caribbean origin use their speaking opportunities to goad each other about their football allegiances; and Khoumba refuses to read aloud in class, a situation that pushes Marin into taking an unnecessarily authoritarian line with her, exposing both the limits of his approach (the class is not interested in his choice of text) and his apparently friendly attitude (he forces Khoumba to apologize, then gets angry when she makes it clear as she leaves the room that she doesn't mean it).

The film privileges a number of scenes that foreground the cultural, and particularly linguistic, differences that separate Marin from his class and account for the precariousness of his hold over them. For example, Khoumba and Esmeralda protest at his sexist, Eurocentric choice of name ("Bill") to exemplify a particular use of vocabulary, offering "Aïssata" as a more appropriate substitute, and Marin is forced to resort to "intuition" to explain how the class are supposed to know what register of language they should use in any given context. Most importantly, however, Marin's shortcomings are exposed in his inept handling of the fallout from a staff meeting at which he inadvisably describes Souleymane, his most disruptive pupil, as "academically limited." When he realizes that Esmeralda and Louise, the two class representatives, have passed on his comment to Souleymane, Marin accuses them of behaving like "pétasses" [slags].[12] His shockingly ill-judged, sexist remark, which highlights the social and generational gap between him and his class (and suggests that he might have done well to learn the semantic nuances of his pupils' language), immediately causes him to lose face. At the same time, his description of Souleymane provokes the latter into hurling abuse and leaving the classroom in a violent rage, thus conforming to negative stereotypes of ethnic minority youths.[13] Marin's shabby treatment of Souleymane is subsequently underlined by his attendance at Souleymane's disciplinary committee (the unethical nature of which is pointed out, to no avail, by an observer from l'Education nationale) and his support for Souleymane's expulsion, this despite the dignified pleading of Souleymane's mother (who speaks no French and is not even offered the services of a translator) and even though he learns from Khoumba that Souleymane's father will send him back to Mali. The incident foregrounds not only Marin's personal limitations but also the unacceptable level of symbolic violence exercised by the school in disciplining its ethnic minority others.[14]

The film's insights into the unequal power relations between Marin and his class end on an apparently good-natured scene of staff and pupils playing football together in the courtyard at the end of the year. However, the sense of community portrayed is as uneasy and ambiguous as that in *L'esquive*. Marin has distributed bound copies of the class's self-portraits, to their evident pleasure (though it is not clear if Souleymane's is included). And when he asks the class what they have learned that year, Esmeralda, one of the "pétasses," reveals that she has been reading Plato's *Republic*. However, any suggestion that Marin's teaching methods might be comparable to those of Socrates is deliberately undercut by her sarcastic tone, and the fact that she has been reading the book (belonging to her sister, a law student) outside the classroom. Furthermore, the last girl to leave confesses that she has understood nothing of her schoolwork, underlining the overall failure of the classroom as a space for education. Although the film centers on the charismatic teacher (and made a media star out of Bégaudeau), it does not represent the exemplary, inspiring teacher familiar from Hollywood fiction. Rather, Marin's flawed, often ineffective, attempts to negotiate the contradictions involved in imposing the curriculum required by republican ideology, while recognizing the diversity of his lively but resistant pupils, provide yet another illustration of the shortcomings of the French education system.

This review of representations of education and (non)integration in French cinema demonstrates that the issue is being addressed in increasingly complex, multivoiced ways. If *L'esquive* focuses on nonstereotypical performances of pupils in the multiethnic *banlieue*, *Entre les murs* foregrounds the problematic role of the teacher in the multiethnic republican classroom in inner Paris. But Marin is not simply a would-be authority figure as in *Le plus beau métier*, nor a walkover as in *L'ecole pour tous*. Unlike the teachers of *Ma 6-T va crack-er*, *Le plus beau métier*, *L'esquive*, and *L'ecole pour tous*, who uncritically impose a Eurocentric diet of Western historical and literary culture (the American and French revolutions, the plays of Marivaux and Molière), Marin is plagued by self-awareness and self-doubt, never totally in control, and makes mistakes that he regrets. Whatever its limitations, then (the privileging of the teacher's point of view, the lack of an ethnic minority voice in the staff room, and the stereotyping of the most disruptive pupil), *Entre les murs* vividly illustrates the contradictions inherent in the republican model of education and hints that regardless of their ethnic origins, pupils have a right to an education with which they can identify. However, it also underlines the continuing disciplinary power of the education system to produce failure and exclusion.

Notes

1. *L'esquive* won four Césars (the French equivalent of the Oscars) in 2005 for best film, best director, most promising actress, and best screenplay, and attracted over 470,000 spectators. *L'ecole pour tous* attracted over 340,000 spectators, *Entre les murs* over 1.5 million spectators.

2. The latest film in this series, *La journée de la jupe* (Jean-Paul Lilienfeld 2009), stars Isabelle Adjani as a caring but vulnerable, frustrated French teacher who takes her recalcitrant multiethnic pupils hostage when one of them introduces a gun into the *banlieue* classroom. Borrowing from the American school hostage drama, the film builds on the tension between the teacher and her most (stereotypically) violent, misogynist pupils, while police vainly try to resolve the situation. The teacher, who turns out to be of Algerian origin, uses her moment of power to defend the secular state education system, give a class on Molière, expose the misogyny of male *banlieue* youth culture, and exhort her pupils to make the most of their education because of the sacrifices made by their immigrant parents. Her most radical demand before tragedy strikes is that an annual "skirt day" should be introduced to allow girls to wear skirts without being considered sluts.

3. This law was introduced by a group of right-wing Union for a Popular Movement (UMP) deputies.

4. The value of Rachid Bouchareb's film *Indigènes* (2006), which reconstructs the hitherto neglected roles of colonial North African Arab (or Berber) soldiers in the liberation of Italy and France during the Second World War, lies precisely in the way it counteracts

the marginalization or erasure of France's ethnic minority others from dominant French history and highlights the injustices of the colonial régime.

5. See also Falaize (2009), a study inspired by the opening of the Cité nationale de l'histoire de l'immigration in Paris.

6. See also Brouard and Tiberj (2005) for a discussion of the term "New French."

7. Since it is concerned with secondary state schooling in contemporary France, this article does not address Bertrand Tavernier's *Ça commence aujourd'hui* (1999), set in a primary school in the deprived postindustrial north of France, or Nicolas Philibert's nostalgic documentary *Etre et avoir* (2002), set in a village school in rural France. Nor does it address school films set in the past, like Jean Baratier's *Les choristes* (2004), or in nonstate schools, like Jean Odoutan's *Djib* (2000), in which a Beninese grandmother sells her refrigerator in order to send her grandson, Djib, to a Catholic boarding school.

8. The film's violence can be compared with the anarchic explosion of white working-class violence that confronts the school-aged protagonist of Jean-Claude Brisseau's *banlieue* film, *De bruit et de fureur* (1988).

9. *Samia* is a loose adaptation of Soraya Nini's novel *Ils disent que je suis une beurette* (1993), in which the Maghrebi-French protagonist is able to escape from the *banlieue* and her restrictive patriarchal Maghrebi family, thanks to the French education system. The novel thus echoes the positive representation of the school as the path to integration in Azouz Begag's *Le gone du Chaâba* (1986), made into a film by Christophe Ruggia in 1998. In contrast, Farida Belghoul's novel *Georgette!* (1986) expresses the confusion of cultural values in the head of a little primary school girl of Maghrebi descent. According to Samia Chala's documentary *Sauve qui peut!* (2008), Belghoul, a lycée teacher in a Parisian *banlieue*, decided to educate her own children at home. She has since set up an organization to address illiteracy among school-leavers.

10. Debates about the French education system's ability to deliver equality, respect, and by extension, integration, have been occasioned since the late 1980s by the infamous "foulard" affairs. The consequent banning of the Islamic veil in school in 2004 (along with other ostentatious signs of religious and political affiliation) underlined the system's desire to erase "difference."

11. Kechiche correctly assumed that participation in the making of the film might help his young amateur *banlieue* actors acquire "une conscience de leur propre potentiel artistique, et par conséquent, une revendication des moyens d'expressions" [an awareness of their artistic potential, and consequently, their right to the means of expression] (cited in Mélinard 2004). Sarah Forestier, Sabrina Ouazini, and Rachid Hami have all gone on to enjoy careers as actors, and Hami has directed a short film, *Choisir d'aimer* (2007).

12. Although the meeting involves pupil representatives, there seems to be no effort to educate them as to what that kind of responsibilities might be involved. The difficulty of finding an adequately nuanced English translation of *pétasse*, rendered as "skank" in the American subtitles, was demonstrated by the extensive discussion that took place on the Francofil electronic discussion list from November 12, 2008, through March 4, 2009.

13. National Front leader Jean-Marie Le Pen described the film as "showing what these Parisian schools are really like, their [ethnic] composition" (Vincendeau 2009, 36).

14. In contrast, the staff wholeheartedly demonstrate their support for Wei, the stereotypical "good" boy of the class, whose Chinese mother gets deported in the course of the school year and who is himself also at risk of deportation. Unlike Suleymane, Wei is not of postcolonial immigrant origin.

References

Begag, Azouz. 1986. *Le gone du Chaâba*. Paris: Éditions du Seuil.

Bégaudeau, François. 2006. *Entre les murs*. Paris: Éditions Gallimard.

Belghoul, Farida. 1986. *Georgette!* Paris: Barrault.

Bourdieu, Pierre. 1979. *La distinction, critique sociale du jugement*. Paris: Les Éditions de Minuit.

Brouard, Sylvain, and Vincent Tiberj. 2005. *Français comme les autres? Enquête sur les français issus de l'immigration maghrébine, africaine et turque*. Paris: Presses de Sciences Po.

Code de l'éducation. 2007. Article L121-1. http://www.legifrance.gouv.fr/initRechCo deArticle.do (accessed January 28, 2009).

Esclangon-Morin, Valérie. 2003. "Pour une relecture de l'histoire coloniale." http://www.ldh-toulon.net/spip.php?page=imprimer&id_article=811 (accessed March 30, 2009).

Falaize, Benoît, ed. 2009. *Enseigner l'histoire de l'immigration à l'école*. Coll. Éducation, Histoire, Mémoire. Paris: INRP/CNHI.

Guénif-Souilamas, Nacira. 2006. "La française voilée, la beurette, le garçon arabe et le musulman laïc: Les figures assignées du racisme vertueux." In *La république mise à nu par son immigration*, ed. Nacira Guénif-Souilamas, 109–32. Paris: La Fabrique Éditions.

Mangeot, Philippe. 2008. "Entretien avec Laurent Cantet et Francois Bégaudeau." In *Entre les murs: Un film de Laurent Cantet*, 6–24. Pressbook. Paris: Haut et Court.

Mélinard, Michaël. 2004. "'Cette jeunesse n'a pas de place dans le paysage audiovisuel': Abdellatif Kechiche, *L'Esquive*." *L'Humanité*, January 5.

Nini, Soraya. 1993. *Ils disent que je suis une beurette*. Paris: Fixot.

Ott, Laurent. 2006. "Pourquoi ont-ils brûlé les écoles?" In *Quand les banlieues brûlent . . .*, ed. Véronique Le Goaziou and Laurent Mucchielli, 120–38. Paris: Éditions de la Découverte.

Rancière, Jacques. 2005. *La haine de la démocratie*. Paris: La Fabrique Éditions.

Swamy, Vinay. 2007. "Marivaux in the Suburbs: Reframing Language in Kechiche's *L'Esquive* (2003)." *Studies in French Cinema* 7 (1): 57–68.

Tarr, Carrie. 2005. *Reframing Difference: Beur and Banlieue Filmmaking in France*. Manchester: Manchester University Press.

———. 2007. "Reassessing French Popular Culture: *L'Esquive*." In *France at the Flicks: Trends in Contemporary French Popular Cinema*, ed. Darren Waldron and Isabelle Vanderschelden, 130–41. Newcastle: Cambridge Scholars Publishing.

Vincendeau, Ginette. 2009. "The Rules of the Game." *Sight and Sound* 19 (3): 34–36.

Filmography

Baratier, Jean, dir. *Les choristes*, 2004.

Blain, Gérard, dir. *Pierre et Djemila*, 1987.

Bouchareb, Rachid, dir. *Indigènes*, 2006.

Brisseau, Jean-Claude, dir. *De bruit et de fureur*, 1988.

Cantet, Laurent, dir. *Entre les murs*, 2008.

Chala, Samia, dir. *Sauve qui peut!*, 2008.

Charef, Mehdi, dir. *Le thé au harem d'Archimède*, 1985.

Faucon, Philippe, dir. *Samia*, 2001.

Génestal, Fabrice, dir. *La squale*, 2000.

Hami, Rachid, dir. *Choisir d'aimer*, 2007.

Kassovitz, Mathieu, dir. *La haine*, 1995.

Kechiche, Abdellatif, dir. *L'esquive*, 2004.

Lauzier, Gérard, dir. *Le plus beau métier du monde*, 1996.

Lilienfeld, Jean-Paul, dir. *La journée de la jupe*, 2009.

Odoutan, Jean, dir. *Djib*, 2000.

Philibert, Nicolas, dir. *Etre et avoir*, 2002.

Richet, Jean-François, dir. *Ma 6-T va crack-er*, 1997.

Rochant, Eric, dir. *L'ecole pour tous*, 2006.

Ruggia, Christophe, dir. *Le gone du Chaâba*, 1998.

Serreau, Coline, dir. *Chaos*, 2001.

Tavernier, Bertrand, dir. *Ça commence aujourd'hui*, 1999.

8

DON'T TOUCH THE WHITE WOMAN

La journée de la jupe or Feminism at
the Service of Islamophobia

Geneviève Sellier

The success of the Rachid Bouchareb's film *Indigènes* (2006),
both at the Cannes Film Festival and in theaters, as well as the
growing popularity of its producer, the stand-up comic Jamel Debbouze and his program, Jamel Comedy Club on Canal+ (2006), all
seemed to point to a new positive visibility of the French minority
of postcolonial immigrant origins. However, the Franco-German
cultural television network Arte's 2009 broadcast of Jean-Paul Lilienfeld's *La journée de la jupe* starring Isabelle Adjani reactivated
the debates that had shaken the country in 2004 when the law on
religious signs in public schools, better known as the "law against
headscarves" (or "against the veil") came up for a vote. This of
course was before a group of deputies from all political persua-
sions raised the "burka problem" in June 2009, which was then
immediately picked up by the media and then by the president
of the Republic in his June 22 address to the joint session of the
French Parliament at Versailles. The implication therein was that
republican secularism would be threatened by the few women who
cover themselves with the full veil.[1] This regular reactivation of a

threatening figure of otherness tied to Islam allows the creation of a sacred union around the defense of "republican" and "secular" values that subsequently makes it possible to dispense with any concrete struggle against, on the one hand, all forms of discrimination to which French citizens of colonial heritage are subject, and on the other, against the persistent inequalities between men and women in French society.

Arte, High-Brow Culture, and Islamophobia

The film, telecast on Arte on March 20, 2009, tells the story, almost in "real time," of a female French teacher in a suburban middle school (Maxime Gorki Middle School) who takes her students (almost exclusively Muslims and/or of Maghrebi or African origin) hostage with a handgun confiscated from one of them.[2] The school authorities and the police sent to the scene initially believe that it is a student who has taken the class hostage. When they come to realize the truth of the situation, the special unit negotiator relays Sonia Bergerac's demands: the organization of a "skirt day" in all educational institutions to teach boys respect for girls.[3] When the Minister of the Interior arrives on the scene (in a pantsuit), she believes that she is dealing with a crazy woman, while Bergerac's colleagues trot out sardonic double talk concerning her rigidity and her "look" so poorly adapted to the suburbs. Cross-cutting between the action in the class and what is taking place outside (in the middle school and on the street) allows the audience, in the tradition of action and suspense films, to follow the hostage-taking until its tragic conclusion: Sonia Bergerac is shot by RAID agents.[4]

It seems paradoxical that the telefilm was produced by Arte — a cultural channel that privileges auteur cinema — but was directed and written by Jean-Paul Lilienfeld (theretofore unknown in cinephile circles), who had previously distinguished himself (as both screenwriter and director) with a genre of cinema that could be classified as vaudeville or "Broadway" comedy, in which he addressed social questions in a rather heavy comic tone.[5] For this occasion Arte put aside its modus operandi — productions with high cultural value — which serves to alert us to the particular stakes attached to this telefilm. On March 20, 2009, the film drew more than 2 million television viewers, a record audience for Arte. Released in theaters shortly thereafter (an exceptional operation in a country where films and telefilms are separated by an impermeable economic and institutional divide), the film marks Isabelle Adjani's return to cinema; her last notable role was in 2003 with Jean-Paul

Rappeneau's *Bon voyage*.[6] If Arte had already associated its name with a film star, it was under completely different circumstances. For example, Arte's biography on Marie Bonaparte, one of the founders of psychoanalysis, played by Catherine Deneuve, was directed by Benoît Jacquot, a cineaste labeled "auteur."[7]

Jean-Paul Lilienfeld describes having sent the script to Isabelle Adjani, who immediately signed on to the project. I will closely analyze the choice of an actress whose ethno-cultural heritage (she is the daughter of a mixed couple: her father is Algerian and her mother German) had until recently been concealed, and whose star image has been built as the antithesis of that identity. Her blue eyes and white skin, as well as her classical training (the Conservatoire and then the Comédie-Française), as well as the totality of her roles, all give credence to the viewer's belief in her "Frenchness." In the same manner, in the film Adjani's character, Sonia, constantly reaffirms her "pure" French identity until, in the last five minutes, we hear her speaking Arabic to her father.

La journée de la jupe comes on the heels of two memorable films on schools in "difficult" neighborhoods: Abdellatif Kechiche's *L'esquive* (2004), which won four Césars in 2005 (the French Oscars) and attracted 450,000 spectators, and especially *Entre les murs* (2008) by Laurent Cantet, which won the Cannes Film Festival's 2008 Palme d'Or award and drew some 2 million spectators to theaters (Sellier 2009). In the former, a French professor succeeds in getting her junior high students to put on Marivaux's *Le jeu de l'amour et du hasard*; in the latter, a junior high French professor has difficulty getting his class to read *The Diary of Anne Frank*. In both films, the directors' gaze on the students, whether succeeding or failing in school, is an empathetic gaze, and yet it does not vilify the teachers.[8] Both films adopt the tone of social commentary, use no known actors, and employ many nonprofessionals. Contrary to *L'esquive*, *Entre les murs* does not follow the students (nor the teachers) outside their school, but it does give us access (more so than François Bégaudeau's novel from which it is adapted) to the students' point of view (Vincendeau 2009). These two films construct a representation of students from an underprivileged middle school that endeavors to avoid vilification as well as idealization, in as much as the boys and girls present markedly diverse personalities that cannot be reduced to either their ethnic-social background, nor their gender.

La journée de la jupe breaks with this position. The students are presented as an undifferentiated mass, boys on one side, girls on the other, whose French professor tries unsuccessfully to make them recite Molière's *Le bourgeois gentilhomme* (*The Bourgeois Gentleman*). She finishes by contenting herself with making them say the "true name" of the author, Molière, under the threat of a handgun![9]

Many critics have presented Lilienfeld's film as the antithesis of *Entre les murs*. For instance, Danièle Heymann states: "Right away we see that next to these kids those of *Entre les murs* are cherubs straight out of the Countess of Ségur" (2009); David Fontaine speaks of "the brilliant fervor that would make *Entre les murs* practically pass for a fairy tale" (2009); for *Témoignage chrétien*, *La journée de la jupe* is "much more powerful than the consensual *Entre les murs*" (F.Q. 2009). In newspapers like *L'Humanité* (Vergnol 2009), *Le Nouvel Observateur* (Pliskin 2009), and *L'Express* (Festraëts 2009), we also find long political interviews with Isabelle Adjani on her Algerian origins, her support for the law "against headscarves in school," and her character's "passionate and stakhanovite upholding of secularism." She is clearly solicited to give her "immigrant child" stamp of approval to the film.[10]

But despite Arte's emblematic prestige, film critics were lukewarm at best: *Les Inrockuptibles* admits that "the film has hardly convinced our editorial staff" (Delignières 2009). For *Libération*, "the uneasiness sought would have been alternatively heavier and more interesting if the message had not been taken over by a contextualization intended to produce this collective disaster through, in no specific order, demagogic teachers, a cowardly principal, bellicose cops, cynical politicians and parents of a rare intellectual dishonesty" (Icher 2009). On the other hand, *Le Monde* and *Libération* address the film's reception in the "society" pages: in both cases, it is a question of having junior high teachers and their students confirm the validity of the situations that the film presents (see, for instance, "investigations" by Catherine Simon [2009] and Stéphanie Binet [2009]).

Moreover, the film provoked intense activity in the blogosphere, in particular with the defenders of "secularism."[11] For example, one of their most active representatives, Jean-Paul Brighelli, writes the following in his blog: "*La journée de la jupe* is an important antiracist film. . . . The type of film that self-righteous organizations vomit. . . . Politically incorrect, say the journalists! . . . One finds them drooling in front of *Entre les murs*, a sanctimonious film like those made under Vichy" (2009).[12] *Riposte laïque*'s blog-entry title reads, "*La journée de la jupe*: THE movie that pulverizes the Islamically correct" (2009).

More surprising yet, the film also received the enthusiastic support of Philippe Meirieu, the best-known spokesperson of "active pedagogy," while the film seems to align itself rather overtly with the partisans of a traditional education based on classic authors.[13] For Meirieu, beyond "the stereotyped characters who get under the skin of the self-righteous," the film denounces "the violent chauvinistic and archaically virile behavior of a certain number of boys (of different ethnic origins and religious beliefs). . . . It champions the legitimate demands of girls and women for a 'dignified equality' that is far from being achieved" (2009). The film thus succeeds in creating a sacred union between the tenants of traditional education and the partisans of a pedagogy centered on the student, thanks to the designation of a mutual enemy: the Muslim boy.[14]

There are some texts, however, that break with this consensus: from a pedagogical standpoint, middle school teacher Christophe Chartreux denounces this representation of the suburbs as the "site of perdition, of violence, of burnt cars, of gang-bangs, of the massacred French language, of extortion, and of drugs" (2009). Bernard Girard remarks as well that "a film on chauvinism, sexism, stupidity, and intolerance could be made anywhere: in the small, rural middle schools in the backwoods of France, in the high schools in upscale neighborhoods, private or not, and in the *grandes écoles* (elite schools)" (2009). As for Mona Chollet, she places the film in relation to the stigmatizing discourses surrounding French citizens of colonial heritage: "Faithful cinematic adaptation of *Les territoires perdus de la Rébulique* [Brenner 2002], *La journée de la jupe* carefully brings together all of the clichés that the ferocious propaganda of the last few years has firmly seated in the minds in the guise of evidence. The characters don't have any defined depth, or any individuality; they are there to incarnate stereotypes" (Chollet 2009). In fact, there is not the slightest doubt that this film takes a didactic position characterized by the instrumentation of all narrative and formal elements for the purpose of an ideological demonstration.

The "Muslim Boy": Barbarian Personified

From the outset of the film, the theme of violence and insecurity in the suburbs, and its impact in schools, is conveyed through the identification of the spectator with the female teacher, who is presented as though she were a missionary (white) trying to bring civilization (Western) to a threatening horde of barbarians (African). In order to accomplish this, the mise-en-scène, cutting, and editing use extremely old cinematic narrative codes: those that were invented by D. W. Griffith in the 1910s to recount the tales of confrontation between good and bad, white and black, honest citizen and outlaw, victims and aggressors, in order to transmit a Manichean vision of a world where the relations of class, sex, and race are masked (as much as is possible) by WASP morality. In Lilienfeld's film, from the very first sequence, which brings the teacher and her students together, Adjani's small white silhouette in the background must confront the somber mass of larger boys — whose backs are framed in a close-up shot — who constantly threaten to invade her personal space, while she finds herself cornered, pressed flat against a wall. This eminently anxiety-producing mise-en-scène is repeated on several occasions: in the hallway where she tries to get them to calm down; in the theater during a supposed rehearsal of *Le bourgeois gentilhomme* when she attempts to make them sit down; and later, when she confiscates the gun that she discovers in one student's bag. Moreover, the theater — whose stage is raised in relation to the grave-like orchestra pit — does not have any windows, which accentuates the sensation of claustrophobia (we learn later that the theater is soundproof, which is to say completely isolated from the outside world). The feeling of claustrophobia is so intense that even the spectators, like the teacher, have a difficult time breathing and are relieved when she brandishes the gun and forces a large black boy by the name of Mouss (short for Moussa, or Moses in Arabic) to back up. Mouss responds by threatening her with the worst of retaliations (gang rape). Bergerac has to fire the gun in order for Mouss to take her order seriously, thus suggesting that "those people" only respond to violent action and threats.

From the beginning of the sequence everything is done to instill a feeling of oppression in the audience: contrary to what is typically observed in middle school classrooms, the boys hurry forward while the girls lag behind. The theater is situated at the base of a stairwell that forms a cul-de-sac. The camera first captures the stairwell with a low angle shot as it follows Bergerac, who has a difficult time clearing a path amidst the throng of students who are bigger and more massive than she. The image recalls Blandine in the pit of lions! Her outfit accentuates her vulnerability: not only is she in a skirt (beige), but she is wearing a white jacket over a white blouse, whereas all of the students are dressed in dark and shapeless clothes that cover them entirely. Her white complexion, so often highlighted in her previous films, from Andrej

Zulawski's *Possession* (1980) to Patrice Chéreau's *La reine Margot* (1994), successfully completes the portrait of her vulnerability as it stands in contrast to the more or less dark hues of brown-complexioned boys who attack her; strangely, the girls, who will show themselves to be more "civilized," have lighter complexions.[15] This harkens back to a Hollywood film tradition that persists to this day wherein the lighter the skin tone of women "of color" the more they are shown in a positive light, whereas the (bad) black men who lust after them are generally much darker.[16] However, the "whiteness" of Adjani also refers, as Richard Dyer (1997) has analyzed, to the norm, to a nonmarked category in relation to the "brown," the "yellow," or the "black," which signifies otherness. The spectator, and especially the female spectator, can more easily identify with Adjani since she has abandoned the features that made her an "exceptional" being in most of the films that largely contributed to her fame; in fact, her shapeless but short haircut (while in the past, her long black hair served to frame her delicate face and formed a major part of her image) hides, in part, her slightly swollen face (she has visibly gained weight); her curves are in no way accentuated by the combination of her straight-cut jacket, a blouse buttoned to the top, a wraparound skirt, and heeled, knee-high brown boots. There is nothing here that connotes a star, but rather the assignation to an ordinary yet vulnerable femininity: the high heels and the skirt, which restricts movement and forces one to sit knees together. Qualified by Pierre Bourdieu as an "invisible corset," the skirt is a reminder to women of the confinement and subjection of their bodies, which is placed at the disposition of the other sex (Portevin 1998). In the film, Adjani's outfit makes her easy prey for the hulking brutes in pants who confront her.

Adjani distinguishes herself from her distant cinematic ancestor — the frail young woman from *Birth of a Nation* (D. W. Griffith 1915) who prefers to throw herself from atop a cliff rather than be raped by a black soldier who has deserted from the Northern army — in her capacity to respond to the aggressor by turning his weapons against him. In this regard, she is the direct descendant of *Thelma and Louise* (Ridley Scott 1991) and of all women in contemporary action films (American) who brandish a gun in order to hold violent men at bay. The choice of a student aggressor, as well as the sexually explicit nature of the insults and threats directed at Sonia Bergerac ("Ya got an idea of what it'll do to ya to feel two dicks — two big black nigger dicks [*deux belles bites de bamboulas*] — clean ya out at the same time, bitch!"), adds a racial and sexual dimension to the authority crisis that teachers of both genders are experiencing.

The second theme more directly concerns the school, the culture that it transmits, the methods that it employs, and the respective place of students, teachers, the administration, and the regulatory authority. The vision of school that the film proposes is shockingly conservative. Paradoxically, the fact that the class takes place in a theater and not in a classroom becomes a disturbing element in the film instead of being the means to a more attractive and creative pedagogy. In allowing the students to climb onto the stage in diametrical opposition to Bergerac, who finds herself on the floor, it is as though the film is suggesting that the topography of the room undermines the teacher's authority (this is reinforced by the sequences shot-countershot from a high and then low angle). The rehearsal of the scene, moreover, is an absolute fiasco because Bergerac cannot watch the other students who are behind her while she speaks to those on stage. Here, the teaching philosophy seems to be derived from the old principle of "discipline and punish" that, as Michel Foucault (1975) has shown, has spread from prison to school. Sonia Bergerac's problem is that the layout of the theater space does not allow her to exert a panoptic gaze on her students and thus to "keep her class in line"! Thanks to the gun that she finds in one of the bags, she succeeds in reestablishing enough control by making them first lie on the ground and then sit in the places that they had been assigned. We are clearly within a carceral vision of school!

An Archaic Reaffirmation of "Feminine Vulnerability"

In the extensive series of French films about school, the last two exceptionally successful avant-garde and experimental (*art et essai*) films — *Être et avoir* (Nicolas Philibert 2002) and *Entre les murs*, each with more than 2 million spectators — have a male figure play the role of the teacher, in a primary school in the former and in a junior high in the latter, despite the fact that there is an almost complete feminization of primary school faculty and the majority of teachers in middle school are women.[17] The small rural schoolteacher in Philibert's documentary is a traditional patriarchal figure, whereas François Bégaudeau — who plays himself in Laurent Cantet's adaptation of Bégaudeau's autobiographical book — is a modern version of masculine authority who uses humor and mockery to establish a complicity with his students and minimize conflicts and pedagogical problems. On the other hand, Isabelle Adjani, the French teacher in *La journée de la jupe*, is an exemplary incarnation of feminine vulnerabilities: not only through the physical and vestimentary traits that I have discussed above, but by her image as a "fragile, perturbed or mysterious heroine" (Wikipedia 2009), with strong connotations of neurosis and insanity (*Adèle H.*, *Possession*, *Camille Claudel*), nymphomania (*L'eté meurtrier*, *La reine Margot*), and death (*Mortelle randonnée*). This vulnerability is ambiguous. On the one hand, the film seems to acknowledge the suffering that male and female teachers endure in the everyday exercise of a profession that has lost all of its social prestige, including in the eyes of the students. On the other hand, the vulnerability that the actress projects through her image and her role (she seems to suffocate from the first sequence) conjures up the traditional vision of fragile femininity, incapable of coping with the difficulties of the profession as soon as it is no longer easily assimilated to motherhood.

This impression is reinforced by the cut editing with Labouret, RAID's "negotiating" officer, played by Denis Podalydès. As the figure of an actor, Podalydès is the polar opposite of Adjani. Although both Adjani and Podalydès entered the national French theater company Comédie-Française, Podalydès, unlike Adjani, became a member in 2000 and has been successful in juggling careers both in theater and film. Adjani, by contrast, had to step down from the Maison de Molière in 1975, three years after her admission, because her career (in cinema) was judged to be "all consuming" (and surely too showy) by the other members. Brother of director Bruno Podalydès, in whose films he acts regularly, Denis Podalydès is associated with auteur cinema (Desplechin, Ducastel, Bourdieu, Guédiguian, Haneke) and "his fragile, hesitant, and 'spacey' air earns him the right to play characters lost in situations that they do not control" (Bifi 2009). So, we could say that he is cast against expectations in this role of a RAID officer in charge of negotiating with the hostage takers. His image, however, allows him to humanize a role that the audience is used to seeing in American action films (Sonia Bergerac and her students mention the film *The Negotiator* [F. Gary Gray 1998] when they discover that RAID slipped a camera into their room by going under the stage). He plays the role of the "good cop" versus Yann Collette's "bad cop," the officer who wants to give the assault order and who, in the end, is vindicated.[18] In order to truly stress his humanity, the film depicts Labouret, in between two negotiations with Sonia Bergerac, attempting (also by telephone) to wheedle his wife, who, fed up with having been sacrificed to his professional responsibilities, has just left him. In comparison to the unpredictable behavior of Isabelle Adjani's character, who is completely overwhelmed by the shockwave that she has unleashed, Denis Podalydès plays a watchful authority figure in the vein of Harvey Keitel in *Thelma and Louise*. He is the one who calms Bergerac's husband after the latter physically assaults the principal, for, according to Monsieur Bergerac, the former is guilty of having ignored his wife's cries for help. Labouret is the one who agrees to undress in order to meet and discuss with Madame Bergerac and subsequently manages to get her to free one of the students as a gesture of good faith. His plain physique, his slight build, and his expanding baldness, allow him to play the scene in his underwear while avoiding the trap of ridicule and eroticism. Their numerous telephone exchanges, filmed through cut-editing and close-ups, are constructed in opposition, between his calm and the teacher's bafflement, perceptible by her heavy breathing and her incoherent and stammered responses. Even if the officer's negotiation efforts are not crowned with success (like with Harvey Keitel in *Thelma and Louise*), in the film he represents the only element, apart from Sonia Bergerac, with which the spectator can identify. All other representatives of authority (the minister, the RAID officer), of school (the principal, her colleagues), or of civil society (the parents, the journalists, the neighborhood inhabitants) are more or less heavy caricatures that the film turns out one after another. As for the husband, who we understand has just left his wife (Bergerac) because he could no longer put up with her professional suffering, he is simply pitiful.

The asymmetry between Isabelle Adjani and Denis Podalydès also stems from the fact that they are not at the same point in their careers. The star, born in 1955, is on the wane: her last notable role in a film dates back to 2003 (*Bon voyage*) and she received her last award in 1994.[19] Denis Podalydès, born in 1963, has on the contrary become more and more active in the field of elitist culture, as much in the theater as in the cinema (he has been in six films since 2007). Furthermore, he has broken out of the realm of auteur cinema to play in mainstream films (*Embrassez qui vous voudrez*, *Laissez-passer*, *Palais royal!*, *La vie d'artiste*, *Coluche*) and even in international blockbusters like *The Da Vinci Code*. As Raphaëlle Moine (2007) has shown, French actresses are seen principally to incarnate sexuality, whereas the image of male actors is much richer and more socially and culturally complex. Adjani represents an "eternal femininity" comprised of seduction and vulnerability and whose attractiveness is extremely limited by age. Podalydès, on the other hand, incarnates the modern form of the French cultural elite, lacking in pedantry and arrogance, and whose seduction only increases with age. Their asymmetry exposes the manner in which French culture continues to construct the inequality between the sexes and masculine domination. The film perpetuates the idea that women's "natural" fragility is poorly adapted to the violence of the modern world, while men's "natural" authority can cloak itself in tenderness in order to adapt to the complexities of a democratic society.

Moreover, the film instrumentalizes Isabelle Adjani, herself the daughter of an Algerian immigrant, in order to create an icon of the so-called good integration (in the film, her name is Bergerac — like Cyrano — and she refuses to teach anything other than Molière); two-thirds of the way through the film she is suddenly isolated in the frame, in a frontal medium shot without reverse shot, for a monologue addressed as much to the students as to the film's audience: "Your parents, they left home in order to offer you a better life . . . it's your duty to succeed . . . you must give a sense to their sacrifice, you understand . . . you have the deck stacked against you, but it's no reason to say 'I'm a victim! It's not my fault!' You can't put the responsibility on others like that in your life! . . . I beg you [she joins her hands], don't think like that! It's not because one is a victim that one can't be an assailant."

This monologue reactivates the meritocratic discourse of the republican education model based on an ostensible notion of equal opportunity, which ignores the importance of social structures, the dysfunction of school, and the symbolic violence that it exerts. It places the responsibility for the "problems" that their integration poses on the immigrants themselves.

Retrospectively, this discourse is all the more poignant when Sonia Bergerac, to the stupefaction of her students (and the spectators), begins to speak Arabic to her father on the phone: she had succeeded in completely hiding her Maghrebi origins! As if it were a shameful secret, a stain that would have kept her from being a credible French teacher! But the film, instead of deconstructing the interiorization of the stigmatization, makes us adhere to the pathetic effort of Sonia Bergerac to be "whiter than the whites" to the very end. At this moment in the film the audience discovers that Sonia's Algerian family ostracized her for having married a European "Frenchman." The film also tells us that her *pétage de plombs* (cracking up) is not explained by the discrimination that immigrants and their children suffer, but rather stems from the suffering provoked by her family situation and by the intolerance of Muslim parents who do not permit their daughters to "truly" integrate by marrying "true French" (that is to say, non-Muslim) boys.[20] Behind Sonia

Bergerac, the French norm of integration begins to take shape. A requisite step is the total abandonment of one's cultural heritage, even going so far as effacing the family name. To this end, only girls, by a marriage that allows them to abandon their father's name for that of their husband, can integrate "completely." Boys do not have any possibility of total integration since they cannot "get rid of" their family name. In other words, the traditional patriarchal system as it continues to function in French society, in particular through the adoption of the groom's name (although no longer an obligation, it continues to be practiced by the majority of women who marry), is presented as the model to adopt for "Muslim" girls who desire emancipation. Just as the skirt, an ostensible sign of the difference between the sexes in Western society (that is to say, relegating women to a kind of dominated femininity), is posited by the film as the ultimate proof of emancipation, the adoption of the husband's name is suggested, through Sonia Bergerac's character, as the "good" solution for girls of immigrant origin who want to become undetectable French women.[21] One understands better why this "feminism" so pleases the defenders of "secularism" who denounce, moreover, all struggles against sexual discrimination as a battle of the sexes, and against racial discrimination as communitarianism.

This telefilm effectively reactivates the fears of the "cultured" middle class (Arte's audience) for whom the social ladder has ceased to function, and who fear being swallowed up by the (lower) social strata of immigrant origins. At the same time it diverts the question of inequalities between men and women — an area in which France lags behind relative to her European neighbors as much on a political level as on the level of salaries and the distribution of tasks — toward the questions of cultural difference.[22] By focusing on cultural difference, the telefilm is then able to stigmatize Muslim communities as the primary element responsible for the discrimination against women.[23] Finally, by waving the red flag of secularism, the common standard for both the French Right and Left, the film creates a consensus concerning the ills suffered by the education system. This move completely ignores the social discrimination that transformed suburban middle schools into ghettos for the poor while inner-city high schools retained their status of ghettos for the rich. As we see, we are dealing with a three-pronged operation whose cultural mediocrity goes largely undetected, since it so effectively panders to the social fears reactivated by the latest economic crisis.

Translated from the French by Joel Strom.

Notes

I would like to thank Sophie Broza, Delphine Chedaleux, Astrid Condis, Mehdi Der-foufi, Gwenaëlle Le Gras, and Charlotte Sanson for their remarks that enriched this article.

1. According to Isabelle Mandraud in *Le Monde* on July 29, 2009, two reports submitted to the government by the French police concluded that wearing the burka is a phenom-enon practiced by an ultra-minority. The report from the DCRI (Direction Centrale du Renseignement Intérieur [Central Directorate of Interior Intelligence]) estimates that some 367 women wear the burka in France. The figure is drawn from observations made across the whole of France by teams of intelligence agents. "The majority of the women identified wear the full veil voluntarily; the majority of them are less than 30 years old; 26% of them are French women who have converted to the Muslim religion."

2. The name of the middle school suggests that it is situated in a "red" suburb — a municipality that is or was run by the Communist Party. Thus, for the French public, all of the social dysfunction that the film shows is associated with the real or supposed failure of the Communist Party's municipal policies which, for the longest time, it prized as its greatest success.

3. As Mona Chollet (2009) remarks, the choice of the characters' proper names system-atically reinforces the opposition between "European French" and French of immigrant origin. Here, the reference to Cyrano de Bergerac, an emblematic work of educational culture in middle schools, functions even more efficiently since the revival of the play by Rappeneau's 1989 cinematic adaptation with Gérard Depardieu.

4. RAID is an elite unit of the national police, used in hostage crises and terrorism (unlike the GIGN, the intervention group of the National Gendarmerie). The terrorism to which the RAID responds since the 1995 attacks in Paris is systematically associated with Islamic extremism, an association only reinforced by the attacks on September 11, 2001.

5. As director: *HS* (2000), *Quatre garçons pleins d'avenir* (1997), *XY* (1995), *Il n'y a guère que les actions qui montent ces temps-ci* (1990); as screenwriter: *Génial, mes parents divorcent* (Patrick Braoudé 1991), *La contre-allée* (Isabel Sebastian 1991), *Et moi et moi* (Guy Mouyal 1989), *Sale destin* (Sylvain Madigan 1987); *L'œil au beurre noir* (Serge Meynard 1986), *L'été en pente douce* (Gérard Krawczyk 1987).

6. Despite the fact that all television stations are required to contribute a percentage of their sales to a fund that supports cinema, public and private financing for cinema and television do not come from the same institutions. Moreover, films slated for a theatrical release adhere to a "media chronology" that ensures staggered release dates for theaters, on DVD, and their broadcast on pay-per-view and free channels.

7. *Princess Marie*, a telefilm broadcast in two episodes in 2003.

8. Clearly these two works do not hold the same cultural status; the first is a mono-lith in the pantheon of French theater associated with libertine and social contestatory movements of the seventeenth-century Enlightenment; the second is the autobiographi-cal account of a Jewish German adolescent who was the victim of Nazi genocide and whose value is above all ethical. The choice of *The Diary of Anne Frank* is typical of an education more oriented toward pedagogy than the transmission of cultural heritage.

9. Part of the most traditional corpus of works taught in middle school, *Le bourgeois gentilhomme* is most often read as a farce against the new social climbers. The "orientalist" dimension of the play as anything more than a comic drive is rarely considered. Generally, Molière, like the majority of canonical authors, is never subjected to critical analysis when he is taught in middle school.

10. According to Wikipedia (2009), Isabelle Adjani was born on June 27, 1955, in the seventeenth arrondissement of Paris to an Algerian father (Mohamed Chérif) and a German mother (Augusta, called Gusti, who died in 2007). She grew up with her younger brother (Eric, who later became a photographer) in Gennevilliers, a northwestern suburb of Paris, and she went to middle school in Courbevoie.

11. Among the identifiable blogs that have devoted a consequential article to the film, we find "pedagogical" blogs (Philippe Meirieu; blog éducation *LeMonde.fr*; les Cahiers pédagogiques; Zéro de conduite); "secular" and "antipedagogical" blogs (Bonnet d'âne; Riposte laïque; Jean-Paul Brighelli; le Volontaire; Athéisme); "political" blogs (Rue89; Bakchich; le Monde diplomatique; Marianne; Indigènes de la République); "citizen" blogs (Agoravox), but none on blogs by "cinephiles."

12. A high school French professor, Brighelli published *La fabrique du crétin* in 2005, followed by *À bonne école* (2006a), *Une école sous influence ou Tartuffe-Roi* (2006b), and most recently *Fin de récré* (2008). He campaigns for a return to school's traditional function, the transmission of knowledge, against the options of "pedagogists" represented by Philippe Meirieu.

13. Meirieu, a specialist in the educational sciences, pedagogy, and creator of numerous pedagogical reforms, is a professor of educational sciences at the Université Lumière-Lyon 2.

14. The amalgam between the boys of Maghrebi origin and those of sub-Saharan Francophone Africa is made in the film across their supposed communal religious identity: Islam. This is something that is questionable in reality but corresponds perfectly to the Islamophobic fantasies that have recently predominated in France. For more, see Guénif-Souilamas and Macé (2004).

15. The poster for Chéreau's film showed Adjani in a beautiful white robe caked with blood.

16. For an example, see Régis Dubois (2000).

17. One must also cite Christophe Barratier's *Les choristes* (2004), with more than 8 million spectators. However, this film, which recounts the story of a music teacher in a boys' boarding school in the 1950s, draws from another sociocultural genre, the heritage film. The film addresses the general public as opposed to *La journée de la jupe*, *Être et avoir*, or *Entre les murs*. For a sociological analysis of *Les choristes*, see Jean-Pierre Garnier (2004, 69–91).

18. We know that the actor Yann Collette lost an eye; his hawk-like profile, his shaved head, and his glass eye have earned him some scary roles — *La journée de la jupe* doesn't break this pattern!

19. Adjani received a César for best actress in 1994 for *La reine Margot* and in 1989 for *Camille Claudel*, for which she also won the same award at the Berlin International Film

Festival; a César for best actress in 1984 for *L'eté meurtrier* and in 1982 for *Possession*; and best actress at the Cannes Film Festival in 1981 for *Quartet* and *Possession*.

20. *Pétage de plombs* is a colloquial expression used in many films to signify the moment when someone who, exhausted and exasperated by a dead-end situation, adopts criminal or suicidal behavior.

21. As the historian Christine Bard (2009) reminds us, "The Parisian police ordinance forbidding women to dress like men in the 1800s was never repealed."

22. According to the latest survey of working couples by the National Institute of Statistics and Economic Studies (INSEE), women in France dedicate twice as much time as men to domestic chores and childrearing and the gap increases with the number of children; on average, women's salaries are 27 percent less than those of men. In spite of the law on parity passed in 2000, women in 2009 comprise only 18.5 percent of the National Assembly (Vanovermeir 2009).

23. Fadela Amara, of the association "Ni putes ni soumises," who is the state minister (*secrétaire d'etat*) in charge of urban renewal at the time of this writing, has been crowned the new face of state feminism by the Right, which only cares to denounce the violence of young Arab men and the wearing of the Islamic headscarf by girls who are inevitably oppressed.

References

Bard, Christine. 2009. "La jupe en révolution: Éléments pour une histoire immédiate de la *Journée de la jupe*." *La vie des idées.fr*, April 13. http://www.laviedesidees.fr/La-jupe-en-revolution.html (accessed June 15, 2009).

Bifi. 2009. "Denis Podalydès." Ciné-ressources, Bifi database. http://cinema.encyclopedie.personnalites.bifi.fr/index.php?pk=88718 (accessed November 11, 2009).

Binet, Stéphanie. 2009. "Porter une jupe, parfois ça donne une réputation, les garçons matent." *Libération*, April 19, 17.

Brenner, Emmanuel. 2002. *Les territoires perdus de la république: Antisémitisme, racisme et sexisme en milieu scolaire*. Paris: Mille et une nuits.

Brighelli, Jean-Paul. 2005. *La fabrique du crétin: La mort programmée de l'école*. Paris: Jean-Claude Gawsewitch.

——. 2006a. *À bonne école . . .* Paris: Jean-Claude Gawsewitch.

——. 2006b. *Une école sous influence ou Tartuffe-Roi*. Paris: Jean-Claude Gawsewitch.

——. 2008. *Fin de récré: Pour une refondation de l'école*. Paris: Jean-Claude Gawsewitch.

——. 2009. "La journée de la jupe." *Bonnet d'âne: Le blog de Jean-Paul Brighelli*. http://bonnetdane.midiblogs.com/archive/2009/03/25/la-journee-de-la-jupe.html (accessed April 21, 2009).

Chartreux, Christophe. 2009. "*La journée de la jupe . . .* En finir avec la démagogie sécuritaire." *Le site de Philippe Meirieu*, March 29. http://www.meirieu.com/ACTUALITE/journee_de_la%20Jupe.htm (accessed June 8, 2009).

Chollet, Mona. 2009. "Ils ne comprennent que la force: Sur *La journée de la jupe*." *Le Monde Diplomatique*, April 12. http://blog.mondediplo.net/2009-04-12-Ils-ne-comprennent-que-la-force (accessed April 28, 2009).

Delignières, Clémentine. 2009. "*La journée de la jupe*: Record d'audience." *Les Inrocks. com*, March 24. http://www.lesinrocks.com/cine/cinema-article/article/la-journee-de -la-jupe-record-daudience/ (accessed April 20, 2009).

Dubois, Régis. 2000. *Images du noir dans le cinéma américain blanc, 1980–1995*. Paris: L'Harmattan.

Dyer, Richard. 1997. *White: Essays on Race and Culture*. London: Routledge.

Festraëts, Marion. 2009. "Je ne suis pas ma première fan: Interview avec Isabelle Adjani." *L'Express*, February 5. http:www.bifi.fr (accessed May 5, 2009).

Fontaine, David. 2009. "*La journée de la jupe*: Les cours ou la vie." *Le Canard enchaîné*, March 25. http://www.bifi.fr (accessed April 21, 2009).

Foucault, Michel. 1975. *Surveiller et punir, naissance de la prison*. Paris: Gallimard.

F.Q. 2009. "Collège: Point de rupture." *Témoignage chrétien*, March 19. http://www.bifi .fr (accessed April 21, 2009).

Garnier, Jean-Pierre. 2004. "Le passé radieux: *Les Choristes*, un analyseur des nostalgies populaires. *L'Homme et la société* 4 (154): 69–91.

Girard, Bernard. 2009. "*La journée de la jupe*, la triple imposture." *Rue89*, April 2. http:// www.rue89.com/2009/04/02/la-journee-de-la-jupe-la-triple-imposture (accessed April 19, 2009).

Guénif-Souilamas, Nacira, and Eric Macé. 2004. *Les féministes et le garçon arabe*. La Tour d'Aigues: Éditions de l'Aube.

Heymann, Danièle. 2009. "*La journée de la jupe*, bien troussée." *Marianne*, March 21. http://www.bifi.fr (accessed April 19, 2009).

Icher, Bruno. 2009. "Molière en joue." *Libération*, March 25. http://www.liberation.fr/ cinema/0101557806-moliere-en-joue (accessed April 19, 2009).

Mandraud, Isabelle. 2009. "La police estime marginal le port de la burqa." *Le Monde*, July 29. http://www.lemonde.fr (accessed August 5, 2009).

Meirieu, Philippe. 2009. "*La journée de la jupe*: Meirieu répond à Brighelli." March 31. http://www.marianne2.fr/La-journee-de-la-jupe-Meirieu-repond-a-Brighelli_a177719 .html (accessed May 5, 2009).

Pliskin, Fabrice. 2009. "Le coup de boule d'Adjani." *Le Nouvel Observateur*, March 19. http://www.bifi.fr (accessed May 5, 2009).

Portevin, Catherine. 1998. "Le corset invisible: Entretien avec Bourdieu." *Télérama*, August 5. http://www.homme-moderne.org/societe/socio/bourdieu/Btele983.html (accessed September 15, 2009).

Moine, Raphaëlle. 2007. *Remakes: Les films français à Hollywood*. Paris: CNRS Éditions.

Riposte laïque. 2009. "*La journée de la jupe*: Le film qui pulvérise l'islamiquement correct." *Riposte laïque: Le journal des esprits libres, pour l'égalité hommes-femmes, pour le République sociale*, March 23. http://www.ripostelaique.com/La-journee-de -la-jupe-LE-film-qui.html (accessed April 21, 2009).

Sellier, Geneviève. 2009. "L'ecole, point aveugle de l'universalisme républicain: *Etre et avoir* et *L'esquive*, deux films rassurants." *Tausend Augen* 32 (April): 54–58.

Simon, Catherine. 2009. "Le printemps de la jupe." *Le Monde*, Horizons, April 8, 15.

Vanovermeir, Solveig. 2009. "Regards sur la parité: De l'emploi à la représentativité politique . . ." *INSEE Première* 1226 (March): 1–4.

Vergnol, Maud. 2009. *"La journée de la jupe*: Interview avec Isabelle Adjani." *L'Humanité dimanche*, March 26. http//www.bifi.fr (accessed April 21, 2009).

Vincendeau, Ginette. 2009. "The Rules of the Game." *Sight and Sound* 19 (3) (March): 34–36.

Wikipedia. 2009. "Isabelle Adjani." Wikipedia. http://fr.wikipedia.org/wiki/Isabelle_Adjani (accessed November 4, 2009).

Filmography

Barratier, Christophe, dir. *Les choristes*, 2004.

Becker, Jean, dir. *L'eté meurtrier*, 1983.

Blanc, Michel, dir. *Embrassez qui vous voudrez*, 2001.

Bouchareb, Rachid, dir. *Indigènes*, 2006.

Braoudé, Patrick, dir. *Génial, mes parents divorcent*, 1991.

Cantet, Laurent, dir. *Entre les murs*, 2008.

Caunes, Antoine de, dir. *Coluche, l'histoire d'un mec*, 1998.

Chéreau, Patrice, dir. *La reine Margot*, 1994.

Fitoussi, Marc, dir. *La vie d'artiste*, 2006.

Gray, F. Gary, dir. *The Negotiator*, 1998.

Griffith, D. W., dir. *Birth of a Nation*, 1915.

Howard, Ron, dir. *The Da Vinci Code*, 2005.

Jacquot, Benoît, dir. *Princess Marie*, 2003 (telecast in two parts on Arte).

Kechiche, Abdelletif, dir. *L'esquive*, 2004.

Krawczyk, Gérard, dir. *L'été en pente douce*, 1987.

Lemercier, Valérie, dir. *Palais royal!*, 2004.

Lilienfeld, Jean-Paul, dir. *Il n'y a guère que les actions qui montent ces temps-ci*, 1990.

——, dir. *XY,* 1995.

——, dir. *Quatre garçons pleins d'avenir,* 1997.

——, dir. *HS,* 2000.

——, dir. *La journée de la jupe,* 2008.

Madigan, Sylvain, dir. *Sale destin*, 1987.

Miller, Claude, dir. *Mortelle randonnée*, 1983.

Mouyal, Guy, dir. *Et moi et moi*, 1989.

Nuytten, Bruno, dir. *Camille Claudel*, 1988.

Philibert, Nicolas, dir. *Être et avoir*, 2001.

Rappeneau, Jean-Paul, dir. *Bon voyage*, 2003.

Scott, Ridley, dir. *Thelma and Louise*, 1991.

Sebastian, Isabel, dir. *La contre-allée*, 1991.

Tavernier, Bertrand, dir. *Laissez-passer*, 2000.

Truffaut, François. *L'histoire d'Adèle H.*, 1975.

Zulawski, Andrej, dir. *Possession*, 1980.

9

A SPACE OF THEIR OWN?

Women in Maghrebi-French Filmmaking

Patricia Geesey

In the introduction to a 2004 special double issue of *Contemporary French and Francophone Studies* devoted to *la banlieue*, the editors note that in contemporary media usage in France, the term *banlieue* has come to designate "urban spaces associated with social disadvantage, criminality, and, above all, dense concentrations of working-class immigrant minorities" (Célestin, DalMolin, and Hargreaves 2004, 3). Notwithstanding French media's negative portrayal of the *banlieue*, it is clear that for contemporary music, literature, and film, this so-called marginal space of French culture is also a vital source of rich and varied cultural productions. Films set in France's *banlieues* have often been analyzed by film critics for their construction and use of cinematic space (Jousse 1995; Vincendeau 2000; Tarr 2005). The construction and representation of space in *banlieue* cinema may be linked to literal and figurative relationships that characters in the film have with the urban space they inhabit. Moreover, cinematic space is also defined by the individual and collective mobility of characters within the film. Since *banlieue* film is so closely associated with its portrayal of outlying urban spaces, I propose to examine how filmmakers approach and formulate issues of gender, identity, and belonging, through the depiction of marginalized social and peri-urban spaces, as they are "practiced" and (re) defined by the female characters of their stories. Films by Maghrebi-French directors such as Malik Chibane, Zaïda Ghorab-Volta, Yamina Benguigui, and Abdellatif Kechiche explore the link between cinematic space that represents the figurative and literal margins of French mainstream society, as well as the physical and symbolic relationship female characters have to the spaces they inhabit.[1] The Maghrebi-French filmmakers under consideration here use and often deconstruct the visual (re)presentations of space to establish new forms of self-identification with place.

Ethnographer Marc Augé's observations on Parisian place (*lieux*) and non-place (*non-lieux*) characterize the suburban landscape as *non-lieux* since it has traditionally been associated with what he terms "supermodernity," that is, "spaces of circulation, communication and consumption" (1996, 178): large shopping centers, airports, peripheral highways, and so on. Augé remarks that these areas, which may be viewed as *non-lieux* for Parisians of the center, have become "places" since residents of the housing estates, especially the younger generation, identify with their *lieux* through a sense of belonging. Given Augé's analysis, it is evident that for Maghrebi-French filmmakers new forms of self-identification with "place" are possible because there has been a shift in perspective in French society, making the *non-lieux* of the *banlieues* into spaces of cultural production.

The setting for such films is often the *cités*, social (subsidized) housing estates that are home to a large cross-section of middle- and lower-income French and immigrant populations. For these films, the urban landscape provides a background for an examination of ethnicity, identity, belonging, and exclusion, and for films produced in the 1990s, male protagonists were often central characters. Carrie Tarr and Ginette Vincendeau have pointed out that women have often been secondary characters in films set in the *banlieue*.[2] In this essay, I focus more closely on films that do offer significant roles for female protagonists and examine the construction and uses of cinematic space as a metaphor for agency and mobility by female protagonists in Maghrebi-French films, by both male and female directors. Cinematic space can be constructed and presented in such a way as to highlight strategies of spatial appropriation by female protagonists. These strategies, in turn, illustrate ways in which a character can assert her belonging to the culturally dominant French society and her claims to agency within this social space. Making a place for herself, then, does not mean sacrificing the specificities of her identity in order to "feel at home" in the world. In other words, the way in which a female character inhabits the "space" of the film on her own terms is often a metaphor for making herself a "place" within French society. Not only have Maghrebi-French directors explored more culturally based notions of space and gender as they relate to North African cultural paradigms in which women may be traditionally restricted to domestic, nonexterior space (Mernissi 1987), but they have also explored the urban spaces in France associated with Maghrebi immigrant housing through a prism of gendered space.

In her study *Reframing Difference:* Beur *and* Banlieue *Filmmaking in France*, Carrie Tarr notes that as *banlieue* filmmaking has evolved away from an emphasis on gangs and police violence, female characters have found greater visibility. Yet, for Tarr, their presence evokes a different range of issues than those associated with men: "As well as negotiating a place for themselves within a fundamentally male-dominated French cinema industry, films which centre on realistic representations of young French women of Maghrebi descent need to situate themselves in relation to Republican discourses on assimilation as the route to integration, and to orientalist discourses, islamophobia and anti-Arab racism" (2005, 87). Although some films portray Maghrebi immigrant families and focus on issues that affect women in particular, often this portrayal borders on the sensationalistic, such as domestic violence, forced marriages, the veil, and limited access to space outside the home.[3]

Whereas young French men of Maghrebi heritage have long been a frequent focus of analysis in research on immigration in French society, young women of North African ancestry have also, more recently, become "visible" as subjects of sociological and cultural discourse. Yet the alleged attributes of women differ from those associated with young men, especially concerning their greater potential for integration into French society. One of the most important aspects to note concerning the mainstream media portrayal of Maghrebi-French women is that it is often more positive. As Nacira Guénif-Souilamas observes: "Les femmes dans l'immigration subissent à priori moins le marquage ethnique que les hommes. Elles apparaissent moins que ces derniers 'de nature' à troubler l'ordre public. Elles sont perçues comme actrices d'un processus d'intégration tranquille" [Women of immigrant origin are supposedly less subject to ethnic labeling than men. By nature, they appear less likely than the latter to disturb the public order. They are perceived as agents of a peaceful integration process] (2000, 87). Young Maghrebi-French women may even, as Guénif-Souilamas suggests, "redeem" the negative image of their brothers thanks to French society's tendency to view them as agents of cultural integration. However, the alleged goodwill on the part of French society does not apply to young women who wish to wear the *hijab*, or headscarf, while attending French public schools. In that instance, a woman is more likely to be viewed by mainstream French media as either a victim of patriarchal and religious forces, or she may be considered a militant seeking the overthrow of a humanistic and secular social order. The French law of 2004 banning "ostentatious" religious symbols such as the headscarf has been viewed as a paternalistic attempt of the state to protect young women from a retrograde religious and cultural practice (Weill 2006; Bowen 2007).

Even if women in *Beur* and *banlieue* cinema in the 1990s played secondary roles to those of male protagonists, some portrayals from this era are nonetheless striking, as for instance in the work of Merzak Allouache. Although not Maghrebi-French himself, Allouache has lived alternately in France and Algeria for the past several decades, and several of his recent films examine life in France for Algerian émigrés and their children. In his 1996 film *Salut cousin!*, Malika (Dalia Renault) — who plays the role of the sister of the protagonist, Mok (Mess Hatou) — supplies the film with an amusing opportunity to overturn a negative stereotype about difficulties facing young women in the gritty *banlieue*. Much of the comedy in the film derives from Alilo's (Gad Elmaleh) — Mok's cousin from the *bled* (Algeria) — misunderstanding of life in France and the his naïve acceptance of everything his pathological liar cousin, Mok, has told him about his family's situation. Visiting Paris for the first time, Alilo has already listened to Mok's disparaging remarks about his own family, that his older brother is in prison, his father is unemployed, his mother takes antidepressants all day long, and his sister Malika has become a prostitute. None of Mok's ravings are accurate; in fact Malika drives a taxicab in and around Paris. The ensuing conversation between Alilo and his aunt and uncle about the sheer "physicality" of her work, and the difficulty Malika has dealing with her demanding "clients," causes a great deal of embarrassment and confusion for the country cousin. His obvious relief when he finally understands what her job really entails belies not just his culturally determined concern about women's sexual purity but his own naïveté in sexual matters, which is another theme of Allouache's film. Malika's brief appearance in *Salut cousin!* and the joke about her line of work underscore the director's intent to challenge viewers' perceptions about expectations concerning young Maghrebi-French women's role in French society. In contrast to Mok, who expresses only hatred toward the neighborhood in which he grew up, Malika's freedom to come and go as she pleases in her family home, and her mobility within and outside of her neighborhood thanks to her cab-driving career, illustrate that she is at ease with her life in the present moment. Malika thus represents a success story of the generation born to Maghrebri immigrants. That her appearance in *Salut cousin!* is but a brief cameo role, however, reveals a lacuna in the portrayal of Maghrebi-French women in cinema of this period.

Zaïda Ghorab-Volta: Challenging Invisibility

Such near (in)visibility of Maghrebi-French women in the cinema of this era is explicitly challenged in Zaïda Ghorab-Volta's 1996 film *Souviens-toi de moi*. An independent and self-produced work, Ghorab-Volta wrote and directed the film, and plays the role of the lead protagonist, Mimouna.[4] Ghorab-Volta was born in Clichy, to Algerian immigrant parents and grew up in the *banlieue* of Colombes, the setting for both *Souviens-toi de moi* and *Jeunesse dorée* (2002). Her first film depicts a brief period in the life of a young woman from the *banlieue* whose life is in a state of flux due to interpersonal issues involving her family, her non-Maghrebi boyfriend, Jacques, and her female friends. The setting of the film alternates between the domestic sphere of the apartment home with Mimouna's family and the outdoor space of both the *banlieue* and the center of Paris proper where Mimouna strolls with friends. The last twenty minutes of the film take place in Algeria during Mimouna's vacation. In these final scenes shot in Algeria, the settings are interior ones, associated with feminine space, where Mimouna enjoys the company of her female Algerian cousins (in fact, Ghorab-Volta dedicates the film to them: "à mes cousines du bled"). The outdoor tracking shots in the *banlieue* that follow Mimouna as she walks in Paris underscore her desire to be mobile and to navigate the urban spaces of her environment. This desire for mobility is especially evident when Mimouna manages to borrow her brother's car and she and her two friends go out to a club for the night. Seated behind the steering wheel, Mimouna murmurs: "Je peux faire ce que je veux maintenant" [I can do as I please now]. As Dominique Bluher stresses: "L'indépendance de Mimouna s'exprime en particulier dans sa mobilité" [Mimouna's inde-pendence is expressed in particular through her mobility] (2002, 93). In fact, Bluher emphasizes the rhythm of Mimouna's movements as the camera fol-lows her walking, and sometimes rushing, through her urban environment. Her mobility is fueled by a liberating energy that also signifies Mimouna's appropriation of "tout l'espace urbain: le centre de Paris et sa banlieue" [the entire urban space: the center of Paris and its suburb] (93). Mimouna's mobility, as she walks outside in the city and in the suburbs, contrasts visu-ally and thematically with the enclosed space that is coded as "feminine" within the film. However, the section of *Souviens-toi de moi* that takes place in Algeria serves to "enhance Mimouna" (Tarr 2005, 94) and enables her to understand better both her parents and her own dual heritage.

As a filmmaker, Ghorab-Volta has resisted being locked into the role as a spokesperson for Maghrebi-French women from the urban periphery. In an interview with Martin O'Shaughnessy, she indicates that whether as an actress or film director, she has had to fight against the efforts of the French mainstream cinema establishment to "box" her in and to call upon her to play or to film the "little beurette from the outer-city projects" (2007, 52). It is not surprising then that Ghorab-Volta's subsequent project did not focus exclusively on a female Maghrebi-French protagonist. Her 2002 film *Jeunesse dorée* portrays two young, working-class French women, Gwen (Alexandre Jeudon) and Angéla (Alexandre Faflandre), who leave their own *cité* outside of Paris, in Colombes, to work on a project photographing residents and hous-ing projects along their route through rural France. Their photojournalism project allows the two young women to physically leave the space of their own *cité* and set out on a journey of discovery in which their self-reflexive use of the camera will enable them to reflect upon theirs and others' relationships to the urban and rural spaces they occupy. A kind of "road movie," *Jeunesse dorée* subverts the usual paradigm of that genre; first of all, the travelers are young women, they leave their homes (which are depicted as constraining due to family disaccord) in a housing estate, to travel through rural France to photograph housing estates that appear to have popped up out of an idyllic, yet isolated, country landscape. The young women encounter many different people on their journey and all are receptive to posing for the photo essay. Gwen and Angéla are interested in the ways in which residents of various types of dwellings identify with their living space. *Jeunesse dorée* is so mark-edly different in its portrayal of *banlieue* spaces from other films made in the late 1990s, not only because the protagonists are female but because the location of the housing estates shifts from what is perceived by society to be the gray and gritty urban periphery, to a sunny "France profonde." In addition, as Carrie Tarr notes, the people photographed alongside their homes display a range of emotions and moods; the residents are "humanized" by the camera's gaze (which in turn allows Gwen and Angéla to be "the subject of the gaze") and the entire film then reinforces the idea that these locations are indeed "social spaces" (2005, 183). In this way, residents of the housing projects filmed along the itinerary are not "objectified" by a journalistic, media-savvy approach. Hence, while eschewing the pressure to focus exclusively on women protagonists who duplicate her own background, Ghorab-Volta is keenly interested in the complex relationship between gender and place, and socioeconomic levels in French society.

Integration through Mobility in *Inch'Allah dimanche*

The relationship between domestic space and mobility in the outside world is also a theme in another award-winning film by a woman director. In her first fictional feature film, *Inch'Allah dimanche*, released in 2001, Yamina Benguigui creates a portrait of a female protagonist, Zouina (Fejria Deliba), an Algerian immigrant to France. For this young woman, mobility and spatial appropriation become necessary skills for negotiating her new life in France — both within the domestic sphere whose confines she will increasingly challenge as well as the exterior space of a French town that she will slowly claim the right to freely access as an individual.[5]

Inch'Allah dimanche begins in an Algerian port as Zouina boards a ferry to France with her three children and domineering mother-in-law. We see Zouina as she is literally torn from the embrace of her own mother, who stands behind a gated enclosure, a cinematic moment that literally enacts the loss of her mother's support as well as that of an extended network of female relations who surround the wailing mother. Once in France, in the northern industrial town of Saint-Quentin, Zouina is shown in transit, riding in the borrowed truck that takes her and her children to the small, dingy apartment her husband has rented. In this early scene she is framed by the window behind her head, the glaring light, the bumpy ride, and the noise from the truck engine appear to unsettle her. But this scene will be contrasted with that of the film's conclusion in which Zouina and her children have a "private" bus ride offered by a friendly driver back to their home. In that later sequence, Zouina is shown smiling and enjoying the view of the passing city streets as she stands next to the driver in the front of the bus. Before the conclusion of *Inch'Allah dimanche*, as Carrie Tarr points out, Zouina has been able to "negotiate a place for herself within her marriage which also opens up the possibility of integration" (2005, 178).

Zouina's appropriation of a space for herself with her new life in France is not just a matter of physical space; Zouina must negotiate a symbolic place of acceptance and integration, beginning in her rented home. The day after their arrival, her husband tells their children they must not make too much noise at home because "on n'est pas chez nous" [we are not at "home" here]. Zouina's unpleasant and racist neighbors also challenge her right to occupy the space she and her husband have rented in Saint-Quentin when Madame Donze tells Zouina she cannot light her *kanoun* (an earthenware grill) out in the garden to make coffee for her mother-in-law. "Ce n'est pas la Casbah ici" [This isn't the casbah here], Madame Donze yells across the small fence that separates their garden plots. By the film's conclusion, Zouina is able to assert her right to leave the house and to refuse her mother-in-law's demands, to shop for food, and to take the children to school herself. These activities symbolize Zouina's agency and mobility outside the domestic sphere, which she has claimed for herself by the end of the film. In appropriating the right to speak up and to make decisions within her domestic space, Zouina establishes her access to the outside space of the French city she now calls home. For instance, one Sunday morning during her husband's and mother-in-law's absence, and despite her young son's caution ("Mais tu n'as pas le droit de sortir" [But you aren't allowed to go out]), Zouina finally gathers enough courage to take her children out in search of the other Algerian family that she has learned also resides in town. At the end of the film, Zouina announces to her husband that "demain c'est moi qui emmène les enfants à l'école" [tomorrow it is I who will take the children to school], thereby claiming her right to access Saint-Quentin's public space, a right that both her husband and her French neighbor Madame Donze have attempted to curtail.[6] Yamina Benguigui's film concludes, then, with an optimistic, integrationist message. Even the supposedly racist neighbor Madame Donze is not portrayed as irredeemably evil since the film shows her enjoying the same call-in radio programs as Zouina, suggesting the two women might have more in common than they realize if they had a chance to live next to each other as real neighbors.

Cultural and Spatial Negotiations in *Douce France*

Whereas *Inch'Allah dimanche* examines life for a newly arrived woman from Algeria in France of the 1970s, the films of Malik Chibane portray the lives of young men and women born and raised in France. His second feature film, the delightful *Douce France*, released in 1995 (the same year as *La haine*), is set in the Parisian *banlieue* of Seine-Saint-Denis. According to Carrie Tarr, this film "foregrounds the domestic spaces of the Maghrebi family and refuses to focus on the *banlieue* as the site of violence and clashes with the police" (2005, 81). Like Ghorab-Volta's *Jeunesse dorée*, Chibane's film avoids portraying the *cités* as a space of urban poverty, exclusion, and conflicts. As Will Higbee points out, *Douce France* "depicts the *banlieue* as a lived social space defined by its inhabitants rather than the architecture itself" (2007, 40). Several scenes in Chibane's film emphasize the village-like community that is the setting for the film, especially the scenes around the mosque where people have gathered to share a meal. The mosque here is a site of communal gathering, not a politicized venue in which ideological forces play out. Higbee notes that this "ultimately non-threatening portrayal of Islam within the French *banlieue* is the source of gentle humor in *Douce France*" (2007, 41). For example, when Farida (Fadila Belkebla) brings supplies for a free meal for the worshippers, her father, who works a *merguez* pushcart out in front of the mosque, complains that she is ruining his business.

Douce France portrays two sisters, Souad (Selouma Hamse) and Farida, who are romantically linked to two friends, Jean-Luc (Frédéric Diefenthal) and Moussa (Hakim Sarahoui); the strategies of cultural and spatial negotiation employed by the two young women are at the heart of the film's narrative. The viewer first encounters Souad and Farida in the bedroom they previously shared, arguing about borrowed clothes. Farida has recently adopted modest Islamic dress and has exiled her elder sister to the sofa in the living room. Souad has short hair, wears jeans, miniskirts, and makeup, and works in a Quick Burger restaurant. She used to date Jean-Luc but they broke up since he was reluctant to speak to her father in order to make their relationship "official."

What is most refreshing about Chibane's film is the manner in which the two young women succeed in making a place for themselves in French society on their own terms, in spite of several obstacles. Souad, already twenty-three years old, is determined to acquire her own living space, not just because she is feuding with her younger, pious sister but also because she is in conflict with her father, who does not approve of her working late at night. After one such argument, Souad leaves the family home and takes shelter in a friend's beauty shop for the night. The next scene shows Souad accepting a ride from Jean-Luc, who has been seeking to reestablish their relationship. Souad visits an empty apartment in the hope of being able to rent it. The rental agent insists that her pay stubs indicate that she does not earn enough to obtain the apartment. In true "système D" fashion, Jean-Luc enters to play the role of her partner, showing his own pay stubs as proof of sufficient financial means; even so, Souad, on a quest for her own personal space, is not altogether receptive to Jean-Luc's pleas to reestablish their relationship.[7] She tells him, "Si j'ai quitté mon père, ce n'est pas pour vivre avec un autre homme" [If I've left my dad's place, it isn't to go and live with another man].

It proves more difficult for Farida to find a space of her own. She has completed a two-year degree and is looking for work. In addition, Farida volunteers in the kitchen of the local mosque (whose "space" is also a temporary one, used until the real one — minus the minaret so as to blend into the *quartier* — is constructed). In the variety of locations used for scenes that show Farida out and about in *Douce France*, it is clear that the director wishes to illustrate how her character occupies space — both secular and "sacred" — on her own terms. She rides her bike to the mosque to work, she phones about a job prospect from an outdoor pay phone, she meets with a school official to apply in person for a job, and her traditional Islamic dress is not a hindrance. However, at the post office window, trying to cash a check, Farida is asked, "Vous ne pouvez pas enlever votre tchador?" [Can't you take off your chador?], so the clerk can "verify" her resemblance to her photo identification. Farida attempts to negotiate but agrees to remove the *hijab* only in front of a female postal employee. In a scene that shows Farida interviewing for employment at the local social center to provide "soutien scolaire" [help with schoolwork], she is told by the administrator that the center is "un lieu d'intégration et de laïcité" [a place of integration and secularism]. Farida, wearing a *hijab*, according to the school official, symbolizes "le militantisme pour la religion" [religious militancy], revealing the (now infamous) French belief about the incompatibility of headscarves and public schools. Farida stands her ground with the official and responds that while rejecting a qualified young woman in a *hijab* (who precisely is an agent of integration given her successful academic studies and desire to find gainful employment), the school would most likely not complain about a candidate in revealing clothes who could be accused of what Farida calls "le militantisme pour l'industrie du sexe" [activism on behalf of the sex industry].

Farida will finally find employment, teaching French in a place that does not object to her *hijab*, in a school for Jewish children. The contrast of headwear, showing Farida in front of the class of yarmulke-wearing boys, is a visually ironic metaphor for religious understanding—two religious minorities in French society finding perfect symmetry in their working together. The film repeatedly shows Farida in Islamic dress in a range of public and also private spaces to portray how she must at times defend her right to wear it; even her own sister would seem to not fully support her choice to wear it. Farida asserts her right to occupy the space of her own choosing in her traditional garb, even if she too must resort to the "système D." For example, she is briefly shown swimming contentedly in a municipal pool, all alone, wearing her *hijab-maillot*. Farida knows the custodian of the municipal pool and therefore can access it in the off hours. Thus, this scene without dialogue functions to position Farida as an agent of integration who operates on her own terms, maintaining her preference for modest dress in spite of French society's expectations for assimilation of mainstream dress codes. It is thus through Farida's character that Chibane's film addresses notions of tolerance and freedom of expression in French society for young Maghrebi-French women.

The scene in which Farida most clearly expresses her sense of belonging and appropriation of a space for herself in French society is one evening when she describes a dream she just had to Moussa. Farida dreams that she is a large earthenware *poterie maghrébine* (Maghrebi earthenware jar), balancing on a wall. A strong wind knocks her down, shattering her into pieces; it rains and the pieces of hardened clay dissolve into the earth. When the sun returns, Farida dreams she is reconstituted again as a *poterie*, but with a difference. She is, as an elderly haji in her dream explains, "mélangée de la terre de ce pays [la France]" [mixed with the earth of this country]. "Tu ne seras plus jamais une poterie maghrébine" [You will never again be a Maghrebi jar]. Farida's dream symbolizes the appropriation of her own space: she has become a part of France, the land of her birth, and it has become part of who she is. The dream is also an image of a mutual mixing and symbolic blending of earth: Farida leaves some of herself in the French earth as well. In this way, Chibane suggests the notion of "integration" is preferred to that of "assimilation." Assimilation has largely been thought of as one-sided, that is, immigrants and their children assume "French" identity in order to belong. But the image of melted and reconstituted pottery, of two types of earth that melt together as in Farida's dream, shows that the more fertile and harmonious mixture is to be achieved through integration.

At the conclusion of *Douce France*, Farida and Souad accompany Myssad (Nadia Kaci), Moussa's would-be bride, to the airport so she can return to Algeria. Moussa's mother, ostensibly facing a life-threatening illness, had arranged for Myssad to come to France to marry him, but both Moussa and Myssad decide they are not what either one is seeking in a spouse. In the airport restroom, Farida observes several fashionably dressed women, apparently from a conservative Islamic country, changing into long dark robes and headscarves for their return home. As she watches them, the medium close-up on her face would suggest that Farida comes to a realization about her own choices. The filmmaker's goal is to contrast the freedom Farida enjoys in France to adopt modest dress or discard it at will, with what the viewer assumes must be a law requiring returning travelers in the women's own country to cover themselves. On the ride back, Farida removes her headscarf and lets it blow away into the distance; she has tears on her face, indicating her mixed feelings about this decision. In the space of that brief airport encounter, Chibane seems to suggest that Farida has come to an understanding about women's lack of choice in conservative Islamic countries that impose the *hijab* on women. Farida, being a citizen of France, can freely choose the veil as well as choose to remove it. But this scene does not necessarily signify that she has given up on her Muslim identity in the face of pressure from French secular society. Instead, the viewer sees that Farida has reached this decision of her own volition. The final frames of *Douce France* shows Farida and Souad exchange a smile of reconciliation as they speed down the highway, signaling that they have taken their destiny into their own hands.

Appropriating Space through Performance in *L'esquive*

Abdellatif Kechiche's invigorating and award-winning film *L'esquive* (2004) presents a completely different view of young Maghrebi-French adolescents of the *cité* who create a kind of "virtual" space for themselves through a school production of Marivaux's *Le jeu de l'amour et du hasard*. Shot mainly outdoors in the *cité* of Francs-Moisins (Seine-Saint-Denis), the film portrays in several scenes, a group of girls who occupy the space of the steps, usually coded masculine, in front of their buildings, discussing their friendships, schoolwork, and families. Frida (Sabrina Ouazani), a quick-tempered high school student, plays the role of Silvia, the bourgeois daughter, in Marivaux's play. When Lydia (Sarah Forestier) shows up for an outdoor rehearsal with Krimo (Osman Elkharaz), a fellow classmate who is not yet officially in the play, Frida appears anxious about rehearsing her lines in front of him and picks a fight with Lydia over his presence there. The space shown has a low rise of steps surrounding an open space that appears to be a kind of outdoor theater. Ari J. Blatt observes that Kechiche's film has carefully used this space within the *cité* to provide a visual commentary on the relationship between Marivaux's eighteenth-century text and the urban space occupied by the protagonists of *L'esquive*. As Blatt notes, by using the space within the group of HLM (state-subsidized housing) buildings that no doubt was conceived of as a space for public performance, the young characters of the film challenge a stereotypical audience expectation of the kind of "quotidian theatrics" that occur in the *cité* (2008, 518). In other words, it is not inconceivable that "classical" theater could be performed outdoors in the *banlieue*. Later in the film, when Frida is totally alone on this concrete, outdoor stage in the *cité*, she is shown gracefully rehearsing her dialogue, creating a personal space of intense concentration to prepare for her role. The very fact of playing a role on stage gives Frida the opportunity to try on a different identity and reality. Parallel to Marivaux's notion that his characters learn a great deal about what is deep down inside themselves when "disguised" to play the role of another, Kechiche's characters learn to be vulnerable, to open up their feelings about friendship and their desires for the future as they prepare for roles as eighteenth-century characters. In Marivaux's play, ultimately the message is that social origins will win out — the nobles fall in love even disguised as servants, the same for the servants disguised as nobles. Kechiche's film subtly undermines the play's assumptions about the inescapability of social origins, as it also overturns preconceived ideas in mainstream French media that adolescents from *la banlieue* cannot escape their social conditions either.[8]

By foregrounding strong young women (such as Frida) as protagonists, *L'esquive* overturns the preconceived notion that young Maghrebi-French women are victims of oppression. Speaking to journalist Florence Aubenas of *Libération* about the film, Sabrina Ouazani explains the doubts she initially had about the project when she answered the casting call: "je m'attendais au blabla habituel: les tournantes, les grands frères acharnés sur les filles de la famille, la délinquance. Parfois les jeunes sont montrés comme coupables.

Parfois comme victimes. Finalement, ça ne fait pas une si grande différence" [I was expecting the usual blah-blah: gang rapes, older brothers policing their sisters, delinquency. Sometimes young people are shown to be the guilty ones. Sometimes they're the victims. In the end, it doesn't make much difference] (Aubenas 2005, 4). This young actress from La Courneuve admits that she hesitated about accepting a role in the film for fear of the kind of portrait it would give of *la cité*. Frida, along with her *potes* Nanou, Magalie, and Lydia, are repeatedly shown outside of interior (domestic) spaces. Aside from Krimo's apartment, the classroom, and the school performance space, the scenes of the film are mostly all shot outdoors. In addition to learning their lines for the play, Frida, Lydia, and the other young women engage in verbal jousts, well-peppered with *verlan*, concerning "qui kiffe qui" [who has a crush on whom] and which couples have or have not broken up. David Lepoutre's study of social codes and language in the *banlieue* addresses this aspect of young women's behavior. He notes that boys engage in verbal jousts, show-ing off their talent for rapid putdowns and insults, but for girls, the insults and the replies to them revolve around their reputation and the pressure to conform to ideals of female sexual purity (Lepoutre 1997, 280–83). This is apparently the case in the scene in which several girls press Lydia to decide whether or not she wishes to date Krimo. Magalie, who still believes she and Krimo are dating, tries to warn Lydia away from her boyfriend. The social codes and verbal banter of Marivaux's universe find their modern reflection in Kechiche's portrait of this group of friends as they display their talent for *tchache* and *la vanne* (chatting and putdowns).

The filmmaker's desire is to enable his characters to break out of a clichéd cinematic representation that has plagued other films set in the *banlieue*. In an interview, Kechiche explains that in Marivaux's time, it was revolutionary for valets and peasants to express their feelings and ambitions: "Leur fonction sociale ne suffisait plus à les définir: ils accèdent au rang d'hommes ou de femmes à la fois complexe et universel. Il y a davantage d'audace dans cette représentation des 'petites gens' que dans celles des minorités aujourd'hui" [Their social function was no longer sufficient to define them: they attained the level of men and women both complex and universal. There is more audac-ity in that representation of modest classes than in that of minorities today] (Aubenas 2005, 4). Linking Marivaux's innovative portrait of non-nobles in the eighteenth century to what Kechiche, as the director of *L'esquive*, tries to do for adolescents in the *banlieue* helps the viewer understand that his intent in this film is to establish a kind of "ownership" (i.e., appropriation) of a "classical" French play by young people from what is normally viewed as a site of cultural exclusion, that is, *la cité*. The young protagonists of *L'esquive* make the classical text their own, much in the same way as they assert ownership of their school life and social life that unfolds in their *cité*, with its attendant joys and dramas.

Maghrebi-French women have played different roles and occupied "spaces" of both inclusion and exclusion in films directed by Maghrebi-French filmmakers throughout the previous decades. The dilemma for Maghrebi-French directors has previously been how to depict female characters without recourse to tired clichés of representing them as victims of family violence and religious-cultural oppression. Recent developments in French politics illustrate that Maghrebi-French women occupy significant positions of political, economic, artistic, and cultural weight. In French cinema, Maghrebi-French women protagonists who truly occupy a cinematic space of their own and become agents of their own narrative destiny will certainly be more visible in the future, as a reflection of what is already a reality in French society. In short, films such as *Souviens-toi de moi*, *Inch'Allah dimanche*, *Douce France*, and *L'esquive* illustrate that Maghrebi-French women have finally begun to occupy a space of their own both in front of and behind the camera.

Notes

1. In this essay, the term "Maghrebi-French" will be used to designate these directors to underscore their dual heritage — their parents were from North Africa but they were born in France or, in the case of Kechiche, arrived there as a child. The hyphenated term attempts to address the notion of a double heritage, following a recent trend in cinema studies (see, for example, the special issue of *Cineaste* 33 [1] [Winter 2007]), without assigning a hierarchical value to either label.

2. See Vincendeau (2000) for an analysis of Mathieu Kassovitz's successful film *La haine* and the way in which it focuses almost exclusively on "a male world." As she notes, the few women present in the film reveal a traditionally gendered approach to the portrayal of space: sisters and mothers are at home, not outside. Women who are in a public space (i.e., the art gallery opening) are merely targets of the three boys' inept sexual advances (see especially pages 314–16).

3. Two films that fall into this category include *Des poupées et des anges* (Hamidi 2008) and the made-for-television film *Leïla née en France* (Courtois 1993), based upon the book by Aïcha Benaïssa and Sophie Ponchelet (1990).

4. According to the Web site http://lumière.obs.coe.int, *Souviens-toi de moi* had only 6,623 entries at the box office. While the film is by no means a "mainstream" success given the small audience, it is a significant filmic text that has garnered subsequent critical attention.

5. Benguigui is well known for her award-winning documentary *Mémoires d'immigrés: L'héritage maghrébin* (1998). In that film, Benguigui devotes an entire segment of the three-part series to women who immigrated to France to join their husbands. Maghrebi women immigrants have played significant roles in earlier films, where their specific concerns as "first-generation" women immigrants to France center on nostalgia for the homeland and bitterness that their children raised in France are becoming strangers to them. In *Souviens-toi de moi*, Mimouna's mother sadly recounts to her relatives in Algeria that she is "coupée en deux" [cut into two pieces]; she wants to return home to Algeria but could not leave her French-born children over in France. In Mehdi Charef's 1985 film *Le thé au harem d'Archimède*, Majid's mother Malika speaks little French; she is depicted as a strong woman who struggles to support her family and to inspire her eldest son to look for work and make something of himself. Her character is that of a woman worried about her family's future in France and nostalgic for the country she has left behind.

6. Angelica Fenner notes that to a certain extent, Zounia's (re)appropriation of agency and space comes at the expense of her unpleasant mother-in-law, who is ordered by her son to remain silent from now on and to let Zounia have her say (2007, 116). The ending of Benguigui's film thus allows the audience to feel that Zounia's suffering at the hands of her mother-in-law is partially avenged as her husband finally asserts himself and demonstrates loyalty to his wife in rebuking his own mother.

7. In French, "système D" refers to getting around bureaucratic rules and procedures through the use of connections or sometimes a more sneaky approach. "D" stands for the verb *débrouiller*, meaning to untangle or sort out a problem. In both the films *Hexagone* and *Douce France*, Malik Chibane shows young Maghrebi-French people who employ the "système D" to circumvent the ordinary obstacles they encounter in achieving their goals.

8. The motif of adolescents from *la cité* performing classical French theater appears to have gained some currency of late. In Faïza Guène's best-selling 2004 novel *Kiffe kiffe demain*, the narrator relates the tale of a young woman from the same *cité* who ran away from her family to pursue her desire to act on stage and has finally entered the Comédie-Française. Guène has also used this story line as the subject of her *moyen-métrage* titled *Rien que des mots* (2004). When Maghrebi-French female protagonists in film and literature perform as characters from France's classical theatrical repertoire, it relays a message of a successful appropriation of some of France's most esteemed cultural artifacts, symbolizing an integration that transcends boundaries of urban and cultural space.

References

Aubenas, Florence. 2005. "La banlieue par la bande." *L'Avant-Scène Cinéma* 542 (3) (May): 4–5.

Augé, Marc. 1996. "Paris and the Ethnography of the Contemporary World." In *Parisian Fields*, ed. Michael Sheringham, 175–79. London: Reaktion Books.

Benaïssa, Aïcha, and Sophie Ponchelet. 1990. *Née en France: Histoire d'une jeune beur.* Paris: Éditions Pocket.

Blatt, Ari J. 2008. "The Play's the Thing: Marivaux and the *Banlieue* in Abdellatif Kechiche's *L'Esquive*." *French Review* 81 (3) (February): 516–27.

Bluher, Dominique. 2002. "Les 'Meufs rebeus' ou la représentation des femmes maghrébines dans le cinéma français hip-hop." *L'Esprit Créateur* 42 (1) (Spring): 84–95.

Bowen, John Richard. 2007. *Why the French Don't Like Headscarves: Islam, the State,
and Public Space*. Princeton NJ: Princeton University Press.

Célestin, Roger, Eliane DalMolin, and Alec G. Hargreaves. 2004. Introduction to *Contemporary French and Francophone Studies* 8 (1–2): 3–7.

Fenner, Angelica. 2007. "Aural Topographies of Migration in Yamina Benguigui's *Inch'allah
dimanche*." *Camera Obscura* 66 (3): 93–127.

Guène, Faïza. 2004. *Kiffe kiffe demain*. Paris: Hachette Littératures.

Guénif-Souilamas, Nacira. 2000. *Des "beurettes" aux descendantes d'immigrants nord-
africains*. Paris: Grasset.

Higbee, Will. 2007. "Re-Presenting the Urban Periphery: Maghrebi-French Filmmaking
and the Banlieue Film." *Cineaste* 33 (1) (Winter): 38–43.

Jousse, Thierry. 1995. "Prose combat." *Cahiers du Cinéma* 492:32–35.

Lepoutre, David. 1997. *Coeur de banlieue: Codes, rites et langages*. Paris: Éditions Odile
Jacob.

Mernissi, Fatima. 1987. *Beyond the Veil: Male Female Dynamics in Modern Muslim Society*.
Rev. ed. Bloomington: Indiana University Press.

O'Shaughnessy, Martin. 2007. "The Experience of a Maghrebi-French Filmmaker: The
Case of Zaïda Ghorab-Volta." *Cineaste* 33 (1) (Winter): 52–53.

Tarr, Carrie. 2005. *Reframing Difference: Beur and Banlieue Filmmaking in France*.
Manchester: Manchester University Press.

Vincendeau, Ginette. 2000. "Designs on the Banlieue: Mathieu Kassovitz's *La Haine*
(1995)." In *French Film: Texts and Contexts*, ed. Susan Hayward and Ginette Vincendeau, 310–27. 2nd ed. London: Routledge.

Weill, Nicolas. 2006. "What's in a Scarf? The Debate on Laïcité in France." *French
Politics, Culture and Society* 24 (1): 59–73.

Filmography

Allouache, Merzak, dir. *Salut cousin!*, 1996.

Benguigui, Yamina, dir. *Mémoires d'immigrés: L'héritage maghrébin*, 1998.

———, dir. *Inch'Allah dimanche*, 2001.

Charef, Mehdi, dir. *Le thé au harem d'Archimède*, 1985.

Chibane, Malik, dir. *Hexagone*, 1994.

———, dir. *Douce France*, 1995.

Courtois, Miguel, dir. *Leïla née en France*, 1993.

Ghorab-Volta, Zaïda, dir. *Souviens-toi de moi*, 1996.

———, dir. *Jeunesse dorée*, 2002.

Guène, Faïza, dir. *Rien que des mots*, 2004.

Hamidi, Nora, dir. *Des poupées et des anges*, 2008.

Kassovitz, Mathieu, dir. *La haine*, 1995.

Kechiche, Abdellatif, dir. *L'esquive*, 2004.

10

SEXUAL/SOCIAL (RE)ORIENTATIONS

Cross-Dressing, Queerness, and the Maghrebi/
Beur Male in Liria Bégéja's *Change-moi
ma vie* and Amal Bedjaoui's *Un fils*

DARREN WALDRON

In her pioneering monograph *Reframing Difference:* Beur *and*
Banlieue *Filmmaking in France*, Carrie Tarr includes three chapters that specifically address portrayals of gender (2005, 86–123).
However, while she discusses some mediations of transvestism
and cross-dressing, particularly in her studies of *Origine contrôlée*
(*Made in France*) (Ahmed Bouchaala 2001) and *Chouchou* (Merzak Allouache 2003), this area of representation receives limited
attention. This is no fault of Tarr herself since, before the huge
commercial success of *Chouchou*, the Maghrebi transvestite or *Beur*
cross-dresser had generally been a much maligned and marginalized figure in filmic depictions.[1] Yet, despite the fact Liria Bégéja's
Change-moi ma vie (*Change My Life*) (2001) and Amal Bedjaoui's
Un fils (*A Son*) (2003) significantly address this absence, they
receive only a brief mention in Tarr's work — in either a subordi-
nated clause or endnote (2005, 172, 207). This chapter seeks to
attend to this absence by furnishing a more detailed comparison of
the representations of cross-dressing among Maghrebi immigrants
and *Beur* men in both films. It reveals that, by contrast to *Chouchou*,

which constructs its hero, Choukrane (Gad Elmaleh), as virtuous and eager to assimilate the dominant values of his adopted country (his name means "thank you" in Arabic), the Maghrebi/*Beur* cross-dressers in *Change-moi ma vie* and *Un fils* are constructed in less idealistic terms as sex workers, and in some cases, alcoholics and drug users. The interplay between gender, sexuality, and ethnicity is central to the analysis of these characters, which include Sami (Roschdy Zem), Fidel (Sami Bouajilah), and Leïla (Arié Elmaleh) in *Change-moi ma vie*, and Selim (Mohamed Icham) in *Un fils*. Informed by theories of "category crisis" (Garber 1992) and the performativity of gender (Butler 1990), this discussion examines the extent to which these figures imbricate both masculine and feminine codes of gendered behavior and the inflections of ethnicity on their performed identities.

In an article published two years after Tarr's book, Denis M. Provencher characterizes both films as portraying "'queer' sexual citizens who continue to survive outside the dominant French social space but who are still able to create meaningful friendships and often times even new forms of kinships and queer affiliations" (2007, 48). For Provencher, the directors "have deliberately placed the experiences of queer Maghrebi characters at the center of their own stories" (49). Yet this label of the "queer citizen" is a more adequate descriptor of Selim in *Un fils* than Sami in *Change-moi ma vie*. This article will argue that, despite some elements in *Change-moi ma vie* that clearly evoke the countercultural dissidence of queerness, they are peripheral, contained, and diminished by the narrative's alignment with its European-French heroine, Nina (Fanny Ardant).[2] Indeed, Nina's role as the audience's guide is central to the film's portrayal of ethnicity, gender, and sexuality, and Sami, Fidel, and Leïla's status as illegal immigrants position them as clandestine figures in relation to both French citizenship and Nina. The sense of marginalization in *Un fils*, however, remains constant and consistent throughout the diegesis, and is enhanced by the proximity of the spectator in relation to the *Beur* cross-dressing protagonist, Selim.

Oriental Adventures and the De-Queering of the Maghrebi Transvestite in *Change-moi ma vie*

By aligning the spectator with Nina, Liria Bégéja generally maintains the audience at a distance from the represented lives of her Maghrebi transvestite prostitutes. *Change-moi ma vie* follows Nina's trajectory from failing actress to successful performer, a journey initiated by her chance meeting with Sami, a cross-dressing prostitute working the Parisian boulevards. The marginal, nocturnal universe in which Sami and the other North African immigrant sex workers exist provides the background to the development of Nina's problematic relationship with Sami. They become the objects of our curious and scrutinizing gaze as it is refracted through Nina's own uninformed, voyeuristic eyes; we are, then, like Nina, externally positioned with regard to their marginal universe. This exterior viewpoint replicates the director's own self-declared stance; when asked by critic Gwen Douguet about how she was perceived by some of the real-life transvestites Bégéja casts as extras in her film, she repeatedly refers to them in the third person: "Ce ne fut pas facile. Il a fallu que je gagne *leur* confiance, *leur* respect. En *leur* parlant. Beaucoup" [It wasn't easy. I had to earn *their* trust, *their* respect. By speaking to *them*. A lot] (Douguet 2001, my emphasis).

Nina is not, however, constructed as wholly conventional. The opening scene at the terrace of a sidewalk café presents her as a neurotic, desperate, unemployed, middle-aged actress who has just returned to Paris after an eight-year stay in Russia. Moreover, Nina has not fulfilled her normatively defined gender role as wife and/or mother; in fact, she expresses resentment at having been a maternal figure for her fellow actors in Russia. Nevertheless, Nina is a French citizen who, by contrast to Sami and his clandestine immigrant friends, has the right to reside and work legally in France, with all the security and opportunities such a privilege allows. Furthermore, Bégéja implies that the classically bourgeois central Parisian world to which Nina has returned is not one from which she intends to escape, but one to which she aspires. Consequently, rather than being positioned at odds with hegemonic morality, Nina is portrayed as striving to conform to some of its central modes of cultural taste and moral ethics.

In interviews, Bégéja conveys her empathy with Nina's predicament. In fact, her own background mirrors elements of Nina's fictional past. She was born in Paris to a French mother and Albanian father, thereby suggesting a dual influence between her country of birth and residency, and the eastern European culture of her father. Agreeing that the theme of exile is a central thread of her work,[3] Bégéja adds that "trouver sa place ou non dans le monde, l'intégration qui peut en découler, sont des sujets que j'aime explorer, que j'ai besoin d'explorer" [to find one's place in the world or not, the integration that can result from it, these are the themes that I like to examine, that I need to examine] (Douguet 2001). Bégéja locates this discovery of the self, this reintegration of the exiled figure, in the body of her European-French heroine; Sami, on the other hand, is confined to a perpetual state of disaffection, unable to break free from his marginalized existence, that is, until his premature death as the result of a drug overdose.

The mediated construction of the Maghrebi characters is first introduced in the scene in which Sami enters the narrative. Bégéja sutures the spectator's gaze with that of Nina through a series of point-of-view shots, the third revealing Sami as he jogs through Parc Monceau in the chic part of Paris's seventeenth arrondissement. While Nina's vision in the two preceding shots has been shaky, it momentarily stabilizes as she observes Sami run past, his proximity briefly returning her to some form of consciousness, which is also conveyed by the widening of her eyes. Through these techniques, it is implied that Sami has become the object of Nina's curiosity and perhaps desire, his conventionally masculine allure emphasized by his taut upper arms. The soundtrack — that we later discover to be the music Sami is listening to on his Walkman and that which he uses to revive Nina — conveys his ethnic identity as Maghrebi and thus marks him as exotic and distinct from Nina. The song is performed by leading *Raï* star Cheb Mami, who, as Thibaut Schilt remarks, "seeks to make *Raï* music an international phenomenon by opening the genre up to Western influences" (2007, 366). This merging of occidental and Maghrebi sounds and rhythms can be described as a "hybrid" cultural artifact that generates an "ambivalence [that] enables a form of subversion" from which minorities "intervene in the unifying and totalizing *myths* of the national culture" (Schilt 2007, 364, based on Bhabha 1994, 112, 249). Yet in this scene the music is kept in its original melancholic mode, with only a suggestion of Western percussion and electronic instruments entering at the point that Sami places the headphones into Nina's ears.

However, Sami's role extends beyond the passive object of Nina's gaze. As the subsequent series of shots showing Nina being discharged from hospital confirms, Sami has served as Nina's rescuer, his attempts at keeping her awake having seemingly staved off her descent into unconsciousness. This act provides the catalyst that sets in train a series of events that will eventually lead to Nina finding her "dream" acting role and consequently achieving some form of social normalization. Nina's reorientation toward a better life becomes the central thrust of the narrative, as the title *Change-moi ma vie* indicates, and Sami plays a decisive role in this redirection.

In her work on *Queer Phenomenology*, Sara Ahmed provides a fruitful account of the verb "to orientate" and its etymological origins in linguistic and cultural constructions of the Orient.[4] Ahmed notes that "to orient(ate)" is built upon the substantive stem of "the Orient," which takes the East as its horizon (2006, 113). Ahmed reminds us of Edward Saïd's work on orientalism (1978) in which the Orient "does not simply refer to a specific place" but is a European construct to describe that which is "not Europe" or that which is not the Occident (2006, 114). Ahmed observes that this Orient is made oriental as a "submission to the authority of the Occident" but which, in its not being Europe, "points to another way of being in the world" that includes fantasies of "romance, sexuality and sensuality." The Orient possesses that which the West is "assumed to be lacking" and the fantasy is thus based on "what is 'not here'" and "shapes desire for what is 'there'" (114). In the park scene, Sami alerts Nina to this vision of "what is 'there,'" both through his physical attractiveness and the *Raï* music. Sami's effect on Nina is the point at which he appears as an object on her "horizon" (to use Ahmed's term, 113), on the edge of her gaze.

From this key narrative moment, the film ostensibly becomes the story of the movement of Nina's European-French, heterosexual female body across a series of borders as she follows her impulse to pursue Sami, the practical necessity to return the Walkman providing a pretext for her discovery of the "new (oriental) world" in which he resides. As Ahmed argues, "lines of desire take us in certain directions," they "direct bodies towards objects" (2006, 114). The root of the verb to orient(ate) in the geographically and culturally marked spatial signifier of the Orient is given visual signification in the film as Nina is literally drawn toward the East. The journey takes her northeastward from the affluence of Parc Monceau to the shabby, rundown, and multiethnic Porte de Clichy and Boulevard Bessières. Porte de Clichy has everything that the rest of the arrondissement lacks, and much of this is bound up with notions of the exotic and erotic. Yet, Bégéja's film privileges Nina's reactions as she encounters the unfamiliar and alluring individuals who populate the neighborhood. In the sequence showing Nina's first visit she occupies the center of the shots that record her responses as she exits the metro and walks along the boulevard — the various Maghrebi outlets and passersby are confined to the margins of the screen space with the exception of one short take showing a grocery store. The emotions inscribed upon Nina's face range from bewilderment to fascination and culminate in astonishment and fear in the ultimate scene in which she is confronted with Sami's identity as a cross-dresser and sex worker in a telephone booth. Sami is dressed in his full transvestite gear, including a wig of long, straight black hair, a shiny black PVC bustier and miniskirt, a transparent black body-stocking, and long black thigh-high boots. Sami's act of removing his wig to confirm his identity serves as a springboard, generating a series of facially and corporeally inscribed responses that, once again, return the focus to Nina. She is seen stumbling backward, breaking her heel as she slips off the curb, refusing his invitation to go for a drink and hastily hailing a taxi as a means of escape.

Yet it is not Sami himself that Nina is shown to fear, but the connotations of unorthodox gender and desire associated with his nocturnal alter ego. The potency of transvestism as a queering strategy that destabilizes the normative gendered codes of appearance and behavior has been recognized by Marjorie Garber in her work on cross-dressing and cultural anxiety. Garber describes "vestimentary codes" as a "system of signification" that speaks "in a number of registers: class, gender, sexuality, erotic style" (1992, 161). Transvestism uses clothes as one of its most palpable and pivotal signifiers of resistance to heteronormativity and thus engenders what Garber characterizes as a "'category crisis'"— that is, "a failure of definitional distinction, a borderline that becomes permeable, that permits of border crossings from one (apparently distinct) category to another" (1992, 16). Read along these lines, Nina's discovery of Sami in the telephone booth is the catalyst for her acknowledgment of the crossing of yet another frontier, this time sexual, which distinguishes between straight gender identities and queer subjectivities.

The ultimate shot of the sequence in which Sami returns Nina's gaze registers his own aversion to the queer connotations of his subcultural identity. By contrast to Provencher's description of Sami as a "queer sexual citizen," Bégéja constructs him as aspiring to a normative model of masculinity. She conveys this on the level of his appearance — even when in transvestite attire — and his forceful interaction with his clients. If, as Garber warns, "part of the problem — and part of the pleasure and danger of decoding [vestimentary codes] — is in determining which set of referents is in play in each scenario" (1992, 161), the "set of referents in play" in Sami's transvestite outfit serves as a repudiation of his feminization. Sami's clothes function as his suit of armor that deflects any reading of his identity as passive and unmanly. Consequently, his hard, shiny black PVC bustier becomes his breastplate, his thigh-high stiletto boots his greaves, and the black mesh of his transparent fishnet body-stocking his chain mail shielding his body from emasculation. This projection of virility is reinforced by his assertive behavior with his clients. He barks at one, "Si tu veux toucher, tu paies" [If you want a feel, show me the money], and later indifferently confirms another's assumption that he takes both male and female clients: "Les hommes, les femmes, tout ce que tu veux, puis je ne me fais pas enculer" [Men, women, anything you want, but I don't get fucked]. Refusal to play the receptive role in male-to-male sex is a cliché of perceptions of homosexuality within Arabic cultures in which, as Jarrod Hayes has noted, "Arab men, as long as they are penetrators, even with men, are still manly; the passive partner is either a boy or is feminized" (2000, 4). Sami's comment thus transmits his compliance with this virile mode of Arabic masculinity.

Difference in relation to sexuality is incarnated by the more marginal characters who exhibit almost no anxiety about their transvestism and, in the case of Fidel, status as prostitutes. For instance, Fidel is heard rebuking Nina's assumption that no one is a sex worker for pleasure: "Qu'est-ce que t'en sais, toi, si on le fait par plaisir ou pas?" [How do you know whether we do it out of pleasure or not?] Furthermore, Fidel and Leïla are almost always dressed in their transvestite attire, while Sami is often seen wearing his running gear. The birthday scene provides an unequivocal example of this juxtaposition between ("masculine") Sami and his ("feminized") friends; he is seen dancing in his jogging suit opposite Leïla, who, donning feminine garments and accessories, mimics the moves of the *Raqs sharqi* or belly dance, "her" hips shimmying in rhythm to the Arabic music. This pairing briefly illustrates what Malek Chebel has described as the "entire continuum of sexualities" that exist in Arabic cultures and which includes "drag queens" and "active bisexuals" (1998, 17). Moreover, through "her" act, Leïla exemplifies the extent to which, as Judith Butler argues, drag reveals that gender "is a kind of imitation that produces the very notion of the original as an *effect* and consequence of the imitation itself" (1990, 313, her emphasis).

Yet, despite these brief interludes into a way of being that is ethnically and sexually distinct from the prevailing moralities of Western culture, the film constantly returns to the emotions and experiences of Nina. Nina is seen often returning to the area and integrating into the subcultural milieu of its inhabitants. We watch her breaking fast with Sami and the other Maghrebis during Ramadan, and she is an observant in the birthday party scene. She is also shown developing a strong bond with Fidel and brokering a deal with

Sami that aims at saving them both. However, the film ascribes success in escaping from a desperate existence to Nina. While the cumulative effects of Sami's long-term drug habit bring about his death, Nina finally breaks onto the Parisian stage, as the lead in a theatrical performance of Sami's life. As a European-French, heterosexual woman literally "playing" the role of a Maghrebi transvestite prostitute, the potential of Nina's act to reveal that sexuality, gender, and even ethnicity are performatively constituted is great. Nevertheless, as argued, it is Sami's status as Nina's savior that is identified as having enabled her to achieve a sense of purpose and recognition from her audience, explicitly portrayed in Nina's theatrical narration of her late lover's existence. As Ahmed remarks in her account of orientation, "desire involves a political economy in the sense that it is distributed: the desire to possess, and to occupy, constitutes others not only as objects of desire, but also as resources for world-making" (2006, 115). Since the film posits Sami as Nina's resource — or what Ahmed elsewhere terms "supply point" (114) — for the rebuilding of her own life, the construction of Nina as someone who seeks to integrate and live like the inhabitants of Sami's subcultural community is superseded by the far less salutary figure of the colonizer who conquers non-Western civilizations. The mise-en-scène of the theatrical performance conveys this clearly; Nina occupies center stage, the Maghrebi prostitutes are displaced to the margins of the space, just visible against the walls of the reconstruction of the Boulevard Bessières. Consequently, Nina appropriates the ways and wares of the Maghrebi transvestite community in order to confirm and reaffirm her own legitimacy within a dominant, European-French social space, the film thus replicating the distribution of power within the territories of the Maghreb during the period of colonization by the European-French.

Queer Affiliations: Proximity and Dissidence in *Un fils*

Like *Change-moi ma vie*, *Un fils* is not a film about cross-dressing. Rather, its central narrative focus is the relationship between its cross-dressing, sex-working hero, Selim, and his father, Omar (Hammou Graïa). Hence, while Selim is the main protagonist for two-thirds of the narrative (until his unpremeditated death by a drugs overdose), Omar becomes the agent of the final section as we observe how he comes to terms with the discovery of his late son's unconventional identity and lifestyle. However, unlike Bégéja, Amal Bedjaoui conveys a strong sense of affiliation between herself, her audience, and her cross-dressing protagonist. She avoids portraying him through the inquisitive and objectifying gaze of an intermediary character, and in so doing, creates the impression of granting viewers a more direct access to the marginal world he inhabits. This perception of an absence of mediation is accentuated by her filming style and aesthetics. Bedjaoui's camera follows her characters rather than leading them, thereby conferring an organic, improvised quality onto the film. Moreover, she enhances the veneer of objectivity in the image by avoiding subjective tracking and point-of-view shots, privileging a stable and, at times, fixed camera and favoring long takes and depth of field. Mise-en-scène is thus given priority over editing as the chief location of textual meaning-making. For instance, when Selim has lunch with Omar, the camera is positioned just beyond the end of the small dining table and thus records them as they finish their meal, mainly in silence. The depth of field allows us to observe Omar as he stands up and walks to the back of the living room (and thus shot), turns on the stereo and sits down in his armchair. Similarly, in the next scene at his friend Louise's (Isabelle Pichaud) apartment, the camera is fixed at a distance simply recording Selim sleeping on his side and Louise casually painting her toenails.[5]

Yet, for all her apparent objectivity, Bedjaoui rarely allows Selim to stray from her close and insistent gaze, until, that is, after his death. As Frédéric Strauss writes, "Elle ne le quitte pas des yeux" [She doesn't take her eyes off him] (2004). This immediacy is evidenced in the predominance of medium close-ups focusing on Selim's head and upper torso, an example of which opens the film. The shot is taken from just behind Selim's naked shoulder, his face clearly reflected in the large mirror of the bathroom in which the scene unfolds. The mise-en-scène of his head and body and the diegetic sound serve to introduce and reveal the character to the spectator. The bright white strobe surround of the mirror illuminates Selim's lowered face from underneath, while the back lighting bounces off his shoulders and arms. A connection is established between the incandescent light, the glossy mirror, and Selim's smooth, unblemished skin.

Seconds into the scene, however, Bedjaoui introduces a sound offscreen of heavy panting that troubles this initial representation of her protagonist. The breathing begins almost exactly at the point when Selim suspends his meticulous cleaning of the sink and fixes his gaze on an object reflected in the mirror, which is beyond the frame and thus the audience's view. The image track cuts back to a medium long shot to reveal that the source of the sound is an anonymous client (Xavier Maly) who is having sex with Louise in the bath. A strange juxtaposition therefore separates the initial images of Selim and the explicit sexual exchange occurring alongside him. Yet matters are complicated in that the client's erotic gratification is enhanced by Selim's conventionally handsome looks; he is seen staring insistently at Selim from the rear, then steps out of the bath and stands behind him, placing his left hand over Selim's, and follows his slow movements as he cleans the sink. As such, *Un fils* deploys the narrative device of revelation, which, as Judith Halberstam has argued in her work on representations of transgender characters, "causes the audience to reorient themselves in relation to the film's past in order to read the film's present and prepare themselves for the film's future" (2005, 77–78). Here, it is Selim's status as a sex worker that is being exposed, principally by his lack of protest at the client's physical advances. Reorientation is thus mobilized in a dynamic between the audience and the queerly positioned protagonist rather than being located in a diegetic relationship between main and secondary characters as in *Change-moi ma vie*. Unlike Sami, Selim is not a "resource for world-making" that sets a perplexed occidental heroine on a normative life course, but functions as a constant challenge to prevailing orthodoxies of desirable and undesirable subjectivities, behavior, and lifestyles. Furthermore, while Bedjaoui offers Selim for the erotic and sensual visual pleasure of her audience — particularly when juxtaposed with the trick's limp, coarse, hirsute body — she thwarts stereotype by making him the agent of the narrative, until his untimely end. This is confirmed in the sequence that follows the bathroom scene in which he is filmed collecting his keys and returning to his hotel room in the Porte de Clichy, counting his money and lying on his bed, and then traveling on the RER to visit his father, Omar.

Bedjaoui affirms her empathy with her fictional hero in press interviews. For instance, when asked about her motivations for examining Selim's relationship with Omar, she replies: "Je ressens beaucoup d'émotions face à ces rapports, de pudeur, de honte, d'incommunicabilité. Je m'y identifie de manière familière et intime. Je pense que c'est parce que tout ce à quoi mes origines me renvoient ne me convient pas. Je suis autre, et appréhende bien ces relations entre père et fils" [I feel many emotions in front of these relations, of modesty, of shame, of a breakdown in communication. I identify with them in a familiar and intimate way. I think I don't agree with everything that my background represents. I am other, and understand very well these relations between father and son] (Levieux 2004).

Bedjaoui's self-defined status as other is explicitly articulated in this last affirmation. She describes her migratory trajectory, recounting how she was born in Algeria and then moved to France with her family at a young age in order to study. Although she spent three years in New York, she returned to France in the mid-1980s to enroll at the prestigious film school, the IDHEC (Insitut des hautes études cinématographiques). Hence, while not born in France, Bedjaoui can be described as *Beur* by virtue of her socialization and acculturation within the French system. Given such repeated crossing of both national and cultural boundaries, it is hardly surprising that Bedjaoui asserts a sense of empathy with Selim's feelings of disconnection with the culture of his parents. She echoes what Carrie Tarr notes is a broader sentiment among the young *Beur* generations who "have been brought up in ignorance of their family and community histories" given that their parents "tended not to transmit their histories to their offspring" (2005, 5). For Tarr, such silences have had a "disempowering" effect on the "second (and later third) generation" (5). It is this disconnection, this silence that Bedjaoui claims to understand well.

A close study of the arrangement of the family home reveals that, while there are some signifiers of Omar's ethnic background and family history, these are by no means obtrusive. A short verse of the Koran hangs on the wall of the hallway, two postcards depicting men in *djellabas* are attached to the refrigerator door and a *tajine* dish sits on the shelf behind the dining table. Moreover, Omar is seen praying on only one occasion and visiting his wife's grave in the local Muslim cemetery twice. Beyond these subtle referents, Omar's existence is stripped almost completely bare of objects and customs that hail from the Maghreb. The only language of communication between Omar and Selim is French, and the music of preference is American blues (topically Luther Allison's *Love Me Papa*). Bedjaoui claims that she intended to enhance the universal appeal of her father-son narrative and to avoid ghettoizing her story and characters within a minority Maghrebi community. Such an approach might reflect, as mentioned, her personal disaffection from the culture of her parents. Yet in diluting the ethnic specificity of both Omar and Selim, Bedjaoui could be criticized as failing to break the silence around the "family and community histories" that, as Tarr notes, many young Maghrebi-French citizens find so "disempowering" (2005, 5).[6]

Nevertheless, *Un fils* succeeds in constructing an image of its *Beur* hero as having integrated a non-Maghrebi milieu. Selim is depicted as having established new relationships away from the family home, embodied most obviously by Louise and also to a degree by Max (Aurélien Recoing), his client and object of his romantic aspirations. Moreover, Bedjaoui's sensitivity toward Selim is also evident in the paucity of conventional visual markers of vice and seediness. In fact, Bedjaoui distances her protagonist from the racist jibe that attributes the qualities of the soiled and the immoral to Maghrebi prostitutes by inserting relatively long takes of Selim washing his face and body, cleaning his teeth, wiping down surfaces (as in the opening scene), or doing the washing up, almost always in silence. This apparent attraction for cleanliness is not explained in simplistic terms as a means through which Selim can purify himself of his nocturnal encounters. Although he says to Louise early on, "Je ne vaux pas grand chose à part le prix de mon cul" [I'm not worth much, apart from the price of my ass], the film implies that this gloomy self-assessment is an internalization of his father's criticism of his apparent lack of ambition and not his own evaluation of his existence and status. Beyond this particular instance, Selim is depicted as indifferent to his line of work. It is Louise, not Selim, who eventually urges that they put an end to their prostitution, uttering the line "Tu sais, je crois qu'il serait peut-être temps qu'on arrête ces conneries" [You know, I think it's perhaps time we stopped this crap]. Furthermore, the film challenges the clichés that sex workers sell their bodies to feed either a drug habit or alcohol addiction and that they are incapable of maintaining filial relationships and forming senti-mental attachments. *Un fils* strives to offer a morally acceptable justification for Selim's status as a prostitute — as his attempts to raise money to finance his father's back operation — and, despite the depiction of his death by a narcotics overdose, it includes two explicit denials of his drug dependency. Similarly, the images of sex between Selim and Max are preceded by moments of tenderness — dancing a slow and caressing each other's bodies on their first encounter and having a meal together on their second. Elsewhere, it is the series of rejections to which Selim is subjected, including Omar's refusal of his money, Max's ending of their relationship, and a homophobic beating by a group of young *Beur* assailants, which is represented as the events lead-ing him to swallow the drugs. Given his fastidious attention to hygiene and altruistic concern for others, Selim complies with some of the attributes of a "good French sexual citizen."

However, *Un fils* avoids simplification by sustaining Selim's dissidence in other areas as central to his character and lifestyle. Paradoxically, then, although his ethnic difference is diluted, his queerness — through his occupation, sexuality, and lifestyle — is constantly maintained. This is further evidenced in his performance of his gender, which in contrast to Fidel and Leïla, cannot be allied with any one of the two conventional poles of sexed physicality and conduct. He wears some women's garments, which have a necessary narrative function since it is their discovery that elicits the homophobic attack and leads his father to learn of his son's cross-dressing. More importantly, though, Selim's appearance fuses both male and female physical and vestimentary signifiers, to recall Garber's point mentioned above (1992, 16). Selim's short hair and faded, close-fitting jeans that emphasize the musculature of his legs connote a virile model of masculinity that is contradicted by the figure-hugging red sequined vest he has borrowed from Louise. Moreover, his slouch on the seat of the nightclub conveys his casual assuredness which is underlined as he confidently returns Max's gaze. This agency is then questioned as he acquiesces to Max's request that he "make out" with Louise on the sofa. More than *Change-moi ma vie*, then, *Un fils* renders explicit the "failure of definitional distinction," the "borderline that becomes permeable" that Garber sees as the central destabilizing force of cross-dressing (16). Selim provides an illustration of what might be called a "third space" of gendered and erotic behavior — not the third gender of nineteenth-century sexology but a sexual subjectivity and mode of desire along the lines of Bhabha's conceptualization of new forms of ethnic identity, constructed at the interstices between dominant and minority cultures (1994, 4). This unorthodox gender identity is forged through a merging of both manly and womanly codes and stands as an androgynous and unaligned figure between the poles of masculinity and femininity, agency and passivity.

There can be no doubt that representations that tie sexual non-normativity among North African immigrant and *Beur* populations to prostitution and vice are problematic. Prevailing discriminatory discourses risk being maintained rather than challenged, and the extent to which such images defy existing modes of representation is highly questionable, particularly when, as in *Change-moi ma vie* and *Un fils*, the main cross-dressing character dies. That this is Selim's end is particularly disappointing given that, as argued, Bedjaoui's protagonist manages to find a sense of self in a non-ethnically-defined space and establish strong relationships. This has been interpreted in part as emanating from the director's sensitivity for and empathy with Selim, which she conveys by making him her central protagonist. The approach is crucial, and while *Change-moi ma vie* does depict ways of living that stand outside heteronormativity, the close affiliation between spectator and externally positioned character displaces these unorthodox images to the periphery of the narrative by making them the object of a (our) voyeuristic gaze.

When we compare these films with the other major recent portrayal of a Maghrebi transvestite, *Chouchou*, we can conclude that all three films offer only two options for cross-dressers of Maghrebi descent: assimilation or removal through death. Both incur silence of sorts. Perhaps this is simply a product of a culture that officially privileges assimilation as its approach to the integration of its multiethnic and multisexual communities (McCaffrey 2005, 33–40). Such a polarization leaves ample space for more nuanced representations in which, at the very least, the cross-dressing Maghrebi/*Beur* figure is no longer doomed. A model for such a character might be Fidel since he is not constructed as feeding a drug habit or alcohol addiction, and talks of a future in which his transvestism will still play an integral part. Yet, quite apart from being a secondary character, Fidel's aspirations are restrained to the realm of hypothesis. The challenge for filmmakers might thus be to provide material depictions of these characters' futures and to make these the center of their narratives.

Notes

1. I use *Maghrebi* and *Beur* as shorthand in order to differentiate between the characters of the films I study (Sami, who, as an immigrant, is not French, and Selim, who is French of Maghrebi descent). Similarly, I use the term "European-French" in reference to the ethnic origins of the majority population.

2. Michele Aaron defines queer as representing "the resistance to, primarily, the normative codes of gender and sexual expression [and to] the restrictive potential of gay and lesbian sexuality.... In this way, queer, as a critical concept, encompasses the non-fixity of gender expression and the non-fixity of both straight and gay sexuality" (2004, 5).

3. See *Avril brisé* (1987) and *Loin des barbares* (1994).

4. "To orientate" is a synonym of "to orient" that does not require any syntactical modification from the noun form "the Orient," rendering the connection even more explicit.

5. By allowing the characters to "exist," as fellow director Laurent Cantet remarks in an interview that accompanies the DVD release of the film, Bedjaoui recalls a realist tradition in French cinema, famously championed by André Bazin (Lapsley and Westlake 1988, 159–60) and which can be found in the early films of Jean Renoir (Bazin 1971, 76–84). Equally, she nods to the "natural" atmosphere of Jean Eustache's cinema, particularly in his epic *La maman et la putain* (1973). Eustache's definition of the subject of his film as "la façon dont les actions importantes s'insèrent à travers une continuité d'actions anodines ... sans le raccourci schématique de la dramatisation cinématographique" [the

way in which important events are inserted into a series of banal actions . . . without using systematic shortcuts imposed by cinematographic dramatization] (Weyergans 1973, 56) might apply to the style of *Un fils*.

6. Laurent Cantet evokes this issue by singling out the very last shot of Omar in a Muslim cemetery as projecting a particularly strong political image: "Même si la vie de ce père et ce fils peut ressembler à la vie de pas mal de gens en France, le cimetière lui ne ressemble pas à un cimetière 'français'" [Even if the lives of this father and son might resemble the lives of a lot of people in France, the cemetery itself does not resemble a "French" cemetery]. The politics are conveyed by the Islamic status of the cemetery and also by the fact that it is displaced to what Cantet refers to as a marginalized, industrial zone. Perhaps here, then, Bedjaoui attempts to voice ethnic difference in her film, although she associates this with the older generation and, in response to Cantet, is evasive; she steers the conversation to her choice of American blues over Algerian music, adding — somewhat flippantly but nonetheless controversially — that "les noirs, le blues, c'est un peu l'équivalent, enfin, si on transpose, ce sont les Algériens des Américains" [black people, blues (music), it's like an equivalent, well, if we transpose it, they are the Algerians of the Americans] (2005, interview with Laurent Cantet, *Un fils* DVD).

References

Aaron, Michele, ed. 2004. *New Queer Cinema: A Critical Reader*. New Brunswick NJ: Rutgers University Press.

Ahmed, Sara. 2006. *Queer Phenomenology: Orientations, Objects, Others*. Durham NC: Duke University Press.

Bazin, André. 1971. *Jean Renoir*. Paris: Éditions Champs Libre.

Bhabha, Homi. 1994. *The Location of Culture*. New York: Routledge.

Butler, Judith. 1990. *Gender Trouble: Feminism and the Subversion of Identity*. New York: Routledge.

Chebel, Malek. 1988. *L'esprit du sérail: Perversions et marginalités sexuelles au Maghreb*. Paris: Lieu Commun.

Douguet, Gwen. 2001. "Liria Bégéja, plus près des autres." http://www.bifi.fr (accessed November 3, 2008).

Garber, Marjorie. 1992. *Vested Interests: Cross-Dressing and Cultural Anxiety*. London: Penguin.

Halberstam, Judith. 2005. *In a Queer Time and Place: Transgender Bodies, Subcultural Lives*. New York: New York University Press.

Hayes, Jarrod. 2000. *Queer Nations: Marginal Sexualities in the Maghreb*. Chicago: University of Chicago Press.

Lapsley, Robert, and Michael Westlake. 1988. *Film Theory: An Introduction*. Manchester: Manchester University Press.

Levieux, Michèle. 2004. "Rencontre: Amal Bedjaoui's intéresse au 'plus grand mystère du monde,' la relation qui unit père et fils." http://www.bifi.fr (accessed November 3, 2008).

McCaffrey, Enda. 2005. *The Gay Republic: Sex, Citizenship and Subversion in France.* Aldershot: Ashgate.

Provencher, Denis M. 2007. "Maghrebi-French Sexual Citizens: In and Out on the Big Screen." *Cineaste* 33 (1) (Winter): 47–51.

Saïd, Edward. 1978. *Orientalism.* London: Routledge and Keegan-Paul.

Schilt, Thibaut. 2007. "Hybrid Strains in Olivier Ducastel and Jacques Martineau's *Drôle de Félix* (2000)." *Contemporary French and Francophone Studies* 11 (3) (August): 361–68.

Strauss, Frédéric. 2004. "*Un fils*: Regard sensible sur un prostitué face à son père." http://www.bifi.fr (accessed November 3, 2008).

Tarr, Carrie. 2005. *Reframing Difference:* Beur and Banlieue *Filmmaking in France.* Manchester: Manchester University Press.

Weyergans, François. 1973. "Lettre de François Weyergans à Jean Eustache." *L'Avant-Scène Cinéma* 142 (December): 56–60.

Filmography

Allouache, Merzak, dir. *Chouchou*, 2003.

Bedjaoui, Amal, dir. *Un fils*, 2003.

Bégéja, Liria, dir. *Avril brisé*, 1987.

——, dir. *Loin des barbares*, 1994.

——, dir. *Change-moi ma vie*, 2001.

Bouchaala, Ahmed, dir. *Origine contrôlée*, 2001.

Eustache, Jean, dir. *La maman et la putain*, 1973.

11

(RE)CASTING SAMI BOUAJILA

An Ambiguous Model of Integration,
Belonging, and Citizenship

MURRAY PRATT AND DENIS M. PROVENCHER

Born in Isère in 1966 of Tunisian heritage, Sami Bouajila appeared
on the big screen in 1991 and hit the road to French stardom with
an acting career that spans more than forty movies and a variety of
roles. Some of these, like his portrayal of Abdelkader in *Indigènes*,
situate the character's place of birth in North Africa while others, notably his performance in *Bye-Bye*, *Drôle de Félix*, *Vivre me
tue*, and *Les témoins* see Bouajila starring as "French" characters
of Maghrebi (North African) descent. Yet other films, such as
Embrassez qui vous voudrez and *Pas si grave*, deploy Bouajila with
little or no reference to his character's ethnicity or heritage. Many
of Bouajila's roles engage to varying degrees with issues of nation
and family, biological or constructed kinship. In this chapter we
consider the screening of Bouajila as a cinematic pathway toward
belonging within contemporary imaginaries of the French nation
as a family (see discussion below). The chapter proceeds via an
analysis of the familial, gendered, and sexual roles he has played
in this representative cross-section of films — as partner, father,
"brother" (whether biological or not) — enjoying varying box

office success based on European ticket sales, receiving different receptions, and spanning a range of genres and sociocultural geographies.[1] Bouajila has appeared in other films that address related issues, including *La faute à Voltaire* and *Change-moi ma vie*.[2] However, our analysis concentrates on films where he plays roles in which he achieves forms of integration into the larger social system.

In *Les féministes et le garçon arabe*, Nacira Guénif-Souilamas and Eric Macé critique the (hetero)sexualized and ghettoized partitioning of gender roles in contemporary imaginaries of immigrants and their children in France, and call for more open and democratic symbolic spaces of representation (2004, 21). In tandem, we explore, in each of Bouajila's roles in the above-mentioned films, the versions of (semi)integrated Frenchness that emerge in relation to issues of gender, sexuality, family, affiliation, and *filiation* (parent-child link) — and the contradictions inherent within them, drawing on relevant theoretical perspectives. In particular, Bouajila's portrayals of gendered and sexual subjectivities, embodying characters across a range of sexualities and cast as biological or imagined family members, offer alternatives to conflations of *Beur* masculinity (*le garçon arabe*) with hyperheterosexual or misogynistic traits, and in turn challenge the symbolic order of gender differences, heteronormativity, and masculine domination within the prevailing French familial model.[3] Throughout his career, the actor embodies a range of subject positions that, when coupled with an ambiguous ethnic background or heritage and tied to issues of kinship, allow both the character and the star to be read as a site where ethnicity, masculinity, sexuality, belonging, and citizenship can be reimagined. The masculinities Bouajila performs can be seen as a variation on Ginette Vincendeau's observation that French stars who function as "ambassadors of France" (2000, 31) can help to "naturalize" or validate the "social roles of men and women at key historical moments" (35). In this particular case, this means a greater national readiness to accept an extended set of forms of being both *Beur* and a French man in contemporary and recent past contexts.

The nation has been conceptualized as an "imagined community" (Anderson 1983), and in parallel, theorists have examined the family as a social construct or "fiction" linked to the broader social order. Pierre Bourdieu argues that families are units supported by the state (1993, 36), which in turn serve to maintain the general social and symbolic order through various "reproduction strategies," including biological investments, that propagate forms of social capital (1994, 5–12).

The family therefore reinforces a dominant symbolic social order that maintains forms of gender differences, heteronormativity (i.e., male-female couple), and masculine domination that reflect the state's values.[4] Eric Fassin argues that this symbolic order is fundamental to French kinship models and illustrates how issues of homosexuality, gay marriage, and any sign of unisex *filiation* such as *homoparentalité* are seen as undermining the symbolic order of the French family and society (1998, 229). Hence, by examining the films in which Sami Bouajila is cast into non-normative male roles within the biological or constructed family, we see how characters begin to recast the symbolic order on screen and make room in the French republican space for new (*Beur*) masculinities and sexualities.

While Carrie Tarr maintains that actors such as Bouajila and Roschdy Zem "improbably embody" immigrant transvestite prostitutes (2005, 172), we stress that it is precisely because an actor like Bouajila plays roles that defy concrete typecasting about *le garçon arabe* that he can harness an expanding awareness of how hegemonic notions of national identity are questioned (Fassin 1998; Papanikolau 2008) and how integration gets configured. Hence, this chapter considers Bouajila's capacity to serve as a model to French audiences for new modalities of belonging, although by attending to the ways in which his roles function as signs, it also traces hesitations about the viability of cinematic encoding of templates for an integrative or secularizing mission within contemporary republican French discourse. Thus, the chapter deploys the notion of the "star as sign," according to which stars contribute to cinema's part in "enunciating the national" (Hayward 2005, 8) insofar as they are "the mediators between the real and the imaginary" (Hayward 2005, 12), alongside existing research that points to the increasing diversity and success of actors of Maghrebi descent in French cinema (Tarr 2005, 12–13, 168). Importantly, since the chapter includes analysis of films dealing with social and political conflicts — including the role of North African soldiers freeing France from German occupation during the Second World War and the place of *Beur* bodies in the AIDS and post-AIDS eras — we look beyond narrow definitions of the politics of integration in France to consider the actor's body as a site where evolutions in French thinking and memory about immigration and integration can be traced.

In these films, neither of which achieved considerable box office success, Bouajila plays the big brother who helps the younger avoid the dangerous streets, or mediates the younger's machismo. First, *Bye-Bye* (with ticket sales of 11,346) by Franco-Tunisian director Karim Dridi presents two brothers of Maghrebi descent, Ismael (Bouajila) and Mouloud (Ouassini Embarek), who leave Paris and head to Marseille to live temporarily with their father's brother and his family. *Bye-Bye* belongs to a series of mid-1990s films that displace *Beur* characters beyond the "multi-ethnic gang of unemployed youth" of the *cités* (Tarr 2005, 79). For Tarr, this newer cinematic trend includes representations of Maghrebi domestic spaces and proposes new agency for the central male figures (2005, 81–82) while concentrating on "interpersonal and intergenerational relationships within the Maghrebi community in France, and the central character's problematic relationship with French society" (2005, 79). In *Bye-Bye*, Dridi operates similar displacements, while also locating the action in Marseilles, a port on the periphery (i.e., not Paris) that has been represented as embracing fluidity between the Maghreb and France (Higbee 2001, 52–54, 56–57).

Dridi uses the brothers to represent two different experiences for *Beur* individuals. Like many male protagonists in *Beur* and *banlieue* filmmaking of this era, the fourteen-year-old Mouloud maintains an estranged relationship with a visually absent father, who only appears via telephone to threaten his son's return to *le bled*.[5] Moreover, Mouloud is associated with the older drug dealer Renard, who although playing a secondary role, represents a stereotypical image of crime in the *banlieue* (Higbee 2001, 55). In contrast, Ismael serves as the "good *Beur* brother" who works alongside Jacky and his (racist) French family in the shipyard and who comes to Mouloud's rescue. The film presents flashbacks in which Ismael cares for their disabled brother, Nouredine, who died in a fire, and Ismael's struggle to come to terms with a sense of culpability for his death. In Marseille, Ismael is determined to be the responsible adult figure to Mouloud by listening to his rap song, giving him spending money, and ultimately saving him from *le bled* and Renard. While Mouloud rejects *le bled* outright, Ismael exhibits a connection to the Maghreb by staring longingly over the Mediterranean in several scenes (Higbee 2001, 58–59). Ismael embodies hybridity and ambiguity with ties to both France and North Africa (Tarr 2005, 81), and by defying his Tunisian father by keeping Mouloud with him, Bouajila's character also offers a reconfiguration of Maghrebi identity and initiates new familial and integrative structures independently from *le bled*. He is a reliable guardian to his onscreen younger brother as the latter begins to envisage less troublesome journeys. In this way, Dridi emphasizes universal messages about an older brother's "guilt and responsibility" over issues of difference and immigration in order to invite French audiences to identify with Ismael's family story (Higbee 2001, 60–61), permitting Bouajila to be read as an actor capable of figuring both cinematic integration and new masculine roles and identities.

Ultimately the film suggests the brothers' potential departure from the socially disrupted and unlivable conjunction of drugs, tradition, family, racism, and crime they discovered in Marseille's "Le Panier" district. Ismael decides to keep Mouloud with him instead of sending him to *le bled*, whether they end up going to Spain as Mouloud suggests or struggle to get that far, given the breakdown of their car. In either case, this ambivalent departure indicates that the hostile workplace, the criminal underworld, or integration within the traditional family are unattractive options, and that for all of France's republican discourse, alternative paths to belonging, if not yet fully mapped, seem more viable.

Like Ismael, who protects Mouloud from street life, the older brother Paul (Bouajila) in *Vivre me tue* (with ticket sales of 39,725) mediates his brother Daniel's (Jalil Lespert) problematic fascination with hypermasculinity. Paul's trajectory can be read as a bid for integration within France, as he is positioned throughout the film as a reasonable or "good" influence while his younger brother descends into infirmity and turmoil due to his abuse of drugs associated with bodybuilding. Applying for jobs for which he is eminently qualified, he is confronted with institutional racism that bars his access to them. The film also presents flashbacks showing how he assists his brother in coping with his deteriorating health and the death of their *cheminot* (railway worker) father. Based on the novel of the same name by Paul Smaïl, the film, like the book, positions itself as an "authentic" representation of *Beur* experiences, while minimizing ethnic differences. However, as discussed in Murray Pratt's account (2006) of the literary impersonation that constructs a pretended *Beur* authorial position as "Paul Smaïl" for the author and polemicist Jack-Alain Léger, the status of the literary text is uncertain and insecure. Claiming that his imposture was supported by *Beur* friends as a blast of reason against the political correctness that tolerates what he sees as the excesses of Islam (Léger 2003, 115–16), Léger sees the persona of Paul as a corrective measure, showing that Maghrebi immigrants and/or their children can lead integrated and secular lives.

At surface level, much of the novel's ambiguity is lost in the screen adaptation of *Vivre me tue*, partly due to the differentiated ascriptions of authorship and directorship in literature and cinema. Equally, though, the film focuses on the fraternal relations of the characters rather than the author's internal meditations on political correctness in France. A key element emerging from Sinapi's adaptation is the extra-French dimension of the brothers' experience, as Daniel's journey takes him to Hamburg, where his hypermasculine body has earned him further career opportunities and the affections of a sex-club owner. Yet if the title of *Vivre me tue* can be parsed as the film's refusal to allocate Daniel a place within the hexagonal family, it nonetheless also refers to Paul's ongoing ambivalence about his place within French normative society. Paul occupies a position outside France as he recollects most of the film from the banks of the Elbe and shares his brother's rootlessness. Furthermore, the decision he takes at the film's conclusion also signals his refusal to accept an integrated French identity. At a final video-recorded job interview, Paul is seen to check all the boxes for his prospective employers before categorically stating "Je ne suis plus candidat" [I am no longer a candidate]. The scene is noteworthy as the culmination of his ongoing hesitations about whether or not to anglicize the name Smaïl as "Smile" and as confirmation of the brothers' attraction to Ishmael's bold proclamation of identity that opens Herman Melville's *Moby-Dick*. At the same time, however, the filming of the interview is framed through a *mise en abyme* as an instance of role play: Bouajila plays Paul playing the archetypal company director of Western capitalism, who in the process realizes his preference for a more life-affirming form of integration, the writing and openness to adventure that captures Melville's audaciousness, rather than a nine-to-five job marketing yogurt. Auditioning, then, for a role within French business life, Bouajila here as Paul (as Ishmael, and on some level as the figment of Léger), through his assertive integrative ethos coupled with his continued allegiance to his heritage (through his academic research and the value he places on his family) contrasts markedly with the life choices and fate of his brother. Each film therefore multiplies rather than limits the scope for integrative possibilities beyond restrictive either/or models.

Sexual Difference, Mitigated Masculinities, and
Reimagined Kinship in *Drôle de Félix* and *Les témoins*

This pairing of films starring Bouajila is distinct from the previous section on biological brotherhood and integration in that it relies on sexual difference and mitigated masculinities more than ethnic differences as ways to reimagine the place of Beur characters in the family. *Drôle de Félix* (with ticket sales of 134,165) chronicles the life of Félix (Bouajila), a man born to a Norman mother and an unknown Maghrebi father, who shares an apartment in Dieppe with his boyfriend, Daniel (Pierre-Loup Rajot). After his mother's death, Félix embarks on a road trip to find his biological father and meets a "surrogate" French family instead.

Since 2001 *Drôle de Félix* has received much critical attention (Rees-Roberts 2008, 105), and scholars highlight the film's treatment of belonging and citizenship in France, evident in how Félix negotiates his identity in relation to the French "family" (Tarr 2005, 148–50; Swamy 2006, 61; Grandena 2006, 64–70; Pratt 2004, 95–97; Provencher 2008, 52–55). Many of Félix's newfound "relatives" teach him about self-reliance and alternative kinship: Antoine, for instance, teaches Félix about flexible fatherhood and even imagines him in that role. Moreover, Félix is comfortable with his sexuality and HIV-positive status, sustaining an open, healthy relationship with Daniel (Pratt 2004, 88–90; Tarr 2005, 147–50; Swamy 2006, 61; Grandena 2006, 64–70). Hence, the film deals effectively with sexual otherness and its place within the nation as family, and in fact, Félix resembles the "good" French sexual citizen documented elsewhere who does not highlight sexual difference in conversations with family (Provencher 2007b, 2008). Félix also plays the "good citizen" to his kid brother Jules by helping him finish his sketches for art class and escorting him, albeit prematurely, to his first gay bar. Indeed, Félix shows the youth the way of the gay world, but he never sleeps with him, despite Jules making sexual advances toward him. Importantly, when Félix later has sex with his nameless "cousin," he defies outdated stereotypes of the *garçon arabe*, because when they emerge from the brush where they have been having sex, it is the masculine cousin who has been wearing the condom, suggesting his active role and Félix's "passivity" during sex.

The film deals less definitively, however, with Félix's integration based on ethnic origins (Provencher 2008), as he has difficulty serving as the witness to a racist lynching in Rouen because of his own *gueule arabe* (Arab face).

Félix has trouble seeing himself as anything other than "Norman" despite his ongoing search for his father, and ultimately abandons this quest. Consequently, he is an orphan with no real ties to the Maghreb, the city, or even the violent images of the *banlieue* (Tarr 2005, 17–21), and he remains the happy, moderately sexual, masculine, and assimilated *Beur* citizen who functions at a distance to overt reference to ethnic or sexual difference. To an extent, his trip returns Félix to the republican space of the middle-class French family, where at least temporarily he plays each role required of him. However, the unresolved search for his biological father effectively "interrogates the nexus of paternity, state, authority and race that determines the terrain of his own identity" (Pratt 2004, 99). Within the film's diegesis, the destination of the ship on which Félix and Daniel sail off, equally, is left unresolved. This suggests that Félix, like Ismael in *Bye-Bye* and Paul in *Vivre me tue*, will forge his own place within the French family without being constricted or solely defined by his biological *filiation*.

In a different way from the character of Félix, Mehdi (Bouajila) in André Téchiné's 2007 film *Les témoins* (with ticket sales of 450,719) embodies an interesting confluence of ethnic and sexual differences that calls into question restrictive integrative models for *Beur* men within French social space. *Les témoins* provides the viewer with a flashback to 1984–85 at the rise of the HIV pandemic with a story divided into "Les beaux jours," "La guerre," and "Le retour de l'été" ("The Good Times," "The War," and "The Return of Summer"). As is typical of Téchiné's œuvre, *Les témoins* presents a range of sexualities and masculinities in its male characters (Adrien, Mehdi, Manu). Adrien (Michel Blanc), a medical doctor, meets a young Manu (Johan Libéreau), later to be diagnosed as HIV positive, while cruising in Paris's Bois de Boulogne, and takes him on vacation where he is introduced to Sarah (Emmanuelle Béart) and Mehdi (Sami Bouajila), a young couple who have just had a baby. Adrien and Mehdi both develop a romantic interest in Manu, and in a scene where they fight for Manu's attention, Mehdi accuses Adrien of being an effeminate homosexual, while Adrien accuses Mehdi of being a sexual predator. Though Mehdi exhibits sexual interest in both his wife and Manu, his character never identifies with any particular term to describe his sexuality. While it may appear at first blush that he is bisexual, Téchiné's avoidance of any discourse on Mehdi's sexuality allows him to play an ambiguous character. Moreover, while he is initially depicted as the macho *inspecteur général* who knows no homosexuals in the police force, he eventually reaches a more nuanced subject position. Also, *Les témoins* sets up an older-younger brother dynamic that allows the two unrelated men (Mehdi and Manu) to form an imagined kinship while downplaying suggestions of Mehdi's sexually aggressive potential. However, Téchiné does not highlight either character's Maghrebi origins, and accordingly he does not spell out whether their mutual attraction is ethnically based or not (Rees-Roberts 2008, 120). Thus, Téchiné's representation of Mehdi discards the stereotype of *le garçon arabe* in the story line and Mehdi's ambiguous sexuality further questions this stereotyping.

Mehdi also redefines paternity for *Beur* characters by playing the attentive father, who takes care of his newborn son while his more socially well-off companion is preoccupied with her writing. Hence, Mehdi's character accumulates roles as police officer and older brother or lover to Manu, but also crosses class lines and navigates the positions of the "good father" and (relatively) reliable life companion (to Sarah), in ways other *Beur* or Maghrebi characters have not yet accomplished: with reference to Félix in *Drôle de Félix*, Tarr observes that "the surrogate family he acquires on the road does not present him with the opportunity to meet 'Mon enfant' ('My child')" (2005, 150). At the same time, given that Sarah, like Myriam in Léger's *Vivre me tue* (although the film adaptation does not stress this), is Jewish, Téchiné's portrayal of this relationship can be seen as expanding the metaphorical field of national and familial belonging in other interesting directions. This confluence of ethnicity, alternative masculinity, disregard of convention, and queerness allows Mehdi's character to chart new ground for the *Beur* protagonist within the family.

Given Bouajila's star trajectory, it is unsurprising that this 2007 film casts him in the role of Mehdi, since the character's sexual fluidity is in keeping with the flexible gender and sexual identities the actor has been rehearsing throughout his career. At the same time, however, like Félix, Mehdi shows little interest in the broader political issues of the day (e.g., France's problematic response to the HIV pandemic or the emergence of SOS Racisme, neither or which are foregrounded). In the end, the story line returns to the earlier vacation spot and to a witnessing of Manu's life and death when the reconvening characters remember him. The spectator discovers over the course of the film that the narrative voice belongs to Sarah (the writer), who is chronicling Manu's life on the written page, including his experience with HIV and his unfolding love for Mehdi. Ironically, it is Sarah, as a white, wealthy, French,

HIV-negative heterosexual female, who can witness issues of differences in this film, while Mehdi, for all the social flexibility he demonstrates in other ways, does not approve of her work of remembrance. So, while some of Bouajila's protagonists chart new ground on the big screen for *Beur* citizens, these representations are not free from contradictions, conflicting social investments, or limitations in establishing voices and visibilities based on ethnic and sexual differences.

Passing under the French Radar in
Embrassez qui vous voudrez and Pas si grave

In tandem with Bouajila's performance in *Les témoins*, his casting in *Embrassez qui voudrez* and *Pas si grave* is ethnically unspecified, suggesting a sense in which his star value within the French entertainment industry has become detachable from the actor's own heritage and that there are, increasingly, spaces available in French (and in the second instance Franco-Belgian) cinema for *Beur* actors to embody "everyman" characters whose ethnicity or race are not uniquely defining characteristics. An evolution of this sort could be seen as socially progressive in that it opens possible spaces for plenary belonging within postcolonial Europe to generations of immigrants. Yet there is a built-in specular limitation to this kind of reading. For, while Bouajila's "*Beur*ness" might not figure overtly in the script or on screen, the persistence of spectator identifications of the actor within the normative epistemologies of race and ethnicity that operate among viewing communities mitigates against fully undifferentiated viewing experiences. An examination of Bouajila's characters in these films suggests a more hesitant reading due to a discrepancy between, on the one hand, the overt unremarked belonging (i.e., Franco- or Euro-normativity) of the protagonists, and on the other hand, the less than certain narratological vectors they incarnate.

In the 2002 star vehicle *Embrassez qui vous voudrez* (with ticket sales of 1,835,762), Bouajila plays a secondary part as Kevin, a heterosexual employee of a successful businessman who embarks on what he hopes will be an erotically charged holiday to Chicago with his boss's daughter, Julie. To the extent that *Embrassez qui vous voudrez* can be regarded as a farce, romp, or "romantic comedy," its cast of stars (Michel Blanc, Charlotte Rampling) is relied upon to fulfill the film's titular injunction by finding solace, solutions, or just something different outside their established relationships. Kevin, however, despite initially enjoying a clandestine but mutually satisfying relationship with Julie (Clotilde Courau), sees his stock plunge during the outbound flight when Julie decides to flirt with a random American across the aisle instead of joining Kevin in the mile-high club. From this point on, Kevin's fate is to be plotted, less as the classical *honnête homme* ("honest man" or "plain dealer") than as the *cocu* (cuckold), for his competence, Frenchness, and security capital — all signs of his masculinity — are foiled respectively by a broken suitcase, a penchant for T-shirts proclaiming he "hearts" Chicago, and a mugger who is less friendly than Kevin had supposed.

This sequence culminates in Julie's denial that Kevin had even traveled with her, an erasure compounded by growing speculation that his position in her daddy's company might be at risk, given rumors of financial irregularities in his transactions with clients. If Kevin "just happens" to be a *Beur* character, then it could be argued that the combined star ratings that systematize *Embrassez qui vous voudrez* "just happen" to conspire against him finding someone to kiss within its valued middle-class milieu.[6] Instead, Bouajila's portrayal of Kevin is confined to a character delimited by the hypersexual (at the outset, he feigns normalcy despite being given a blowjob under his desk), the gullible, and the potentially corrupt. Realizing his abandonment at the end of the film, Kevin's response is ambivalent. Although his decision to remove the traces of his intended proposal to Julie could be considered as a sign of his choice to opt out of the family farce (rather than be rejected by it), the way he does so (removing the cassette on which he proposes to her from Julie's camcorder) represents a further erasure, this time a self-erasure from both the French family and the film. Kevin is not kin to anyone, biological or constructed, demonstrating the extent to which Bouajila's place within the extended and sexually charged star family the film depicts remains uncertain.

The emerging theme of biological or constructed families, and the role of brothers and fathers in his star trajectory, however, develops further with Bouajila's heterosexual role in *Pas si grave* (with ticket sales of 204,838). While the film is billed as a road movie, and many of its more picturesque scenes are devoted to the big yellow Volvo (recalling the little yellow 2cv of *Bye-Bye*) in which its protagonists make the round-trip from Belgium to Spain, a competing generic matrix might be that of the traditional, even folkloric, quest. An immigrant (Spanish) father has three sons, and his "dying wish" (the spectator learns that this is a ruse) is that the sons journey to his homeland and retrieve an object (a statuette of the Virgin Mary). As with all good folktales, each son's destiny will depend on his success, but equally, the process of the quest transforms its nature. In fact, much of the impact of *Pas si grave* depends on the twists it brings to the traditional elements of the premise. The sons are adopted, thus explaining why Charlie (Bouajila) can have "white" siblings Max (Jean-Michel Portal) and Léo (Romain Duris), and the grail of the statuette, it is revealed on Charlie's return, turns out to be a pretext for a hidden set of agendas that Pablo and Pilar, their adoptive parents, eventually reveal as a way for each son to find his respective path.

Pas si grave draws on the disadvantaged trio often depicted in *banlieue* cinema — in this case, three orphans of the state — and highlights their sometimes delinquent behavior and displacement into a foreign setting. This includes Max vandalizing a motorcycle that belongs to Charlie's associate before their journey, the three brothers wandering the Spanish beach and streets, participating in a bar brawl, and escaping from the police. Nevertheless, this does not impede them from charting their own respective paths. Moreover, unlike Félix in *Drôle de Félix*, Charlie emerges on equal footing with his brothers because they are all adopted, even if the film neglects direct treatment of Charlie's ethnic heritage. Importantly, however, Charlie is the only son who returns home; this is because Max, unlike Félix, has been reunited with his biological parent, while Léo has moved in with a Spanish police chief, Ramon, who moonlights as Ramona, a drag performer. With Léo happily and unproblematically outed and almost immediately reintegrated in a couple, the film's central mission, to abduct the "virgin" (Angela — the daughter of one of Pablo's civil war comrades, rather than Mary) falls to the remaining two brothers, both of whom find themselves in bed with her. Yet, as Max's epilepsy returns along with his desire to be reunited with his mother, Charlie eventually triumphs in both assuming the mantle of the big brother to the others and winning Angela's affection. Indeed, Charlie is the only son to successfully embody a form of (re)integration here, into the trans-European family, as a clearly positioned masculine figure within the heterosexual couple formed with Angela.

In sum, within the worldview of *Pas si grave*, Charlie's (Bouajila's) ethnic identity goes largely unremarked, with the only specific reference being an early comment about how he is somewhat *coloré* as a brother. Given that he is, at this point, removing the traces of a clown costume and (white-faced) makeup, the sense of even this aside is not entirely unambiguous. However, that Bouajila plays the son who turns out to triumph in the folkloric quest for heterosexual accomplishment, within the broader contexts of his career roles, exemplifies the actor's capacity for embodying normative social positions.

Historical Memory and Integration in *Indigènes*

Indigènes, as much as it is a popular and critically acclaimed film, with ticket sales of 3,171,721, it is also an event, both in terms of the level of media attention it generated and in its reported political impact.[7] Depicting the adventures of a Maghrebi brigade during the final years of the Second World War, it highlights the involvement of North African troops in what is often remembered for French viewers as a European war, as well as detailing the injustices and degradations they endured. Importantly, given the film's closing scene where the now aged Abdelkader (Bouajila) visits the war graves of his fallen comrades, *Indigènes* both revisits events from the past and situates them in relation to contemporary responses, highlighting the continued lack of recognition given to the colonial brigades. Many of these aspects have been considered by the film press in general: here our focus is on the forms of brotherhood, allegiance, military camaraderie, and masculinity incarnated by the main characters, who become "representative" of the types of men who served in the units.

Several of the soldiers who play central roles in the film are recruited from Algeria, and each inhabits a slightly different position in relation to the army, France, their colleagues and superiors. Saïd (Jamel Debbouze) is the semi-emasculated Arab that the other soldiers refer to by the feminine appellation "Aïcha," whereas Messaoud (Roschdy Zem) embodies military allegiance, love, and a desire to integrate into French normative society. Interestingly, the commanding officer Sergeant Roger Martinez (Bernard Blancan) is positioned as French throughout the film, until Saïd discovers that he also has Maghrebi roots. Hence, over the course of the film, the spectator sees a series of alternative and nonhegemonic forms of masculinity unfold, and it is through these interstices that new forms of male and ethnic integration coalesce on screen. So, while the film draws on historical facts, it also contributes to debates about how masculinity and belonging can be configured for the subaltern through a range of cameos. Underlying these representations is the film's strong ethos of political justice for a group of men who were mistreated and given the most thankless jobs in the war. However, equally importantly, Abdelkader (Bouajila) emerges as the leader of the group and articulates their grievances. The film's moments of revolt, and Abdelkader's decisive part in mediating them, in turn are contextualized within the soldiers' military and affective commitment to the France that benefits from their draft, each character working through his ambivalences about belonging, sense of being a man, and relation to the others.

Like many of the protagonists of Maghrebi descent discussed in this chapter, Abdelkader embodies flexibility in his relations to others. The film initially situates French and "non-French" troop leaders on the same level, although Abdelkader's status as a full-fledged equal alongside his peer is thwarted when his French peer is eventually promoted while he is not. Abdelkader also knows how to read and aspires to becoming a *sergent chef*, an ambition borne out by his heroic discourse and leadership. Nevertheless, it could be argued that his heroism is unrecognized, perhaps unrecognizable, within French consciousness at the time the film is set. Despite the film's recourse to the stock emotive clichés of war movie phraseology and cinematography, the "glory" (the film's American title is *Days of Glory*) goes not to Abdelkader but to liberating troops from the regular army. Abdelkader's superior mobility between the linguistic codes of French and Arabic, his insistence on literacy lessons for the North African troops, and the competence he displays beyond the expectations of his commanders, however, each testifies to an agenda according to which (French) education can serve as the leveler of opportunity through which not only integration but success as a male citizen is attainable.

The battleground and the cemetery in *Indigènes* offer a compelling way of anchoring Maghrebi identities in France. This is undeniable both in the battle scene where Abdelkader yells "On va jusqu'au bout" [Let's go all the way] and in the final scene, which is a flash-forward to a cemetery in Alsace sixty years later where Abdelkader visits his compatriots' graves. While these scenes commemorate North African soldiers from the Second World War, they also suggest, through Bouchareb's foregrounding of their patriotism, a reference to France's colonial past and Algerian conflict that allows French cinema to glorify an Algerian as an insider representing *la patrie*. The film's box office success speaks all the more as a barometer of the willingness of filmgoers and critics alike to see this as an acceptable image of Maghrebis in France. In other words, Bouajila's physical incarnation of Abdelkader's aging and persistence marks a national place for North Africans that extends historical references to the present, serving as the "frame that redefines migration, thus creating a new context for its cultural memory" (Papanikolaou 2008, 191).

Queering the French Myth of *le garçon arabe*

Alec Hargreaves contends that *Beur* fiction in the period prior to the 1990s was marked by uncertainty and a concern with the imaginative and narrative process in constructing stable and coherent positions (1991, 2–8). Each of the cinematic roles for Sami Bouajila examined here raises questions about a belonging that is still negotiated with difficulty, a place within the French national imagination that is still uncertain but nonetheless conceivable. Perhaps, unlike the literary text, the identifications at work in cinema, given the particular role of a star in modeling positions of belonging, serve to construct and recast the national family more clearly.

Indeed, Bouajila's roles allow him to emerge as French star and role model for his many "little brothers." In the films examined here, he charts paths toward integration into the French family and nation by destabilizing a number of categories including ethnicity, gender, and sexuality in relation to male roles such as brothers, partners, and fathers. Yet his characters still occupy somewhat ambivalent geographies of belonging, their positions often precarious, their roles mitigated, mediated, or unaccented, as the case may be. Nevertheless, Bouajila's star chart renders social categories porous and fluid, showing that what it means to be both a *Beur* and French man is now capable of being reimagined. In other words, Bouajila's characters, through their ethnic, social, and sexual flexibilities, allow national and familial belonging to be redefined and queered (in the sense that he defamiliarizes normative assumptions about each, revealing what is performative, troubling, or unfamiliar in their everyday operations) — in ways that exert pressure on hegemonic notions of conformity within the French national family (Provencher 2007a, 21). Bouajila's characters also serve to integrate the *Beur* body into an expanded French family as they unite belongings, heritages, and identifications in ways that resignify both the "French male" and *le garçon arabe* within the domestic and national sphere. Moreover, it is through this star's modeling of new pathways and his cinematic role as the good big brother that Bouajila points to possibilities of belonging, on- and offscreen, for an entirely new generation of French characters, actors, spectators, and citizens.

Notes

1. As an indication of this variety, we have included ticket sales information for each film, all drawn from the Lumière database (http://lumiere.obs.coe.int/web/search/).

2. Ticket sales for these films are 92,457 and 76,149, respectively.

3. Following Tarr (2005, 3–4), we use *Beur* to refer to French-born citizens of Maghrebi descent and italicize it to indicate its contested history.

4. See Surkis (2006) for an example of scholarship that illustrates how normative performances of masculinity are tied to acceptable models of male citizenship and belonging and how alternate forms have long been scorned or excluded from the Republic.

5. Following Tarr, we use *"Beur* filmmaking" for films about French-born citizens of Maghrebi descent (2005, 9–17) and *"banlieue* filmmaking" for films about multiethnic French suburbs, often depicting social division (17–21). *Le bled* is slang for "a small place" in French and for "country" in Arabic, often used in reference to remote villages in real or imagined homelands for characters of Maghrebi descent.

6. See Pratt (2004) for a discussion of readings that consider how Félix "just happens" to be gay in *Drôle de Félix*.

7. Jacques Chirac is reported to have changed policy such that foreign veterans' pensions were brought into line with those paid to French soldiers.

References

Anderson, Benedict. 1983. *Imagined Communities: Reflections on the Origin and Spread of Nationalism*. New York: Verso.

Bourdieu, Pierre. 1993. "A propos de la famille comme catégorie réalisée." *Actes de la Recherche en Sciences Sociales* 100:32–36.

———. 1994. "Stratégies de reproduction et modes de domination." *Actes de la Recherche en Sciences Sociales* 105:3–12.

Fassin, Eric. 1998. "L'illusion anthropologique: Homosexualité et filiation." *Témoin* 12:43–56.

Grandena, Florian. 2006. "L'homosexualité en dehors de l'homosexualité: Expressions de l'identité gay dans les films d'Olivier Ducastel et Jacques Martineau." *Contemporary French Civilization* 30 (3): 63–86.

Guénif-Souilamas, Nacira, and Eric Macé. 2004. *Les féministes et le garçon arabe*. La Tour d'Aigues: Éditions de l'Aube.

Hargreaves, Alec. 1991. *Voices from the North African Immigrant Community in France: Immigration and Identity in Beur Fiction*. Oxford: Berg.

Hayward, Susan. 2005. *French National Cinema*. London: Routledge.

Higbee, Will. 2001. "Hybridity, Space, and the Right to Belonging: Maghrebi-French Identity at the Crossroads in Karim Dridi's *Bye-Bye*." In *France on Film: Reflections on Popular French Cinema*, ed. Lucy Mazdon, 51–64. London: Wallflower Press.

Léger, Jack-Alain. 2003. *Tartuffe fait Ramadan*. Paris: Denoël.

Papanikoloaou, Dimitris. 2008. "New Queer Greece: Thinking Identity through Constantine Giannaris's *From the Edge of the City* and Ana Kokkinos's *Head On.*" *New Cinemas: Journal of Contemporary Film* 6 (3): 183–96.

Pratt, Murray. 2004. "Félix and the Light-Hearted Gay Road Movie: Genre, Families, Fathers and the Decolonization of the Homosexual Self." *Australian Journal of French Studies* 41 (3): 88–101.

———. 2006. "Authorship, Impersonation, and the Republic: Outing Ali le Magnifique." *Essays in French Literature* 43 (July): 147–74.

Provencher, Denis M. 2007a. "Maghrebi-French Sexual Citizens: In and Out on the Big Screen. *Cineaste* 33 (1): 47–51.

———. 2007b. *Queer French: Globalization, Language, and Sexual Citizenship in France.* Aldershot: Ashgate Publishing.

———. 2008. "Tracing Sexual Citizenship and Queerness in *Drôle de Félix* (2000) and *Tarik el Hob* (2003)." *Contemporary French and Francophone Studies (SITES)* 12 (1): 51–61.

Rees-Roberts, Nick. 2008. *French Queer Cinema.* Edinburgh: Edinburgh University Press.

Surkis, Judith. 2006. *Sexing the Citizen: Morality and Masculinity in France, 1870–1920.* Ithaca NY: Cornell University Press.

Swamy, Vinay. 2006. "Gallic Dreams? The Family, PaCS and Kinship Relations in Millennial France." *Studies in French Cinema* 6 (1): 53–64.

Tarr, Carrie. 2005. *Reframing Difference:* Beur *and* Banlieue *Filmmaking in France.* Manchester: Manchester University Press.

Vincendeau, Ginette. 2000. *Stars and Stardom in French Cinema.* London: Continuum.

Filmography

Bégéja, Liria, dir. *Change-moi ma vie*, 2001.

Blanc, Michel, dir. *Embrassez qui vous voudrez*, 2002.

Bouchareb, Rachid, dir. *Indigènes*, 2006.

Dridi, Karim, dir. *Bye-Bye*, 1995.

Ducastel, Olivier, and Jacques Martineau, dirs. *Drôle de Félix*, 2000.

Kechiche, Abdellatif, dir. *La faute à Voltaire*, 2001.

Rapp, Bernard, dir. *Pas si grave*, 2003.

Sinapi, Jean-Pierre, dir. *Vivre me tue*, 2002.

Téchiné, André, dir. *Les témoins*, 2007.

12

REPACKAGING THE *BANLIEUES*

Malik Chibane's *La trilogie urbaine*

Vinay Swamy

Since the mid-1980s, *Beur* and *banlieue* filmmaking has traced the
particular histories of immigrant and marginalized populations that
have otherwise gone largely underrepresented in French cinema.[1]
As the terms *banlieue* and *Beur* indicate, this cinema has often
been characterized by the way in which it privileges representations of the mostly unequal relationship between mainstream
France and those in the margins of French society, both quite
literally — given the peripheral locations of the suburbs or *banlieues* — as well as culturally, as indicated by the adjective *Beur* (a
qualifier for descendants of Maghrebi immigrants to France). As
contested as it might be, this term has nevertheless gained currency
and has been frequently used by the media since the last decade
of the twentieth century.[2] While some have chosen to represent in
explicit terms the tension resulting from the imbalance in power
dynamics between the "center" and the "periphery" (Kassovitz's
1995 film *La haine* being the most often cited example), the films
by Malik Chibane can be distinguished by the way in which they
unapologetically focus on the suburb and its denizens. Moreover,

in returning to the *banlieue* setting to develop the subject of each of his three feature films, spanning ten years, Chibane has created a unique, if evolving, perspective on ethnic, class, and cultural difference.[3]

So, in this essay, I would like to foreground Chibane's *La trilogie urbaine*, a newly repackaged triptych — comprising *Hexagone* (1994), *Douce France* (1995) and *Voisins, voisines* (2005) — to consider how, in the eyes of this cineaste, *Beur* and *banlieue* life has evolved from the mid-1990s through the turn of the millennium. In presenting teenagers, young adults, parents, as well as retirees in the three films, Chibane not only emphasizes the particular issues his marginalized protagonists face at each stage of life but also gives us inroads into understanding the changing nature of tradition (be they French, Maghrebi, or other) and its intimate rapport with the politics of identity formation in suburban locales. In particular, focusing on the last film, *Voisins, voisines*, and the way in which it weaves hip-hop culture with its understanding of "Frenchness," I would like to underscore how, while the republican ideal of integration remains at the heart of Chibane's project, his films nevertheless attempt to allow for ethnic, class, and cultural difference as inevitable and even necessary manifestations of a healthy Republic. In so doing, this essay will suggest that Chibane's project straddles the so-called communitarian/republican divide that has been the subject of much debate in contemporary France.

In order to contextualize the themes broached in the *Urban Trilogy*, let us begin by considering Chibane's own career as social commentator, activist, and filmmaker, which spans almost two decades. His extensive presence on television and radio is revealing. Between 1991 and 2009, the radio and television database at the Institut National de l'Audiovisuel (INA) documents fourteen telecasts of documentaries directed by Chibane, three full-length fictional telefilms, and several appearances as a participant in radio (forty) or television (eight) programs either as discussant or to promote his feature films. Furthermore, while mostly shown on France 2 and Arte channels, Chibane's programs on television have also aired on TF1, France 2, France 3, Canal+, TV 5, and M6 channels; the radio stations France Culture and France Inter have regularly featured him, with occasional programs on Radio France Internationale (RFI) and Radio Monte Carlo (RMC).

This survey is notable as much for numerical abundance as the variety of public roles Chibane has undertaken over the years: he has appeared as a participant in social and political debates, documentaries, and talk shows; as a producer of documentaries and films; as a journalist for special programs, and most significantly, as director of both fictional narratives as well as social commentaries. For instance, Chibane participated in a high-profile television debate on TF1 (*Le droit de savoir*, March 26, 1996) with Charles Pasqua — the erstwhile right-wing interior minister (1986–88, 1993–95) and senator since 2004 representing the Hauts-de-Seine department — whose draconian policies on immigration and policing the *banlieues* have been strongly criticized, and his documentary film *Faut-il être blanc pour être élu? (Does One Have to be White to be Elected?)* was broadcast on Arte (June 11, 2002), as was a feature-length drama *Nés quelque part* (Arte, January 19, 1998). Most recently, *Le choix de Myriam*, a three-and-a-half hour fictional narrative, was telecast in two parts on France 3 (May 9, 2009). This film recounts the life of Myriam and her family from her arrival in the 1960s and gradual integration over the next thirty or so years.

Such a quantitative approach to assessing Chibane's contribution assumes that the statistics show the extent to which Chibane (perhaps unlike many other children of immigrants of his age) has been successful in making his voice heard in the debates on integration, and thus, by most measures, has acquired the mantle of public spokesperson. For, following this logic, if the so-called *Beur* generation has matured and many of them have become middle-aged parents of a younger "third" generation (that is to say, those whose grandparents immigrated from the Maghreb), such a generation ought to have by and large found an equilibrium with and in metropolitan French society. Indeed, official recognition and legitimization of Chibane's standing has also been forthcoming: from 2001 to 2004, Chibane served on the *Avance sur recettes* commission (committee responsible for advancing loans based on projected ticket sales) of the Centre National du Cinéma et de l'image animée (CNC) (Lemercier 2003). Given that he himself, like many of his counterparts, had enormous difficulty in finding funding for his first film, Chibane's participation in such a commission is a particularly interesting indicator of integration into the French production system.[4]

In light of this long-standing commitment to the visual medium, Chibane's predilection for engaging with social issues in his interventions also bears comment. Chibane's subject choice is evidently linked to his understanding of the role of cinema in French society, a perspective that is most clearly enunciated in a 2003 article cowritten with his brother and sometime collaborator, Kader Chibane, and titled "Le cinéma postcolonial des banlieues renoue avec le cinéma politique" ("*Banlieue* Postcolonial Cinema Reengages with Political Cinema"). The authors insist on the importance of the role of social cinema as archival resource, a repository of collective memory that bears witness on our times. Moreover, in their words, "Si [les films des banlieues] créent un malaise, c'est parce qu'ils représentent un espace de la société qui n'est pas représenté politiquement" [If *banlieue* films create a sense of discomfort, it is because they represent a social space that is not politically represented] (2003, 37). That is to say, as their 2003 teledocumentary *La France black, blanc, beur, sauf en politique* (*France Black, White, Beur, Except in Politics*) notes cuttingly that, unlike in some other European nations with large immigrant populations — Britain, the Netherlands, Germany, or Belgium — there is yet to be an elected representative of Maghrebi origin in the French parliament, despite the long-standing presence of people of Maghrebi origin in metropolitan France, most of whom have been citizens (either from birth or naturalized) for several decades.[5]

Thus, as the following concluding remarks of their essay indicate, implicitly for the Chibanes, cinema has to bear its fair share of the social burden, even if only through the act of bearing witness, of beginning the immense ideological work necessary for political (and thus social) change: "En captant l'humeur de son temps, en l'immortalisant sur la pellicule, [le cinéma] a avant tout une valeur de témoignage" [In capturing the mood of its times and immortalizing it on film, cinema has value primarily as a bearer of witness] (2003, 38). Given Malik Chibane's commitment to such a political project, I would like to pose the following questions: how does *La trilogie urbaine* in particular represent the director's political impetus, and in what ways do these films not only "witness" but also enter into dialogue with the debate about the successes or failures of French society's goal of integrating all its citizens under the umbrella of the Republic?

Even a cursory survey of *Beur* and *banlieue* filmmaking from the 1980s and 1990s renders evident a particular preponderance for a frank, and perhaps even stark, portrayal of the disenfranchised youth culture in this quasi-subgenre.[6] As Carrie Tarr has aptly recognized, these films seek to demonstrate the basic "humanity" of the *Beurs* (and other ethnically and economically marginalized individuals and groups) (2005, 210), a motive that is consistent with the desire to highlight the problems posed by (and more rarely the successes of) the integration imperative. However, in choosing to focus on the lives of what is essentially one, albeit sizable and highly visible, segment of a diverse *banlieue* population, films that foreground the lives of *banlieue* youth — *Le thé au harem d'Archimède* through *La haine* and beyond — have necessarily had to neglect narrating a variety of other perspectives, be they age-, gender-, or work-related. As a result, some of the stereotypes — of unemployed, drug-peddling delinquent and violent youth, for example — sometimes run the risk of being unfortunately reinforced, if not inadvertently propagated. Even Abdellatif Kechiche's 2005 multiple César winner, *L'esquive*, which attempts (for the most part successfully) to dispel such stereotypes of delinquency, is limited in scope with regard to a representation of *banlieue* life. There is room for only two adults in Kechiche's narrative — Krim's mother and the protagonists' drama teacher — both of whose roles remain peripheral to the diegesis, a position that is indicated also by the fact that they remain nameless.

In contrast, all three films in Chibane's trilogy seem to have been particu-larly mindful of these kinds of issues and have tried to redress such discrep-ancies by carefully giving voice to protagonists at various stages of life. It is in this context that we should understand the trilogy: three films that are marked by their epoch, and at the same time mark the historic moments in which they were produced. Furthermore, the three films were first released separately before they were repackaged as *La trilogie urbaine* (the collective title first appeared only with the boxed DVD set in 2007). Even if it was meant only as a marketing ploy, this re-release invites us to consider whether there has been an evolution not only diegetically speaking, in terms of each film's successive approach to integration, for example, but also in the way in which they can retroactively be seen as part of a coherent (and integrated?) vision of suburban denizens' lives.

Hexagone

Hexagone, the first of the three films, is in this sense perhaps the most social-realist film of the trilogy. A "film du constat et de solidarité" — to make an amalgam of two of the new realist categories suggested by the film critic Franck Garbarz in the review *Positif* (1997, 74) — *Hexagone* focuses on five young adults, including Slimane (Jalil Naciri) and Staf (Hakim Sarahoui) and their friends, and witnesses the suburban lifestyle of the *Beur* youth of the times. Any reference to the older generation only highlights the way in which the youths distance themselves from the traditions adhered to by their parents. Thus, for instance, Slim is very critical of his mother's religious beliefs, and Staf's father is unable to comprehend his son's penchant for fashionable clothes despite being unemployed. The generational gap is also presented as one that is compounded by a growing cultural gap that separates the

French-born youth from the generation of their immigrant parents. Moreover, the young women foregrounded in *Hexagone* take on positions that decry the largely held stereotype that French women of Maghrebi decent are docile, submissive, and ill-treated by the men in the family.[7] For instance, it is Nacéra (Faiza Kaddour), Slim's girlfriend of Moroccan origin, who actively pursues stability, sexual intimacy (she even suggests creative ways to have sex), and public recognition of their relationship, and even dares to confront a reluctant Slim in his own home. If not a runaway success at the box office (47,300 entries), *Hexagone*'s success with the critics can in part be explained by the nuanced positions that its *Beur* protagonists are allowed to take.

The film's critical success is partly related to its frank portrayal of the effects of the socioeconomic crisis in which youth from the *banlieues* found themselves caught as they attempted to find gainful employment. If much of Slimane and Staf's machinations revolve around figuring out the best way to get around the requirements of the ANPE (Agence Nationale pour l'Emploi, the state-run employment agency) to find a job, it is also an indication of the limits of the state in its integration project. For *Hexagone* not only shows Staf's failures at the personal level but we are given to understand that he and his friends have an uphill struggle convincing the laconic state officials to help them. This point is clearly, if not so subtly, developed in a scene in which even Slimane, who is portrayed as the more competent of the two friends, has to rely on the benevolence of an ANPE female employee of Maghrebi descent to ensure that his application for an internship is even read.

Slimane implores the employee for help, claiming that his whole family is on the other side of the Mediterranean and so he does not have relatives to help him network like the French. The woman retorts incisively, "Vous êtes pas français?" [You aren't French?], thus deftly confronting him with thorny questions of citizenship, belonging, and legitimacy. With what amounts to a veiled critique of the republican ideology that the woman implicitly invokes, Slimane quickly replies, "Si, si, vous m'avez compris" [Yes, you understand what I mean]. Thus, Slimane acknowledges the reality (and disadvantage) of being marginalized due to his ethnic (Maghrebi) origins in a supposedly egalitarian Republic, before proceeding to turn his "handicap" into an advantage by establishing a connection and even flirting with her.

Interestingly, although *Hexagone* is successful in foregrounding the interests of the Maghrebi community in France and plays to that audience, it does so, as Tarr observes, by almost evacuating "white French male voices" (2005, 60). It is also perhaps for those reasons that for Tarr, the film portrays the trials and tribulations of its protagonists as "little different from the problems and aspirations of French working-class youth in general" (2005, 60), with added dimensions of racism and questions of inclusion. Read from this perspective, the significance of the film's title, a term often used to refer to metropolitan France as a whole, becomes all the more evident: the story of Slim and his friends is also meant to be a *French* story. Yet, in the end, *Hexagone*'s refreshingly nonviolent representation of *banlieue* youth life could also be its foible. As Mireille Rosello has noted, "Chibane's decision to multiply roles [might] also be translated into a stereotypical list" (1997, 72) — that is to say, the drug addict brother, the *beurgeois* student, the unemployed youth who does not respect the law, a mother who has blind faith in Maraboutism and so on. We can draw from both Tarr's and Rosello's remarks the critique that the film's position risks falling into a progressist logic of integration that posits a future in which a "perfectly" integrated republic is in the offing.

Douce France

The second film, *Douce France*, uses comedy to further Chibane's critical observations of the contemporary French *banlieue*.[8] This time around, we have left the HLMs (state-subsidized housing) for a suburban small-town or village-style environment. Furthermore, in this instance the film highlights not only the lives of the young(er) adults but also those of their parents, as well as the relationship between the two generations. Though the youths of *Hexagone* have grown a little older in this film, there is a continuity that is marked in part through recasting Hakim Sarahoui, who played Staf in the first film, as Moussa in the second.[9] *Douce France* recounts the pressures of work and family life (Moussa's mother goes to great lengths to get him married) forming the battle lines that Moussa has to face. This second film also goes further than *Hexagone* in foregrounding an interethnic friendship and collaboration between the two main protagonists, Moussa and Jean-Luc (Frédéric Diffenthal). Moreover, and perhaps more importantly, in a marked departure from the earlier film, the upholders of Islamic tradition are not just the parents, but the tradition-touting Farida (Fadila Belkebla), who is the sister of Jean-Luc's love interest, the ultra-fashionable and rejecter-of-religion, Souad (Seloua Hamse). In giving the sisters such prominent roles, the film makes more room than *Hexagone* for women's voices to be heard.

In highlighting Farida's insistence on wearing the headscarf, Chibane reflects on one of the main preoccupations of the 1990s, engendered by the "headscarf affair," which first erupted in 1989, a few years prior to the film's release. Farida is portrayed as wishing to retain her identity as a pious Muslim woman, despite being highly educated in the French system: she has a "bac plus deux" [two years of university], is studying for a degree in law (*Licence en droit*), and is superbly articulate. Farida's adamant adoption of the headscarf is not just a religious belief,[10] but a principled stance made on the basis of a well-informed and historicized understanding of the notion of *laïcité*.[11] We learn about her nuanced understanding of this concept when she interviews for a teaching job at the local cultural center. Farida is told that her application would not be successful — although her credentials (*bac plus deux*) are more than sufficient — because her insistence on wearing the headscarf goes against the principles of laïcité: "C'est un lieu d'intégration ici . . . le centre social est un lieu public fondé sur la notion intangible de laïcité" [This is a space that promotes integration . . . the social center is a public place that is founded on the intangible notion of laïcité]. Farida responds by saying: "La laïcité, c'était reprendre les biens du clergé pour avoir collaboré avec la monarchie. L'exclusion pour particularisme, ce n'est pas en phase avec l'esprit des droits de l'homme de 1789" [Laïcité was conceived to strip the church, which had collaborated with the monarchy, of its resources. Exclusion on grounds of particularism goes against the spirit of the 1789 Declaration of the Rights of Man]. Here, Farida is referring to the history of laïcité, the inception of which dates to the 1905 law (*Loi du 9 décembre 1905 concernant la séparation des Églises et de l'État*) that established the neutrality of the state with regard to religious practices. As Bowen elucidates, this separation came about only after a protracted power struggle during the first three decades of the Third Republic (1870–1940) between the church and the anticlerical factions, prompting the latter to lean toward the construction of a secular state (2007, 22–27). Farida's outburst reveals that her perspective is not just founded on a desire to practice her religious "particularism" in the French public space; her argument goes much further in harnessing republican principles to render legitimate her sartorial practice. Thus, the religious-cultural factor, in this instance, is relegated to a secondary position while the political ideological factor (republican) is privileged.

In this respect, *Douce France* constitutes Chibane's intervention in the long decade of debates about the wearing of the *hijab* in public school.[12] However, the film could also be read as ultimately ensconced in a largely endorsed popular viewpoint that ultimately holds a narrow interpretation of the principle of laïcité as integral to French citizenship. This position is clearly indicated by Farida's untying and abandoning of the headscarf in the concluding sequence of the film. Such a dramatic gesture comes across as liberatory, albeit mitigated by the fact that it is perhaps a reluctant and certainly tearful surrendering, on Farida's part, of Islamic sartorial tradition. The film prepares the viewer for this surprising moment by staging, in the penultimate sequence, what ought to be understood retrospectively as a revelatory moment that acts as the trigger for the literal and cinematic dénouement. In an airport restroom, with the classic use of the mirror, Chibane confronts Farida with the image of young women from a traditional Islamic society getting ready to return to their country.[13] The explicit suture shot in this sequence shows the two coquettishly dressed women donning their haiks as they discuss, ironically but fittingly, the latest fashion (Jean Paul Gaultier). Farida watches (herself watching) them in the mirror, prompting her to question the rapport between religious piety, external clothing, and her own relationship to such practices.

At first, Farida's symbolic relinquishing of the headscarf in the next, and concluding, sequence indicates a reconciliation with her sister, Souad, who is shown smiling as Farida tearfully lets go of her *hijab*. More importantly, it suggests that it is Farida's realization (through mirrored metonymic substitution) of the supposed hypocrisy of the two fashionable women that triggers her to abandon her firmly held belief in the external manifestation of her religious piety in a public space. In other words, Farida, who struggled throughout the film to be fully integrated into French society *as is*, ultimately admits that the headscarf, and the difference that it signifies, only hinders her quest for a place within a *douce* France and that the "ideal" it represents has been shattered by the sight of these women. In filming this dramatic conclusion, Chibane indicates his espousal of traditional republican values as the bedrock of French society. Yet, as we shall see in the last film, this does not preclude him from advocating a pluri-ethnic and pluri-religious vision (as indicated also by *Douce France*'s inclusion of the community's plans to build a mosque) for a contemporary France.

Voisins, voisines

In many ways the last film of the trilogy makes most explicit the political position articulated by the Chibanes in their 2003 essay on *banlieue* film. Released in 2005, ten years after *Douce France*, *Voisins, voisines* strays farthest, at first blush, from the burning social questions (unemployment, integration, and Islam, for instance) that form the subject material of the earlier films: its central plot focuses on a rap musician's writer's block. Furthermore, the high production values of this glossy film, which borrows from the genre of the musical, sets it apart from the grittier feel and editing of *Hexagone* and *Douce France*, both of which tend to rely on the use of static shots and of shot-countershot sequences, giving them an amateurish feel at times. *Voisins, voisines* is also perhaps the most sophisticated of the three films in that it marries elements of hip-hop culture and French rap music with the cinematic medium, and so in these ways is the farthest removed from the *film du constat* style of the social realist film.[14] However, it is this very innovation that gives *Voisins, voisines* its critical purchase and the space to explore the question of social belonging and citizenship. Furthermore, it is also the only film in the trilogy that is not specifically centered around *Beurs* or characters of Maghrebi origin. This decentering is no doubt indicative of a social shift, turning the preoccupation of the director's generation from the activist 1980s (of the *Marche des beurs* period) to a more pragmatic approach to integration. In this, *Voisins, voisines* clearly enunciates a perspective informed by the republican ideal of social *mixité*.

Set in the Résidence Mozart, a former state-run HLM turned condominium complex, the film is narrated by a rap singer of some fame, Moussa Diop (played by the slam and rap artist Insa Sané). Moussa's desire to stay true to his suburban roots makes him take up residence in a flat bequeathed to him by his mother in the Résidence Mozart. Battling writer's (composer's) block, try as he might, Moussa is not able to produce an album with ten songs, and the deadline is fast approaching. So Moussa decides to observe his neighbors because, after all, as he puts it, the life and struggles of *banlieusards* are the stuff and essence of rap songs. But much to Moussa's dismay, the mundane reality of quotidian life in the "F" wing of Résidence Mozart yields no inspiration.[15] We hear him rapping, "Mes nuits et mes feuilles sont blanches, blanches, à cause de mes voisins qui se repassent les mêmes disques, revivent les mêmes événements" [My nights are sleepless, as my pages are wordless, for my neighbors' lives are a broken record].

This very observation is in and of itself significant, for the ultra-ordinary that characterizes the Résidence Mozart makes it the antithesis of the dramatic images of the *quartier chaud* ("dangerous" neighborhood) that stand in for the *banlieue* in the popular media, and with which the French public are constantly fed. Chibane's judicious choice of a neighborhood where nothing happens, then, constitutes an intervention in the much-publicized debate about the unsubstantiated connection between newer immigration and the hyperviolent, and thus somehow supposedly un-French, *banlieue*.[16]

To an American public, Chibane's choice of Mozart residents might come across as a caricature, even if it is a symbolic representation of the different immigrant communities that make up much of suburban France today. Among others, there is the Muslim Monsieur Macer (Sarahoui), who is married, against all odds, to a Jewish lady; M. Malouf (Mohamed Fellag), who is from Algeria; or Paco Garcia (Diffenthal), the new building superintendent, whose family, we learn, is from Spain. Then there is Madame Patisson (Sarah Maldoror), who is evidently from the French Caribbean, and the newest immigrant of all, the Pakistani Monsieur Malik (Rajkumar Bhan), who does not speak much French. So why then, we might ask, does Chibane insist on this kind of tokenist representational style? Yet for the French, for whom social *mixité* as a concept is really key to upholding republican values, a scenario such as this one, in which different ethnic groups live together, is not so unrealistic.[17] The so-called *modèle anglo-saxon* or communitarian model is frowned upon in France. In fact, in their essay, Malik and Kader Chibane even harness Spike Lee's wariness of identitarian politics in order to further their argument that the republican ideal of integration through social *mixité* can be achieved *à la française*:

> [le] projet républicain et jacobin [français] semble éprouver des difficultés à s'exprimer dans une société décentralisée, ultra médiatisée, où les images qui par nature sont émotionnelles se multiplient, avec la volonté, entre autre, d'attribuer tel faciès à telle communauté. Cette attitude ressemble de plus en plus au réflexe anglo-saxon d'une société fondée sur le communautarisme. Dans son film, *Do the Right Thing*, qui a profondément influencé les banlieues-films, Spike Lee ne cache pas son profond pessimisme devant ce type de modèle où l'individu n'existe que par et pour son identification au groupe ou à la communauté. [The French Jacobin and republican project seems to be experiencing difficulty in making itself heard in a decentralized media-driven society in which images that are by nature emotional, proliferate, with the urge, among others, to attribute a (racial) profile to particular communities. More and more, this approach resembles the Anglo-Saxon reflex of a society founded on communitarianism. In his film *Do the Right Thing*, which profoundly influenced *banlieue*

films, Spike Lee does not hide his profound pessimism regarding this type of model in which the individual only exists due to and in connection with his identification with the group or community.] (2003, 38)

However, in the film, Chibane makes it clear that in reality, not all identities are perceived equally. The vocal remarks made by Madame Gonzales (Anémone) regarding Paco's heritage are revealing:

— Paco c'est François en espagnol? Moi aussi je suis d'origine espagnole, mais du côté de mon père. Il y a longtemps que ses ancêtres, ils sont partis ils ont fui l'inquisition. Sépharade paraît que ça veut dire espagnol.
— Vous êtes d'où?
— De Tunisie.
[Madame Gonzalez: "Paco is Spanish for François? Me too, I am of Spanish origin, but on my father's side. It's been a long time now that his ancestors left — they fled the Inquisition. Sephardic apparently means Spanish."
Paco: "Where are you from?"
Madame Gonzalez: "From Tunisia."]

Here, despite Madame Gonzalez's almost dismissive statement, the fact that she compares her lineage to that of Paco clearly indicates that, to her, one's origins are important, especially as in her case they invoke closer ties to Europe, even though her Jewish ancestors moved to Tunisia during the Spanish Inquisition, that is to say about five hundred years ago. Later in the film, referring to Monsieur Malouf's Algerian identity, she remarks, "Ils l'ont l'indépendance de l'Algérie. Même à la retraite il reste ici rien que pour m'emmerder" [Algerians got their independence. Although he has retired, he is staying on here, just to bug me]. This comment not only suggests that she considers Muslim denizens of Maghrebi origin in Résidence Mozart not to be quite as French as her, but also invokes the ghost of a colonial past if only to justify a prejudiced present. The double irony of it all is that not only does she not consider her Tunisian roots, but being French affords Madame Gonzales no security in her own retirement. We are given to understand that she and her husband do not have substantial savings, and given that the little she earned as babysitter was paid "under the table," she cannot depend on the national retirement plan. So, we learn that she is in the process of applying for an Israeli passport in the hope that the Jewish state will take care of her.

If Madame Gonzalez's point of view is not so subtly discriminatory, Monsieur Malouf has no trouble in telling his neighbors of the overtly egregious discrimination he has to face even after forty years in France. A significant part of the plot device revolves round him trying to get the mayor's office to sanction a section in the town cemetery for Muslims to bury their dead. He reveals his Algerian identity to us and to Paco early on in the film when he shows a tattoo of a star, only visible when he holds his hand up, shaping his thumb and forefinger in a crescent and thus reminiscent of the Algerian flag. But much to his consternation, Monsieur Malouf discovers that the tattoo is fast disappearing, prompting us to ponder if it is perhaps an all too convenient metaphor for the gradual assimilation of the likes of Monsieur Malouf into French society. After all, his children, much like many others in France, are not inclined to look after him in his old age. So, then, how can one understand Monsieur Malouf's position in French society? At what point can one consider him "French"? Moussa Diop answers in his inimitable hip-hop-style composition that "que l'on soit de Mozart ou que l'on soit d'ailleurs, rebelle ou gangster SDF ou seigneur, du nord ou du sud, de toutes les latitudes, tous du même pays, quand vient la nuit" [whether one is from Mozart or elsewhere, a rebel or a gangster, homeless or a nobleman, from the north or the south, from any latitude, when night falls, we are all from the same country]. Put another way, Moussa expounds on the validity of the motto "Liberty, Equality, Fraternity" in France today. Yet, while this rendering of poetic justice is mellifluous, in this rendition of equality it is only at nightfall that all differences are leveled and when one becomes French, an observation that conspicuously, and perhaps problematically, circumvents the long hours of daytime.

While Farida in *Douce France* had to eventually give up her adherence to overtly Islamic traditions in order to fully claim French citizenship, Moussa, by contrast, seems to advocate a much more tolerant, if not accepting, view of the Republic. And this "evolution," I argue, is in keeping with some of the recent public discussions of French responsibility to acknowledge today's multicultural reality. This debate is most clearly enunciated in the 2005 volume *La fracture coloniale*, edited by Pascal Blanchard and his historian colleagues. They are critical of what they call the false logic of having to choose between, on the one hand, a caricatured, or at least demonized, version of communitarianism that seems invented for the purpose of becoming a foil or counterexample that one has to oppose and, on the other hand, equally artificially rigid interpretations of republican approaches to understanding

French society. For them, much like Monsieur Malouf's assertion, a particular invocation of a minority ethnic group's memories and traditions does not weaken the Republic. Rather, it strengthens French society by recognizing difference to be part of the collective memories that help construct the nation (and cemeteries are after all *lieux de mémoires* [Nora 1984] par excellence). Moreover, such reconciliation is only possible when France confronts its colonial past, so that it can fully deal with its multicultural present, a present rendered multicultural not only by postcolonial migration but also by one that is inflected by globalization, as indicated by the presence of Malik, the Pakistani migrant. In allowing his protagonists to work out a solution for Malouf's conundrum, as improvised as it is, Chibane seems to advocate the kind of legitimization underscored by Blanchard and his colleagues.[18] This is most evident in the concluding sequence of the film in which we learn from Moussa's voice-over that he was successful in composing his music. We leave him dreaming about the day when his CD would be exhibited in a museum: "Si un jour des historiens ou des simples citoyens voulaient savoir comment on vivait réellement à 19 kilomètres de Paris au 21e siècle, ils se rendront sûrement dans un musée pour avoir plus d'information. Moi, je rêve alors que mon album y soit exposé pour être une trace vivante de ce passé" [If one day historians or the public would like to know how we really lived, nineteen kilometers from Paris, in the twenty-first century, they will surely go to a museum to get more information. I hope that my album will be exhibited there as the living trace of this past].

In other words, the rapper's perspective on suburban life is transformed quite literally into a *lieu de mémoire.* The act of physically fixing onto a CD a fleeting temporal art form that is music *and* exhibiting it in a public domain (the museum) doubly renders Moussa's song into a site of explicit collective memory. Put another way, granting Moussa's wish for immortalizing his narrative would turn his artistic contribution into official trace of a *banlieue* life engendered by *mixité sociale* of which the Résidence Mozart is emblematic. Read in conjunction with the Chibanes' essay, this conclusion of *Voisins, voisines* acts like the mirror sequence of *Douce France* in that it uses the trope of metonymic substitution, but this time with the director/auteur as the protagonist. As the brothers' writing indicates, perhaps Chibane hopes that, like Moussa's aspirations for his CD, his films, too, as a trilogy, will ultimately leave the trace of a particular collective memory that would otherwise have been erased. However, if Chibane's political and artistic projects do converge in the

concluding contemporary cinematic moment of *Voisins, voisines*, by definition the jury is still out on the impact of that memorialization. Although thus
far Malik Chibane's films have not enjoyed the same critical acclaim as films
by Abdellatif Kechiche (*L'esquive* [2004] and *La graine et le mulet* [2007])
or receive the same popular endorsement as films by Djamel Bensalah (*Le
ciel, les oiseaux et . . . ta mère* [2003]), they nevertheless present a coherent
perspective on the integration of descendants of Maghrebi immigrants in
France. The explicit retrospective re-presentation of the works as an urban
triptych thus allows Chibane to underscore both temporal links and spatial
continuities in his discussion of integration in France.

Notes

1. I am borrowing the terms "*Beur* and *banlieue* filmmaking" from the subtitle of
Carrie Tarr's groundbreaking 2005 monograph *Reframing Difference*, in which, rather
than using the terms as reified categories (*cinéma beur* for instance), she is careful to
"emphasize filmmaking as a set of changing practices" (2–3). By extension, I argue that
we ought to comprehend both the adjectives in that subtitle as also shifting in signification. To that end, this essay uses the terms *Beur* and *banlieue* not as reified, essential
categories but as shifting signifiers that mediate complex relationships between French
citizens of Maghrebi descent and France for the former, while the latter encapsulates the
experience of denizens of geographically peripheral spaces in their interactions within
an urban topography, whether or not the films include the traditionally (culturally and
physically) dominant center represented by the city in France.

2. For an in-depth analysis of the emergence of the term in the 1980s and its subsequent
contestation, see Alec Hargreaves (1997) and Sylvie Durmelat (2008).

3. *Hexagone* was entirely shot near Goussainville, where Chibane lived as a child and
adolescent. He has publicly acknowledged that film is a result of a desire to memorialize
the neighborhood in which he grew up, before the housing estate (HLM) was torn down
("Beur Is Beautiful" conference, New York, November 6–7, 2007); *Douce France* was
shot close by in Sarcelles, as was *Voisins voisines*. All three locations are in the northern
suburbs of Paris, in the Val d'Oise department.

4. As Bernard Génin notes, *Hexagone* took six years to complete and was produced
by a local association (IDRISS) that Chibane founded (1994, 37).

5. As of this writing in 2009, little over thirty years after France closed its doors to
non–European Union immigration, we witness the political inclusion of the French
citizens of Maghrebi descent only to unelected positions. For instance, Azouz Begag was
minister for affirmative action during 2005–7 in the Dominique de Villepin government,
and Rachida Dati and Fadela Amara were minister of justice in 2007–9 and secretary
of state for urban policies since 2007, respectively, in the François Fillon government.

6. See, for instance, *Le thé au harem d'Archimède* (Médhi Charef 1985) or *Raï* (Thomas
Gilou 1995) and *Ma 6-T va crack-er* (Jean François Richet 1997).

7. For more, see Nacira Guénif Souilamas's 2003 study, *Des Beurettes*, in which she demystifies some of the long-held stereotypes about adolescent girls and young women of Maghrebi origin.

8. The title evokes Charles Trénet's rather traditionally patriotic 1943 song, which was interestingly reprised in 1986 by the *Beur* (and activist) band Carte de séjour.

9. Chibane wagers on continuity in terms of casting for the trilogy: Hakim Sarahoui also appears as Monsieur Macer in the third film, while Frédéric Diffenthal, who plays Moussa's friend and business partner Jean-Luc, is cast as Paco, the building superintendent, in *Voisins voisines*. In addition, Zina Elm'Barki, who plays Slim's sister, Nora, in *Hexagone*, reappears as a minor character (Souad's hairdresser and friend) in *Douce France*. Thus, while we do not follow the particular lives of characters across three films, the links between them and others who belong to the same group are nevertheless advanced.

10. Her *hijab* is also challenged when a postal employee refuses to cash her check, claiming not to be able to verify her identity. Farida is also shown to be wily enough to seek the help of a fellow Muslim community member, who works at the municipal swimming pool, to allow her to swim during the pool's off-hours. A spectacularly silent close-up sequence shows her swimming in her head garb in an otherwise quiet and empty pool.

11. Roughly translated as "secularism," the French notion of *laïcité* is infused with a particular understanding of the separation of religion and state in the public sphere, a space that is understood to be governed by republican principles. For more on the historical development of this concept, see John R. Bowen (2007).

12. In the year following a major episode in 2003, pushed by widespread public support, the Republic proceeded to ban the headscarf (and other ostentatious religious symbols) by law in public schools.

13. A fairly common cinematic trope, such sequences draw upon a very literal and perhaps popular understanding of the mirror phase in Lacanian psychoanalysis, in which the character, like the child, is said to recognize his or her image in the mirror for the first time.

14. If hip-hop denotes the practices of an entire subculture that promotes values such as nonviolence, antiracism, the refusal of drugs and respect for others, rap refers more to the vocal style that embodies hip-hop culture.

15. As Alec Hargreaves remarks in chapter 1 of this volume, the "F" wing is supposedly an allegory for France.

16. It is rather unfortunate that the film was released just a few months before the October–November 2005 riots that swept across much of suburban France, thus drowning in the media coverage of that high-profile event.

17. In fact, achieving *mixité* in subsidized housing is an official, if disputed, policy. For a critique, see Samuel Thomas (2009).

18. Just before Monsieur Malouf unexpectedly dies, he manages to whisper to his neighbor, Alice (Gwendoline Hamon), that anyone who dies in the neighboring town has the right to be buried in its cemetery, where a section for Muslims has been allotted. So, Alice and Paco deposit Monsieur Malouf's body in that cemetery with the presumption that it will be discovered and given a proper Muslim burial.

References

Blanchard, Pascal, Nicolas Bancel, and Sandrine Lemaire, eds. 2005. *La fracture coloniale: La société française au prisme de l'héritage colonial*. Paris: Découverte.

Bowen, John R. 2007. *Why the French Don't Like Headscarves: Islam, the State, and Public Space*. Princeton NJ: Princeton University Press.

Chibane, Malik, and Kader Chibane. 2003. "Le cinéma post-colonial des banlieues renoue avec le cinéma politique." *Mouvements*, no. 27–28 (May/June/July/August): 35–38.

Durmelat, Sylvie. 2008. *Fictions de l'intégration: Du mot beur à la politique de la mémoire*. Paris: L'Harmattan.

Garbarz, Franck. 1997. "Le renouveau social du cinéma français." *Positif* 442:74–75.

Génin, Bernard. 1994. "Cité ciné." *Télérama*, February 2.

Guénif Souilamas, Nacira. 2003. *Des Beurettes*. Paris: Hachette.

Hargreaves, Alec. 1997. *Voices from the North African Immigrant Community in France: Immigration and Identity in Beur Fiction*. 2nd ed. Providence RI: Berg.

Lemercier, Fabien. 2003. "Le CNC étoffe ses commissions." Cineuropa.org, October 3. http://cineuropa.org/newsdetail.aspx?lang=fr&documentID=39079 (accessed September 12, 2009).

Nora, Pierre, ed. 1984. *Les lieux de mémoire*. Vol. 1. Paris: Gallimard.

Rosello, Mireille. 1997. *Declining the Stereotype: Ethnicity and Representation in French Cultures*. Hanover NH: University Press of New England.

Tarr, Carrie. 2005. *Reframing Difference:* Beur *and* Banlieue *Filmmaking in France*. Manchester: Manchester University Press.

Thomas, Samuel. 2009. "Le fichage ethno-racial = Un outil de discrimination." SOS Racisme report handed to Patrick Karam, délégué interministériel pour l'égalité des chances des Français d'outremer, November 4. http://www.latribune.fr/static/pdf/Karam.pdf (accessed November 15, 2009).

Filmography

Bensalah, Djamel, dir. *Le ciel, les oiseaux et . . . ta mère*, 1999.

Charef, Mehdi, dir. *Le thé au harem d'Archimède*, 1985.

Chibane, Malik, dir. *Hexagone*, 1994.

——, dir. *Douce France*, 1995.

——, dir. *Nés quelque part*, 1998 (telecast on Arte, January 19, 1998).

——, dir. *Faut-il être blanc pour être élu?*, 2002 (telecast on Arte, June 11, 2002).

——, dir. *Voisins, voisines*, 2005.

——, dir. *Le choix de Myriam*, 2009 (telecast on France 3, May 9, 2009).

Chibane, Malik, Nadia Hasnaoui, and Kader Chibane, dirs. *La France black, blanc, beur, sauf en politique*, 2003 (telecast on Arte, June 11, 2002).

Gilou, Thomas, dir. *Raï*, 1995.

Kassovitz, Mathieu, dir. *La haine*, 1995.

Kechiche, Abdellatif, dir. *L'esquive*, 2004.

——, dir. *La graine et le mulet*, 2007.

Richet, Jean François, dir. *Ma 6-T va crack-er*, 1997.

FILMOGRAPHY

YEAR	DIRECTOR	TITLE
1970	Drach, Michel	*Elise ou la vraie vie*
1973	Eustache, Jean	*La maman et la putain*
1977	Mizrahi, Moshe	*Madame Rosa*
1980	Le collectif Mohamed	*Ils ont tué Kader*
1981	Belghoul, Farida	*C'est Madame la France que tu préfères?*
1983	Okacha, Touita	*Les sacrifiés*
1985	Bahloul, Abdlekrim	*Le thé à la menthe*
	Bouchareb, Rachid	*Baton Rouge*
	Charef, Mehdi	*Le thé au harem d'Archimède*
	Gilou, Thomas	*Black mic-mac*
1987	Bégéja, Liria	*Avril brisé*
	Blain, Gérard	*Pierre et Djemila*
	Charef, Mehdi	*Miss Mona*
	Meynard, Serge	*L'œil au beurre noir*
1988	Brisseau, Jean-Claude	*De bruit et de fureur*

RELEASE DATE (FRANCE)	DISTRIBUTOR	TICKET SALES (FRANCE)
November 25, 1970	—	d
July 6, 1973	Tamasa Distribution	d
November 2, 1977	Columbia and Warner Brothers	d
—	—	d
—	—	d
March 23, 1983	Armor Films	4,858 a
February 27, 1985	Entreprises Françaises de Production	36,603 a
December 11, 1985	Films du Sémaphore and Films du Scorpion	72,222 b
June 6, 1985	KG Productions	171,221 a
April 23, 1985	Tamasa Distribution	490,686 a
December 9, 1987	Films du Sémaphore	d
May 27, 1987	AAA Classic and Noblesse Oblige	32,944 b
January 28, 1987	KG Production-Distribution	108,863 b
November 4, 1987	AAA-Revcom	235,314 b
June 1, 1988	Les Films du Losange	129,372 b

Unless otherwise stated, all figures for ticket sales are from the Council of Europe's Lumière database (http://lumiere.obs.coe.int).

a = Figures for Paris sales only (from the database of the Bibliothèque du Film [www.bifi.fr]).
b = Figures from Carrie Tarr, *Reframing Difference* (Manchester: Manchester University Press, 2005).
c = Figures from Bibliothèque du Film.
d = Figures not (yet) available or film made for television or Internet.
— = Data not available or not applicable.

YEAR	DIRECTOR	TITLE
1991	Bouchareb, Rachid	*Cheb*
1993	Courtois, Miguel	*Leïla née en France*
1994	Allouache, Merzak	*Bab El-Oued City*
	Bégéja, Liria	*Loin des barbares*
	Chibane, Malik	*Hexagone*
1995	Bouchareb, Rachid	*Poussières de vie*
	Chibane, Malik	*Douce France*
	Dridi, Karim	*Bye-Bye*
	Gilou, Thomas	*Raï*
	Kassovitz, Mathieu	*La haine*
1996	Allouache, Merzak	*Salut cousin!*
	Ghorab-Volta, Zaïda	*Souviens-toi de moi*
	Lauzier, Gérard	*Le plus beau métier du monde*
1997	Hamidi, Youcef	*Malik le maudit*
	Krim, Rachida	*Sous les pieds des femmes*
	Richet, Jean-François	*Ma 6-T va crack-er*
	Rochant, Eric	*Vive la République*
	Zemmouri, Mahmoud	*100% Arabica*
1998	Benguigui, Yamina	*Memoires d'immigrés: L'héritage maghrébin*
	Bouchareb, Rachid	*L'honneur de ma famille*
	Chibane, Malik	*Nés quelque part*
	Ruggia, Christophe	*Le gone du Chaâba*
1999	Bahloul, Abdelkrim	*La nuit du destin*
	Bensalah, Djamel	*Le ciel, les oiseaux et . . . ta mère!*
	Tavernier, Bertrand	*Ça commence aujourd'hui*
2000	Charef, Mehdi	*Marie-Line*
	Ducastel, Olivier, and Jacques Martineau	*Drôle de Félix*
	Faucon, Philippe	*Samia*
	Génestal, Fabrice	*La squale*
	Odoutan, Jean	*Djib*

RELEASE DATE (FRANCE)	DISTRIBUTOR	TICKET SALES (FRANCE)
June 5, 1991	Tadrart Films	62,096 b
May 19, 1993	Telecast on France 3	d
November 10, 1994	StudioCanal	62,000 a
April 13, 1994	KG Productions	2,414 c
February 2, 1994	StudioCanal	40,454 c
January 18, 1995	Tadrart Films	16,000 c
November 22, 1995	Ciné Classic	18,273 c
September 13, 1995	Diaphana	121,309 c
June 28, 1995	Pan Européenne Distribution	126,419 c
May 31, 1995	StudioCanal	1,978,328 c
November 20, 1996	AFMD	73,668
January 24, 1996	Pierre Grise Distribution	6,623
December 11, 1996	AMLF	2,266,511
September 3, 1997	Les Films du Roseau	1330 a
November 26, 1997	MEDIA II Distribution	26,597
July 2, 1997	Bac Films	67,800
November 5, 1997	Mars Distribution	145,822
November 5, 1997	Eurozoom	124,004
February 4, 1998	Cara M	85,266
January 30, 1998	Tadrart Films	d
January 19, 1998	Telecast on Arte	d
January 14, 1998	Océan Films	826,765
May 5, 1999	Les Films sur la place, ArtMattan Productions	1,784
January 20, 1999	Océan Films	1,233,737
March 12, 1999	Bac Films	877,798
December 20, 2000	Rezo Films	302,176
April 19, 2000	Pyramide Distribution	81,284
November 15, 2000	Pyramide Distribution	321,727
November 29, 2000	UFD (UGC Fox Distribution)	53,136
November 29, 2000	45 RDLC	1,246

YEAR	DIRECTOR	TITLE
2001	Bégéja, Liria	*Change-moi ma vie*
	Benguigui, Yamina	*Inch'Allah dimanche*
	Bouchaala, Ahmed, and Zakia	*Origine contrôlée*
	Bouchareb, Rachid	*Little Senegal*
	Kechiche, Abdellatif	*La faute à Voltaire*
	Serreau, Coline	*Chaos*
2002	Ameur-Zaïmeche, Rabah	*Wesh wesh, qu'est-ce qui se passe?*
	Blanc, Michel	*Embrassez qui vous voudrez*
	Chabat, Alain	*Astérix et Obélix: Mission Cléopâtre*
	Chibane, Malik	*Faut-il être blanc pour être élu?*
	Dupeyron, François	*Monsieur Ibrahim et les fleurs du Coran*
	Ghorab-Volta, Zaïda	*Jeunesse dorée*
	Philibert, Nicolas	*Etre et avoir*
2003	Allouache, Merzak	*Chouchou*
	Bedjaoui, Amal	*Un fils*
	Morel, Gaël	*Les chemins de l'oued*
	Rapp, Bernard	*Pas si grave*
	Sinapi, Jean-Pierre	*Vivre me tue*
2004	Barratier, Christophe	*Les choristes*
	Ferroukhi, Ismaël	*Le grand voyage*
	Gatlif, Tony	*Exils*
	Guène, Faïza	*Rien que des mots*
	Kechiche, Abdellatif	*L'esquive*
	Moknèche, Nadir	*Viva Ladjérie*
	Morel, Pierre	*Banlieue 13*
2005	Bensalah, Djamel	*Il était une fois dans l'oued*
	Chibane, Malik	*Voisins, voisines*
	Haneke, Michael	*Caché*
	Jolivet, Pierre	*Zim and co.*
	Legzouli, Hassan	*Ten'ja*
	Tasma, Alain	*Nuit noire, 17 octobre 1961*

RELEASE DATE (FRANCE)	DISTRIBUTOR	TICKET SALES (FRANCE)
November 28, 2001	Pan Européenne Distribution	76,149
December 5, 2001	ARP Séléction	126,846
January 24, 2001	United International Pictures	67,999
April 18, 2001	Tadrart Films	322,905
February 21, 2001	Rezo Films	92,493
October 3, 2001	Bac Films	1,161,494
May 1, 2002	Haut et Court	67,563
October 9, 2002	UGC Fox Distribution	1,472,906
January 30, 2002	Pathé Distribution	14,313,142
June 11, 2002	Telecast on Arte	d
September 17, 2002	ARP Séléction	324,366
February 27, 2002	MK2 Distribution	5,256
August 28, 2002	Les Films du Losange	1,813,520
March 19, 2003	Warner Brothers Pictures	3,961,067
August 24, 2003	Eurozoom	5,534
April 16, 2003	Pierre Grise Distribution	6,439
March 5, 2003	Pathé Distribution	203,497
June 18, 2003	Cinétévé Distribution	39,600
March 17, 2004	Pathé Distribution	8,355,432
November 24, 2004	Pyramide Distribution	76,501
August 25, 2004	Pyramide Distribution	302,356
—	les-engraineurs.org	d
January 7, 2004	Rezo Films	549,171
April 7, 2004	Les Films du Losange	192,471
November 10, 2004	EuropaCorp Distribution	929,971
October 19, 2005	Gaumont Columbia Tristar	876,855
July 20, 2005	Noé Distribution	41,193
October 5, 2005	Les Films du Losange	517,258
August 17, 2005	Bac Films	99,513
February 2, 2005	Pierre Grise Distribution	25,651
October 19, 2005	Les Acacias	921

YEAR	DIRECTOR	TITLE
2006	Ameur-Zaïmeche, Rabah	*Bled number one*
	Bouchareb, Rachid	*Indigènes*
	Faucon, Philippe	*La trahison*
	Herbier, Laurent	*Mon colonel*
	Rochant, Eric	*L'école pour tous*
2007	Charef, Mehdi	*Cartouches gauloises*
	Gilou, Thomas	*Michou d'Auber*
	Kechiche, Abdellatif	*La graine et le mulet*
	Téchiné, André	*Les témoins*
2008	Ameur-Zaïmeche, Rabah	*Dernier maquis*
	Cantet, Laurent	*Entre les murs*
	Chala, Samia	*Sauve qui peut!*
	Faucon, Philippe	*Dans la vie*
	Hami, Rachid	*Choisir d'aimer*
	Hamidi, Nora	*Des poupées et des anges*
2009	Amaouche, Nassim	*Adieu Gary*
	Bouchareb, Rachid	*London River*
	Chibane, Malik	*Le choix de Myriam*
	Laferrière, Gabriel	*Neuilly sa mère*
	Lilienfeld, Jean-Paul	*La journée de la jupe*
2010	Baroux, Olivier	*L'Italien*
	Bouchareb, Rachid	*Hors-la-loi*

RELEASE DATE (FRANCE)	DISTRIBUTOR	TICKET SALES (FRANCE)
June 7, 2006	Les Films du Losange	68,756
September 27, 2006	Mars Distribution	2,995,992
January 25, 2006	Pyramide Distribution	97,945
November 15, 2006	Pathé Distribution	32,022
October 18, 2006	Mars Distribution	326,212
August 8, 2007	Pathé Distribution	94,756
February 28, 2007	EuropaCorp Distribution	981,465
December 12, 2007	Pathé Distribution	738,735
March 7, 2007	UGC Distribution	385,540
October 22, 2008	Sophie Dulac Distribution	31,300
September 24, 2008	Haut et Court	1,561,763
—	Web film (Viméo)	d
March 12, 2008	Pyramide Distribution	85,530
July 2, 2008	Mars Distribution	d
June 25, 2008	Rezo Films	17,302
July 22, 2009	StudioCanal	125,378
April 29, 2009	Tadart Films	d
September 5, 2009	Telecast on France 3	d
August 12, 2009	UGC Distribution	2,452,007
March 25, 2009	Rezo Films	148,330
July 14, 2010	Pathé Distribution	d
September 22, 2010	StudioCanal	d

The following are non-French films and French films with no particular connection to filmmaking by and about descendants of Maghrebi migrants (ticket sales and release dates not included):

YEAR	DIRECTOR	TITLE	DISTRIBUTOR
1962	Varda, Agnès	*Cléo de 5 à 7*	Ciné Tamaris
1963	Cavalier, Alain	*Le combat dans l'île*	Pyramide Distribution
	Godard, Jean-Luc	*Le petit soldat*	Ciné Classic
	Marker, Chris	*Le joli mai*	Sofracima
	Resnais, Alain	*Muriel ou le temps d'un retour*	Tamasa Distribution
	Rozier, Jacques	*Adieu Philippine*	Théâtre du Temple
1964	Demy, Jacques	*Les parapluies de Cherbourg*	Ciné Tamaris
1966	Berri, Claude	*Le vieil homme et l'enfant*	Pathé Distribution
1975	Truffaut, François	*L'histoire d'Adèle H.*	Les Films du Carrosse
1976	Scorsese, Martin	*Taxi Driver*	Columbia Pictures
1980	Zulawski, Andrej	*Possession*	Marianne Productions
1983	Becker, Jean	*L'eté meurtrier*	Société Nouvelle de Cinématographie
	De Palma, Brian	*Scarface*	Universal Pictures
	Miller, Claude	*Mortelle randonnée*	Téléma Productions
1987	Krawczyk, Gérard	*L'été en pente douce*	Acteurs Auteurs Associés
	Madigan, Sylvain	*Sale destin*	Acteurs Auteurs Associés
1988	Nuytten, Bruno	*Camille Claudel*	Lilith Films
1989	Lee, Spike	*Do the Right Thing*	Universal Pictures
	Mouyal, Guy	*Et moi et moi*	Cinexport
1990	Lilienfeld, Jean-Paul, and Jean Schmoll	*Il n'y a guère que les actions qui montent ces temps-ci*	—

YEAR	DIRECTOR	TITLE	DISTRIBUTOR
1991	Braoudé, Patrick	*Génial, mes parents divorcent*	AFMD
	Scott, Ridley	*Thelma and Louise*	MGM
	Sebastian, Isabel	*La contre-allée*	Les Films Ariane
1994	Chéreau, Patrice	*La reine Margot*	Renn Productions
1995	Lilienfeld, Jean-Paul	*XY*	AFMD
1997	Lilienfeld, Jean-Paul	*Quatre garçons pleins d'avenir*	AMLF
1998	Gray, F. Gary	*The Negotiator*	Regency Enterprises
	Spielberg, Steven	*Saving Private Ryan*	DreamWorks and Paramount Pictures
2000	Lilienfeld, Jean-Paul	*HS*	Océan Films
2000	Tavernier, Bertrand	*Laissez-passer*	Les Films Alain Sarde
2003	Jacquot, Benoît	*Princess Marie*	Telecast on Arte
2004	Barratier, Christophe	*Les choristes*	Vega Film
	Lemercier, Valérie	*Palais royal!*	Les Films du Dauphin
2005	Howard, Ron	*The Da Vinci Code*	Columbia Pictures
2006	Fitoussi, Marc	*La vie d'artiste*	Haut et Court
2008	de Caunes, Antoine	*Coluche, l'histoire d'un mec*	Cipango Films

CONTRIBUTORS

HAKIM ABDERREZAK is assistant professor of French and Francophone studies in the Department of French and Italian at the University of Minnesota, Twin Cities. His research centers primarily on Maghrebi and *Beur* literature and cinema. He has published on the Tunisian film *Halfaouine, l'enfant des terrasses* (*Halfaouine: Boy of the Terraces*) and on the work of Algerian director Nadir Moknèche. His publications also include an interview with the Algerian writer Boualem Sansal, as well as an article on clandestine migration in Moroccan and Spanish literature. He is currently coediting a special issue of *Expressions maghrébines* on Maghrebi literature in languages other than Arabic or French. He is also working on a book project that examines contemporary Francophone, Spanish, and Arabic literary, musical, and cinematographic representations of irregular migratory patterns in the western Mediterranean.

MICHEL CADÉ is professor of contemporary history at the University of Perpignan Via Domitia and president of the Jean Vigo Institute, the Euroregional Cinémathèque responsible for the festival of film history and criticism Confrontations. His research focuses on cinema and society, particularly the representation of class and immigration in French cinema, and he has written widely on these and other topics. His publications include *L'histoire de France au cinéma*, with Marcel Oms and Pierre Guibert (Corlet, 1993); *L'Ecran bleu: La représentation des ouvriers dans le cinéma français* (Presses universitaires de Perpignan, 2000); and *La Retirada en images mouvantes* (Trabucaire, 2010).

SYLVIE DURMELAT is associate professor of French and Francophone studies in the Department of French at Georgetown University. She has published articles on narratives of immigration and integration in France, Algerian cinema, and on Caribbean literature. Her research interests, located at the crossroads between cultural studies and the analysis of literary and filmic texts, include colonial legacies and national discourses, and in particular the phantoms of the Algerian War of Independence. Her book *Fictions de l'intégration: Du mot "beur" à la politique de la mémoire* was published by L'Harmattan (2008). Her current book project is titled "The Taste of Empire: Table Matters and Food Exchanges between France and the Maghreb."

PATRICIA GEESEY is professor of French at the University of North Florida. She has published articles on Maghrebi literature and cinema and on North African immigration in France. Her translation of Mouloud Feraoun's *La terre et le sang* is forthcoming from the University of Virginia Press.

ALEC G. HARGREAVES is director of the Winthrop-King Institute for Contemporary French and Francophone Studies at Florida State University. A specialist on political, cultural, and media aspects of postcolonial minorities in France, he is the author and editor of numerous publications, including *Voices from the North African Immigrant Community in France: Immigration and Identity in Beur Fiction* (Berg, 1991; 2nd edition, 1997); *Immigration, "Race," and Ethnicity in Contemporary France* (Routledge, 1995); *Racism, Ethnicity, and Politics in Contemporary Europe*, coedited with Jeremy Leaman (Edward Elgar, 1995); *Post-Colonial Cultures in France*, coedited with Mark McKinney (Routledge, 1997); *Minorités postcoloniales anglophones et francophones: Études culturelles comparées* (L'Harmattan, 2004); *Memory, Empire, and Postcolonialism* (Lexington Books, 2005); *Multi-Ethnic France: Immigration, Politics, Culture and Society* (Routledge, 2007); and *Transnational French Studies: Postcolonialism and Littérature-monde*, coedited with Charles Forsdick and David Murphy (Liverpool University Press, 2010).

WILL HIGBEE is a senior lecturer in film studies at the University of Exeter. He has published numerous articles on contemporary French cinema, with a particular focus on Maghrebi-French (*Beur*), North African émigré, and *banlieue* filmmaking. He is the author of *Mathieu Kassovitz* (Manchester University Press, 2006) and coeditor of *Studies in French Cinema: UK Perspectives, 1985-2010* (Intellect, 2010). He is currently preparing a monograph for Edinburgh University Press titled *Cinemas of the North African Diaspora in France.*

MURRAY PRATT is dean of the School of Arts and Humanities at Nottingham Trent University. His research is situated within the broad fields of French and European social and cultural studies, with a focus on intersections between attributed and lived identifications and belonging. He studied in Glasgow, Lyon, and

Oxford, where he completed a doctoral thesis on autobiography, masculinity, and sexuality in Barthes, Guibert, and Robbe-Grillet. He has published widely on a range of cultural texts, including film, writing, and graphic novels. Current projects include autobiography in the "Bande Dessinée," difference in France, and European cultural identities.

ALEXANDER PRICE has a master of arts in French studies from the University of Washington and works as a lecturer for the University of Washington Extension. He also maintains a blog, *N'importe nawak* (http://portnawak.info/Blog), on French language, culture, and politics.

DENIS M. PROVENCHER is associate professor of French and intercultural communication and affiliate associate professor of language, literacy, and culture at the University of Maryland, Baltimore County. He is the author of *Queer French: Globalization, Language, and Sexual Citizenship in France* (Ashgate, 2007) and coeditor of a special issue of *Contemporary French Civilization* on "France, 1940–44: The Ambiguous Legacy." His research examines the linguistic representation of citizenship, national identity, gender, and sexuality in literature, mass and popular culture (television, film, graphic novels, maps, school manuals), and language data derived from ethnographic fieldwork in France. He is currently working on a new monograph that will examine issues of homosexuality, Maghrebi cultures, and Islam in France.

MIREILLE ROSELLO is chair of the Program of Comparative Studies and coordinator of the Masters Program in Cultural Analysis at the University of Amsterdam. She has authored several monographs, including *France and the Maghreb: Performative Encounters* (University of Florida Press, 2005), *Postcolonial Hospitality: The Immigrant as Guest* (Stanford University Press, 2001), and *Declining the Stereotype: Representation and Ethnicity in French Cultures* (University Press of New England, 1998). She is currently working on a collection of essays on European multilingualisms and on "What's Queer about Europe" (coedited with Sudeep Dasgupta).

GENEVIÈVE SELLIER is professor in cinema studies at the University of Michel de Montaigne Bordeaux 3 and is a member of the Institut Universitaire de France. She is the author of *Drôle de guerre des sexes du cinéma français 1930–1956*, written with Noël Burch (Nathan, 1996), and *La Nouvelle Vague: Un cinéma au masculin singulier* (CNRS Éditions, 2005), translated by Kristin Ross and published in 2008 by Duke University Press as *Masculine Singular: French New Wave Cinema*.

Joel Strom is a PhD candidate at the University of Washington completing his dissertation on the various aesthetics and practices of politically engaged cinema in contemporary France.

Vinay Swamy is associate professor of French and Francophone studies at Vassar College, Poughkeepsie, New York, where he teaches contemporary Francophone literature and cinema. His essays have been published in several journals, including *Studies in French Cinema* and *Yale French Studies*. He is the author of *Interpreting the Republic: Marginalization and Belonging in Contemporary French Novels and Films* (Lexington Books, 2011).

Carrie Tarr is emerita professor of film at Kingston University. She is the author of *Diane Kurys* (Manchester University Press, 1999); *Cinema and the Second Sex: Women's Filmmaking in France in the 1980s and 1990s*, with Brigitte Rollet (Continuum, 2001); and *Reframing Difference: Beur and* Banlieue *Filmmaking in France* (Manchester University Press, 2005). Her publications also include *Women, Immigration, and Identities in France*, coedited with Jane Freedman (Berg, 2000); *A "Belle Epoque"? Women in French Society and Culture, 1890–1914*, coedited with Diana Holmes (Berghahn, 2006); an issue of *Nottingham French Studies* on "Focalising the Body in Contemporary Women's Writing and Filmmaking," coedited with Gill Rye (2007); and a supplement to the film journal *Cineaste* titled "Beur Is Beautiful," coedited with Richard Porton (2007). In 2007 she guest edited an issue of *Modern and Contemporary France* on "French Cinema: Transnational Cinema?" and curated a festival of Maghrebi French ("Beur") Cinema in New York (2007). Her current research is on transnational Franco-African cinematic connections and women's filmmaking in France in the 2000s.

Darren Waldron is a lecturer in French screen studies at the University of Manchester. His research interests include representations of sexuality and gender in contemporary French film comedies and their reception. He has published articles on the films *Gazon maudit* (Balasko, 1995), *Pédale douce* (Aghion, 1996), *Le Placard* (Veber, 2001), and *8 femmes* (Ozon, 2002). He is the coeditor (with Isabelle Vanderschelden) of *France at the Flicks: Trends in Contemporary French Popular Cinema*, published by Cambridge Scholars Press in 2007. His monograph, *Queering Contemporary French Popular Cinema: Images and Their Reception*, was published by Peter Lang in November 2009.

INDEX

women, Maghrebi-French: as actresses, 17; characterization of, 162–65, 176n5; clothing of, 144–45, 164, 170–71, 172, 217–18, 226n10; as directors, 4, 165–68, 188; education of, 129, 132–33; feminine vulnerability and, 151–55, 172–75; feminism and, 154–55, 172; marginalization of, 67–68; and violence and oppression, 148–51

World War II, 103–5, 113–23, 124n7, 140n4, 206–7

Yamakasi, les sept samouraïs des temps modernes, 43, 44, 45

Zeitoun, Ariel, 43
Zem, Roschdy, 101, 104, 179, 196, 206
Zemmouri, Mahmoud, 43, 50
Zim and co., 47
Zulawski, Andrej, 149–50
Zwick, Edward, 36

CPSIA information can be obtained at www.ICGtesting.com
Printed in the USA
BVOW021525051111

275242BV00009B/6/P